# The Belly Dance Reader

From the Editors of
GildedSerpent.com

This book is a publication of

GildedSerpent
P.O. Box 39
Fairfax, CA 94978

editor@gildedserpent.com

Ordering information is available online at
http://www.gildedserpent.com/reader

ISBN - 978-0615735597

© 2012 by Gilded Serpent

All rights reserved. The text of this publication, or any part thereof, may not be reproduced in any manner whatsoever without written permission from the publisher.

Library of Congress Cataloging-in-Publication Data

Cover by Giulio Rosati, "The Dancing Girl".

Dedicated to

My Mentors

Najia: Who has been there from the beginning
of Gilded Serpent.

Dawn Devine: Who pushed me to make this book
and showed me how.

Anton: Who insisted I slow down and
find all the mistakes.

To my family: George, Michel and Sophia

And most of all, to our fascinating community,
including the dedicated volunteers who helped all
the way through to publication!

Najia Marlyz teaches at a Rakkasah Festival Workshop in 1992.
Lynette listens.

# TABLE OF CONTENTS

## Section 1 - An Introduction

*Welcome to Belly Dance!*
    by Najia Marlyz ............................................................................................................ 10

*Belly Dance & Contemporary Dance Studies*
    by Barbara Sellers-Young PhD ......................................................................................14

*Reading like a Researcher,*
    *Can You Trust Your Sources?* by Mahsati Janan ........................................................ 18

*Orientalism,*
    *Zumarrad's Completely Non-scholarly Quick & Dirty Guide* by Brigid Kelly ........................ 24

*The Soul Of Belly Dance,*
    *The Most Important Thing is the Feeling* by Alia Thabet........................................................ 28

## Section 2 - Dancing Through the Stages of Your Life

*Teaching Children to Belly Dance,*
    *Joys and Pitfalls* by Martha Duran...............................................................................40

*A Dancer's Journey,*
    *from Beginner to Semi-Pro* by Elianae Stone ............................................................. 44

*The Teacher-Student Relationship,*
    *A Psychological Point of View* by Izzah PhD ............................................................. 48

*Belly Dance Class or Cult?*
    Artwork by Leela Corman ............................................................................................ 52

*Turning Pro,*
    *From Hobbyist to Star to Teacher* by Lauren and Jillina............................................ 54

*A Boomerang Career,*
    *Life & Dance in the Land Down-Under* by Amera Eid ............................................ 62

*It Ain't Easy Being the Crone*
    by Shelley Muzzy........................................................................................................... 66

## Section 3 - History

*"Harem Girls",*
    *Dance in Historical Harems, Early 1700's-Early 1900's, The Perpetual Masquerade*
    by Andrea Deagon PhD ............................................................................................... 72

*The American Belly Dancer*
    *in Early Burlesque and Vaudeville Theatre* by Catherine Scheelar ........................... 94

*Belly Dance as Performance,*
    *Historical Phenomenon or Logical Evolution?* by Iana ............................................ 100

*Dancer Trading Cards,*
    Artwork by Leela Corman, Stats by Sausan ............................................................. 108

## Section 4 - Biz

*What a Band Needs,*
  *But Doesn't Always Get* by Denise of Pangia ...................112

*Dancing with Live Bands,*
  *The Little Book of Ettiquette* by Leyla Lanty ...................118

*Selling Your Dance,*
  *A Series of Elevator Pitches* by Athena ...................122

*Marketing Belly Dance for Fitness,*
  *Is it a Good Idea?* by Mayada ...................124

*Tip O' the Hat to Tipping,*
  *Practices of Appreciation* by Samira Shuruk ...................126

## Section 5 - Costume and Appearance

*Raqqin' the Retro, Vintage Costume Care*
  by Princess Farhana ...................132

*Omani Jewelry from the Collection of Nancy Hernandez,*
  Photos by Alisha Westerfeld ...................138

*Practice Makes Perfection,*
  *Make up Artists Share Their Secrets* by Davina Dawn Devina ...................142

*A Costume Gallery* ...................146

## Section 6 - Regional Styles

*Beyond Sequins,*
  *Meaning in the Movement* by Yasmina Ramzy ...................162

*Nomads of the Spirit,*
  *The Rom* by Sierra Suraci ...................164

*Romani (Gypsy) History,*
  *An Introduction* by Renee Rothman PhD ...................168

*The Zar,*
  *Dancing with Genies* by Yasmin Henkesh ...................172

*In Search of Zambra Mora,*
  *A Puzzling Dance Mystery* by Dondi ...................178

*Improvisational Tribal Style,*
  *Constructing Self and Community* by April Rose ...................182

*The Ghawazee*
  by Jalilah Lorraine Chamas ...................192

*Two Weddings and a Dancer,*
  *The Beled & The City* by Leila Farid ...................194

*Zeffat Al 'Aroosa,*
  *Ritual Procession for the Egyptian Wedding* by Sahra Kent ...................198

## Section 7 - Theory & Technique

*Belly Dance Motivations,*
   *Context & Content of Performance* by Jezibell ........................................................ 204

*Contextualizing,*
   *Giving Your Dance Context!* by DaVid of Scandinavia.......................................... 210

*Performance Enhancement*
   by Mahsati Janan ................................................................................................................ 214

*How to Balance Anything!*
   by Stasha .............................................................................................................................. 220

*Improvising With Ease,*
   *Strategies That Work* by Anthea .................................................................................. 228

*Shimmylab,*
   *Muscle Activation Patterns in Belly Dance* by Venus ............................................. 232

*Are The Stars Out Tonight?*
   *Fitting Music & Dance to Your Gig* by Najia Marlyz ............................................ 240

## The Backside

Maps ............................................................................................................................................ 246

A Few Maqams & Rhythms...................................................................................................... 250

References................................................................................................................................... 252
    Bibliography Project
    Bonus Material Online
    Disclaimer
    Errata

A Glossary of Common Belly Dance Terms......................................................................... 254

Contributors .............................................................................................................................. 260

Photo & Art Credits ................................................................................................................. 276

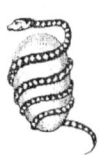

While a condensed biography of each contributor is included at the end of their article,
an expanded biography can be found starting on page 260, which includes their website, where available.
More information can be found on GildedSerpent.com.

# GAMAR*

I learnt to dance like honey falling from a spoon

To curve as smooth as the contours of the moon

I twist my arms then slide my chest to the melody

Intricate as lace, subtle as the waning of the moon

I must not give too much too soon

With a half-sigh my hips circle a harvest moon

I curl my wrist, shoulders ripple then shudder

Each swerve and turn reflects the phases of the moon

The eight twists through the base of the spine

A fish tail in changing tides governed by the moon

Sweet bullets shoot through my hips. Cat-like

My feet, rise one after the other towards the moon

Dum tek, dum dum tek; my wrists snap the air

Staccato drops and falls drift into half-moons

The rhythm is here, I can embrace the earth

Parvenu to myself, in the shadow of the full moon

*Full moon in Middle Eastern Arabic

**Poem by Beatrice Parvin**

# Section 1
# Belly Dance - Introduction

You've heard about belly dance. You've heard that it's an ancient dance of childbirth or that it's a dance of seduction. You may have even seen it at your local Greek restaurant or in a movie where these dancers create a mood of intrigue and sensuality. But really, what is belly dance? Gilded Serpent put out a call to its writers to help answer this question. The essays in this anthology were written by volunteers who were asked to write about what most interested them. The response was wide-ranging, from in-depth histories and how to do research, to how to become a professional performer to personal reflections on issues of teaching and ageing.

Section 1 introduces many issues important to belly dancers but begins with an introduction to the huge range of activities available to today's belly dancer and how to navigate them. For the researcher, learn how the subject of belly dance has been perceived by the scholarly community and how that has changed (a lot as it turns out), as well as how to assess the reliability of research materials much of which were produced by cultural outsiders. Kelly's guide to "Orientalism" is helpful here, as early source material was written (or painted) by Westerners carrying this historical bias. Included is a glossary of theatrical concepts and how they relate to the belly dance community and an exploration of the art of improvisation and self expression.

Whether you are a newcomer to belly dance searching for basic information or you are an old timer brushing up your skills, you can find more about its history and culture at GildedSerpent.com.

**Nakish**

# Welcome to Belly Dance!

*by Najia Marlyz*

You have expressed an interest in learning to belly dance, perhaps because you have seen it somewhere and decided it was personally appealing to you on some level, and it appeared that it might not be too difficult to learn. We welcome you! Many students begin their lessons for many different reasons, but few continue to take lessons because of any desire to become professional belly dancers. Many people see this dance form simply as an activity that they might do instead of jogging or some other form of exercise and they, quite literally, pursue it for years! Nevertheless, if you are looking for exercise or some aerobic movement "to get rid of your muffin-top when you wear your skinny jeans," I suggest that your needs will be served better by enrolling in a swimming class down at the YWCA. It's not that I want to discourage you if you really want to learn how to do a retro dance form with many facets that many dance aficionados think of as an art form. There is much more to Oriental Dance than may meet your eye initially. It can be performed as an art or it can become downright silly, depending upon who is dancing and for what reason she is dancing.

## A Rose by Any Other Name

Belly dancing is also known by the names: Oriental dance, Danse du Ventre, Raqs Orientale, and (the name we dancers would most like to forget) the side-show Hoochy-koochy! Dancers who have spent many years learning, practicing, and performing the belly dance as an art, are uncool and sometimes overly sensitive about what it is called. They are not yet in total agreement with each other on this subject.

Belly dance takes various forms because it has been around a long time and has a somewhat checkered history, not to mention that there has been a considerable amount of fusion and crossover, culturally speaking. There is a great deal of information and misinformation on the form in print as well as imprinted on the minds of the general public.

### True
- Belly dance can be a performance art and as such, a dancer can be a highly skilled entertainer and performer.
- In the Middle East almost everyone belly dances at parties as a social dance (both men and women).
- In the distant past, belly dance may have been a fertility dance, a childbirth dance, a harem or courtesan's dance, a form of exercise, a folkloric dance, a pastime, and a dance of seduction - or any combination of these.
- The belly dance allows for innovation and creativity.

### Partly True
- Men can be professional belly dancers in the Middle East.
- It originated in India and spread throughout Europe, collecting folk-dance steps along the way.
- It originated in Baghdad as a courtesan's dance.
- It is gypsy dancing, and therefore, is a street dance.
- It was used by a band of prostitutes to attract business.
- It is an ancient dance that was performed for the Pharaohs.

### Not True
- Belly dancers need to be fat or thin.

- Belly dance will make you fat or thin.
- Belly dance will make your stomach flat or pooched.
- Belly dancers are all exhibitionists and barflies.
- Belly dancing is from Saudi Arabia.
- Belly dancing will patch up an ailing marriage.

## Choosing a Teacher- Wrong Ideas

- Start with a teacher close to home then, after you become an intermediate level student, you can go to a better teacher.
- The length of the class determines the amount of information you will be taught.
- All teachers teach the same information.
- All teachers share openly and freely share their resources and whatever they know.
- You will become confused if you study with more than one instructor.
- A teacher need not have been a professional dancer to teach all you need to know.
- It is not important that my teacher has never gone to the Middle East to research dance as long as her teacher traveled there.

If you have heard these ideas buzz about in your brain, dismiss them now; as they will lure you into disappointment and difficulty that will get you off to a false beginning with this ethnic dance form. Instead, think of ways that this dance form may enhance your own pursuits.

## Belly Dance May Be Studied on a Hobby Level

Although belly dance can be done as a performance art, it has also been studied since the late 1960s in the US, Europe, and Australia as a tool for women to enhance self-image. They also use it to reclaim their own natural, womanly bodies, feeling that women sometimes are forced to pretend the image of ersatz men in order to compete in the workaday world of business and commerce. Some people find a solace and healing power in the act of dancing and getting in touch with the inner self or creative spirit. Nevertheless, even at the hobby level of study, nothing will happen if you do not plan to practice!

Because fine belly dancing is sensual, it has often been confused with sexual allurement and has often been associated with the dark aspects of social interaction - even in the Middle East (where it originated). However, any art can be used for many social and political statements. Poetry and the graphic arts would be good example of art forms that are used to amuse, to make a political statement, to inspire, or to offend. As a new dance student, you need to think for a moment about what you want out of your lessons so that you can pick and choose from among the many teachers available to you who are good at various aspects of the dance. Some teachers are beautiful dancers, but not good teachers and vice versa. Some are experts at country style dance, some at theatrical performance, some are best at organizing performance troupes, while some are able to coax the best out of your own creativity.

## Choose a Teacher Who Has Studied or Traveled in the Middle East

Though belly dance is called "ethnic" because it arises in a foreign culture and is based in that culture's folklore, it is not the same as learning to folk dance. Parts of it are folkloric in origin and parts of it are now theatrical. It demands creative ingenuity and emotional personal response as it is done in its original cultures. Belly dance is performed in a personal and individualistic style that invites the dancer to interpret the music with her own ability to personify and characterize the music. That music is as varied as the countries from which the dance originates. If you are an American, undoubtedly you will dance with an American accent, just as you would if you studied the Arabic or Turkish languages. After many years of study and experience performing in front of audiences, perhaps you may dance without an American accent, but by that time you will have developed your own personal style and probably will not care whether you have an "accent" or not. Being an American, dancing for other Americans is no excuse for an instructor not to have cared enough about the dance to experience it in its home venue. You would most probably not choose a teacher of Hula dancing who had never traveled to the Hawaiian islands! The Middle East is not on the moon; travel there has been possible and readily accessible for decades. Periodically, there has been unrest in the Middle East and during sensitive times, I would avoid going there unless it is peaceful. Nonetheless, many teachers have been there repeatedly for study and costumes and you should take that experience into consideration when searching for a teacher. The experience of Middle Eastern travel has the power of changing one's dance accent considerably and indelibly. For some students, it has become a deal breaker while, for others, it has been a reliable source of inspiration.

## A Fannana (Arabic for Belly Dance Artist) Must Be an Actress

From an audience's perspective, witnessing perfect dance technique is not as important as seeing the dancer who possesses a full vocabulary of movements, has learned the grammar of stringing it all together so that it makes sense and delivers a non-verbal message that touches the hearts of those for whom she dances. Belly dance, like other forms of dance, is a communications art and each movement should carry some content of meaning on a deep and humanistic level. We work with dance techniques that we hold in common with other forms of public entertainment such as singing, acting, and even clowning! Projection, intent, stagecraft, setup, completion, musical interpretation, creation of an image, costuming and portrayal of emotional character-acting, are just a few of these important concepts that are part of our dance technique.

As you study belly dance, your curiosity may be led to research additional subjects that may, at a glance, seem unrelated. However, belly dance is multi-faceted.

You may find you want to study the following parts of belly dance:

- Finger cymbal and Middle Eastern drum rhythms
- Veil dance movements and styles
- Raqs Assaya (ethnic cane dance)
- Snake dancing (of doubtful authenticity but exciting and provocative, if somewhat reminiscent of our former sideshow aspect)
- Balancing objects while dancing (scimitar, candelabrum, water jugs, or trays containing various objects)
- Special and specific folkloric dances from parts of the Middle East (Depke, Hasaposerviko, Khaleeji, Zaar, Zeffa, etc.)
- Floor dance while prone (demonstrating the strength and flexibility of the dancer)
- Comic and exuberant drum solo dancing

As a student of belly dance, you may find yourself yearning to learn a little more about:

- Foreign history
- Arabic and Turkish words
- Ethnically important rhythms
- Musical forms that are different from Western musical forms and how they differ

**At the Cairo Marriot in 1987, Najia and Mohamad enjoy the singer Fatma Sirhan (Fatma Eid)**

- Middle Eastern cultural differences in gestures and facial expression
- Emotions and creative instincts you had not realized you possess

Do not allow anyone to limit your possibilities!

Your teacher needs to keep you informed of the many events and resources available to you to enhance your total dance experience. Some of these resources are:

- Workshops
- Festivals
- Newspapers and magazines
- Performances
- Videos
- Books
- Internet
- Vendors

Your study of dance should always remain fun (not drudgery or work) even when it is challenging to your physical being. Relentless drilling of technique (called a "workout") is often used by teachers who mean well, not to make you become an exquisite dancer, but to keep you in your place and under a self-limiting control--even those teachers whose dance you most admire may unconsciously employ this technique of control. Remember that the study of belly dance is currently a competitive experience, and you may find yourself competing for attention, titles, gigs, awards, certificates and recognition with the same people who should be there to mentor you in your discoveries.

Never let loyalty to any dance teacher limit your exploration and research into dance in any way--except for critiquing your dance constructively and honestly, explaining the reasoning behind each negative comment. Dishonestly telling you that your dance is superlative when it is not (under the guise of being supportive) can be more devastating to your future as a dancer than the comment that this or that "needs more work, and this is why". Consider yourself forewarned that belly dance has many facets, and you have a right to pursue as many as you can absorb into the shining dance persona that you are hoping to create.

The one caveat I will offer you is: Never try to copy exactly what your special dance role model has accomplished, because it has already been done!

Always, you will be only second-best when you are copying something profound. You will need to create your own dance out of the meager tools of technique and concepts of dance that a competent teacher can pass on to you. However, it is your message that needs to emerge and touch the world through movement; that is the message with which you can become first-best. Do you have an inner message? How would you know if you haven't danced?

**Now, get ready to dance!**

*Najia Marlyz*
*Najia has performed, taught, written, coached, and traveled in the Middle East during her career spanning 45 years. Partnering with her mentor, Bert Balladine, she taught in her Albany, CA, studio, in the 1970s. Masterclass instructor in the '80s through '00s, she is recognized for dramatic improvisation, seamless movement, and inventive technique for coaching pros based on imaginative musical analysis.*

# Belly Dance and Contemporary Dance Studies

## by Barbara Sellers-Young PhD

I remember a story that Morocco once told about her early days as a dancer in New York. She was performing in a Greek restaurant and decided to try out incorporating an arabesque into her improvised performance. Afterwards, the owner of the restaurant came up to her and told her never to repeat such a vulgar movement; instead, she should put her legs together and shimmy. Each time I watch a modern or a ballet dancer using a pelvic variation in front of an audience, I am reminded of Morocco's story and how important it is to understand that what is appropriate in one culture may not be appropriate in another. I am also left with the question of how different we might have perceived North Africa and the Middle East if Flaubert and other writers, artists and politicians of the colonial era could have understood the solo improvisational dances and associated shimmies and hip thrusts within the context of celebration; a context in which the movement vocabulary was a dance of joy in celebration of births, weddings and other events signaled that the family and the community had survived the challenges that face any group. The other side of this query is - if the movement vocabulary of belly dance had been perceived as movements of joy and not movements of seduction, and thus outside of an Orientalist framing — would American women initially, and then, subsequently, women around the globe have adopted and adapted the dance in the 1970s and after as a movement to liberate, and thus, redefine the social/cultural limitations of their bodies? There are numerous questions that can come out of considering the "what if" of history, but what is crucial is that there was the Orientalist construction of the dance created by the colonial moment and this attitude has shaped the dance's reception, and in fact influenced its movement vocabulary, both in imitation of dances of North Africa and the Middle East, most specifically Egypt, and in new styles of bel-

**April Rose writing her master's thesis.**

ly dance - Tribal, Goth, Fusion - that share some of their lineage with this social/cultural area but have created a distinctive costume style, musical accompaniment, choreographic techniques, and movement vocabulary.

For these reasons, since I started my master's degree in dance in 1980, I have been interested in research on belly dance. However, in 1982, I made a proposal to my master's committee in dance to do my thesis on belly dance. It was turned down as I was informed that it was not an appropriate topic for research in dance. Thirty years later, there are undergraduate and graduate students around the world in Asia, Latin America, Europe and North America who are writing a thesis and/or a dissertation based on their individual research of the form. What has changed in those thirty years?

First and foremost, there have been many dancers from the belly dance community who have combined dance with scholarship to publish a series of essays in belly dance publications, and ultimately, academic journals. The early belly dance journals, Habibi and Arabesque, and more recently, Gilded Serpent, have provided an opportunity for this group of dancer/scholars to begin to explore areas of interest from a focus on the history and evolution of the dance in North Africa and the Middle East, to accounts of individual research trips, to questions regarding definitions of femininity in relationship to contemporary issues associated with the feminist movement as well as other areas of research focus. These publications also provided a venue for exchange and networking so that dancer/scholars from various parts of the world became familiar with each other through their writing. Ultimately, they would come together at dance, oral history, and other academic conferences to share new directions in their research and thinking. Finally, they submitted and had essays accepted in the Journal of Popular Culture, Theatre Research International, Women's Studies: An Interdisciplinary International Journal and others.

The essays by dancers and scholars - Andrea Deagon, Anthony Shay, Caitlin McDonald, Donnalee Dox, Donna Carlton, Candace Bordelon, Noha Roshdy, Virigina Keft-Kennedy and many others - create a strong argument as to why belly dance is a legitimate area of dance study. First, their essays incorporate new directions in dance studies that embrace the intersection between ethnographer and dancer. As such, they are "literally dancing through and between ethnography and history" (O'Shea).[1] This approach to ethnography derives from a convergence of anthropology, ethnography and the concept of the performative allied with cultural and performance studies. As such, it unites subjective experience of the dancer with an objective observational stance to reveal the intra-cultural discourses and related cultural flows (using Arjun Appadurai's 1996 conception of the forces of globalization related to technology, transportation, migration and the economy) that are integral to the intercultural adaptation of dance forms across social political boundaries.[2] Consequently, they unite theory and practice to delineate the complex contradictions of a dance form that is a site of appropriation, liberation, and community engagement.

The research of these dancer/scholars also helps us to understand our increasingly globalized world in which images rush at us on the subway and in screens from the Cineplex to the television to the computer. Without the research of Anthony Shay and Stavros Stavrou Karayanni would we appreciate the history and the contemporary positioning of the male dancer? Without Andrea Deagon's poetic account of the classical tradition or the 20th century versions of Salome, would we understand how the feminist movement of the 1970s is related to the classical world and by extension the Salome craze of the early 20th century? Would we know what happened to Little Egypt without the research of Donna Carlton? Can you imagine having a perception of what Baladi is without the research of Noha Roshdy? Would we appreciate the relationship between the dancing body in real and virtual worlds without the insights of Caitlin

McDonald? How many dancers' conception of the aesthetics of an Egyptian solo dance performance has been informed by the presentations of Candace Bordelon? Would we appreciate the nuanced considerations of the dance in terms of contemporary social/cultural theory without the work of Virginia Keft-Kennedy? Or the role the dance plays in the life of the dancer without the work of Donnalee Dox? And, these examples are only a few of the many dancers and scholars from the belly dance community.

The research and writing of these dancer/scholars not only contributes to the belly dance community's understanding of itself and its positioning in global discourse. These dancer/scholars are contributing to the ongoing evolution of dance studies. Their research points out aspects of gender studies and the ongoing dialogue of masculinity and femininity that is a part of political debates and policy-making from Australia to the United States. Their research uncovers and redefines terms often associated with Egypt but rarely understood such as Baladi and Tarab. Their descriptions of the transformations of the dance's vocabulary and style help to reveal the cultural flow of images and how individual communities cope with these images in an increasingly globalized world. The dancing body becomes the site of an interrogation of the meaning of the real and the virtual. Beyond this, the essays often point out how Orientalism still frames the images of North Africa and the Middle East and therefore the political positioning of this area of the world.

If I were to repeat history and ask a dance committee to do a research project on belly dance today, the question would not be "what for?" but "on which aspect of the dance do you want to focus?"; or, phrased another way: "What is the primary question you are interested in investigating?". The one great thing about getting older in this world is watching change take place and getting an opportunity to be an observer of that change, and to observe how knowledge is developed and disseminated. Those early articles in Habibi and Arabesque as well as the ongoing community engagement in Gilded Serpent of dancers' thoughts and stories as well as the determination of early writers Deagon, Carlton, Shay and others, have provided the opportunity for members of the belly dance community around the globe to combine their love of dance with their love of scholarship. I feel privileged to have watched this change unfold.

## References

[1] O'Shea, Janet. *At Home in the World*. Connecticut: Wesleyan Press, 2007. pg 146. Print

[2] Appadurai, Arjun. *Modernity at Large: Cultural Dimensions of Globalization.* Minneapolis: University of Minnesota Press, 1996. Print.

### Barbara Sellers-Young PhD

*Barbara was appointed Dean of the Faculty of Fine Arts and a Professor in the Dance Department at York University in July 2008. Prior to that, she was a professor at the University of California, Davis where she served as Chair of the Department of Theatre and Dance and as executive director of the Robert and Margit Mondavi Center for the Performing Arts. She is an interdisciplinary scholar with an international research profile in the fields of dance, theatre and performance. Her interest in all forms of art and diverse performance styles informs her research on the moving body and globalization, which has taken her to Sudan, Egypt, Nepal, Japan, China, England and Australia.*

**Mahsati's educational and research background focuses on cultural traditions and anthropology.**

# Reading like a Researcher
## Can You Trust your Sources?

*by Mahsati Janan ~ Jessica Brown*

Almost all dancers are passionate about their dance form. For some, this passion extends to learning about the cultures, history, and evolution of their art, but – where to start? There is a lot of information available, but determining how much of it is accurate or reliable can be a difficult task. When you read or hear about this dance form being ancient, what does that mean? How do we know it? What did this dance look like 10 years ago? 50? 100? 1000? This is the first step. As a dancer acting as a researcher, you want to separate your questions into those that are knowable and can be supported with evidence and those that are unknowable and rely on opinions or feelings. Neither should be dismissed, but you will need to approach these kinds of sources differently.

Topics that can be supported with evidence will be the best for your research focus. Topics that cannot be supported with evidence are more philosophical and rely more on feelings and conjecture. While these philosophical questions are valuable, they are far more difficult to judge for validity, accuracy, and reliability. (Pierce, 2008) When we are looking at information sources, the first things to determine are:

- **Accuracy** – This is the one we are most familiar with in our day-to-day lives. Accuracy is how closely your research aligns with reality or other confirmed data. Ask yourself whether this data contradicts or supports the other information you find. If it contradicts the current information, examine both the new and older information for any flaws in logic, reliability, or validity.

- **Reliability** – Is it repeatable? In an experimental research situation, you would determine this by repeating your experiment to see if you find the same results. In this kind of research, reliability is a measure of consistency. Ask yourself if your sources and data points are reliable. If you are using interviews or documents with the views of a specific person, consider whether their telling of events is cohesive and consistent.

- **Validity** – This refers to the appropriateness of the data, information, or evidence to your topic question. Valid information will be reliable, but not all reliable information will be valid. Ask yourself whether the information you have gathered is actually related to the question or topic you would like to research.

If your research is accurate, reliable, and valid, then you have a good foundation to consider it evidence-based and, therefore, knowable.

Another pertinent question is to consider the original source of your resources. Some sources automatically carry more weight in research, such as those from academics in peer-reviewed journals, while others carry considerable less influence, like blog or forum posts. Without knowing where the information comes

**Table top from Nancy Hernandez's lecture on Turkmen Jewelry in November, 2012, for the Ethnic Textiles group at the De Young Museum in San Francisco.**

from, it becomes far more difficult to determine its trustworthiness.

In addition to considering your source, validity, reliability, and accuracy, also keep in mind the difference in types of data, information, and evidence. Data is the raw form of the information as it is received. An example of data would be the responses to a survey or a list of all of the items related to a specific folkloric dance style. Once you review the data, you begin to find and create information. Information is the bridge between data and meaning. An example of information would be using survey data to determine that a specific percentage of dancers are also drummers. This data and information can then be used as evidence. Evidence is generally information used to support a specific theory or conclusion. (Pierce, 2008) Quantitative data refers to data that can be counted, such as how many hip scarves a dancer owns. Qualitative data refers to things that are not countable, even if they may be quantifiable. An example would be a dancer's feelings about each hip scarf owned. Both qualitative and quantitative data are valuable and using a mixed methods approach in your research is advised if information of both types is available.

If you don't have time to conduct extensive research on your own, it is even more important to read critically to judge the quality of the education you are receiving from each source. Otherwise, it would be easy for you to waste a lot of your time learning incorrect, or at least unverifiable, information. Whether you are a student, teacher, or enthusiast, having the best information available is preferable to unreliable information, no matter how enticing the unreliable information may seem at first.

## *Recognizing and Reducing Bias*

We have an amazing resource at our fingertips now, the Internet! Of course, anyone can post anything on the Internet, so you have to take care in which pieces you use. Citations are a logical thing to look for when you start checking the information on a website. If the author of the website can't tell you where that information came from, or if the answer is that it came from another website, hearsay, or a known unreliable source, then you will need to treat anything you gather there as suspect until you can find further verification. This brings us to something extremely important: bias. Nearly everything you find is going to be written from a specific perspective. This perspective is the bias that competent researchers are always trying to reduce. It is almost impossible to eliminate bias, but there are reasonable ways to reduce its impact on your research. First, consider your own bias. This will be based on your own perceptive lens and your perspective. It is informed by everything you have ever done, seen, read, heard, or learned. Some bias is conscious. Other biases are unconscious. In sciences such as chemistry and physics, bias would likely creep in as part of the original research question or design. In social sciences like anthropology, the bias can be identified from the initial question, through your data collection, and in your analysis and interpretation. Unlike something more concrete such as physics where there are constants with which to work, that can help you find and eliminate certain types of bias, in researching history, arts, and experiences, perspective-based bias is simply a fact of life. Minimizing the impact of bias means acknowledging that it exists and then working to present or find multiple perspectives to help triangulate the best information with the least amount of bias interference. (Kiecolt, 1985) Once you have given thought to your own biases, stay alert for the bias in your information sources. Think of it as trying to find the lens that your source is looking through. Some lenses distort a little, others a lot, but if you know what type of distortion to look for, you can filter some of it out to tease out the diamonds of knowledge and pearls of wisdom from the whole mass of raw data.

If bias is everywhere, how can you ever find the truth?

## Truth is a Question of Philosophy

As a researcher, you will always work in a framework of the best available evidence rather than certainty.

Use your research skills to triangulate your data and information. Always keep an open and questioning mind and be willing to let go of your certainty of beliefs and ideas that can't be supported by evidence.

## Orientalism

There is one kind of bias that you will absolutely need to be aware of when studying resources on Middle Eastern, North African, and Mediterranean dance styles: Orientalism. Orientalism is a form of exoticism or "othering " where stereotypes and caricatures are represented as actual life. This specifically looks at the Near, Middle, and Far East (the "Orient") as compared to European or other Western cultural perspectives (the "Occident"). Orientalism can imply a colonialist attitude or perceived superiority. However, any study of the cultures or peoples of these areas by those not a part of the culture can be labeled as orientalist. As such, it is not an automatic negative point, but it gives you an idea of the perceptive lens you can expect in the tone of the research and can pinpoint potential blind spots by the researchers in their data collection or interpretation. Orientalism is a huge topic, so I would recommend reading more about the different forms of orientalist writings, art, and research to help inform your personal studies.

## Data and Sources

Let's say that you have identified your initial set of data sources. Now, you will need to be able to identify the different types of data and the sources you use as reference material. For the first step, you will need to decide if each source is primary, secondary, or tertiary. Each kind of source will have both advantages and disadvantages. Here is a quick guide for identifying primary, secondary, and tertiary sources.

1. Types of Sources
   A. Primary
      i  Original materials being reported by the researcher or participant
      ii Direct evidence, generally judged by how close source is to time, place, and event
      iii Dance Examples:
         a. Sahra Kent's writings on Zeffat al Arous based in part on her firsthand research in Egypt.
         a. Morocco's (dancer) writings about her firsthand experiences from her travels and dancing.
   B. Secondary
      i  Interpretations of primary sources
      ii Discussion and evaluation of primary sources
      iii Dance Example:
         a. Shems' or Shira.net's articles on different dance styles. These articles tend to focus on pulling together data from primary researchers and adding value through discussion and evaluation of both the sources and information.
   C. Tertiary
      i  Compilations of data from primary and secondary sources
      ii Brings together multiple types of data sources from multiple research types into a single document. Filtered and interpreted in many cases
      iii Dance Example:
         a. Gilded Serpent's collection of articles would be a tertiary source, but the individual articles may be primary, secondary, or tertiary depending on their content.

A lot of researchers look for shortcuts to help them initially classify the level of trust to extend to different data sources. The easiest of these is to learn the basic types of publications and other resources and to use that to help you choose which types are best for your research needs. A doctoral dissertation will require a much stronger set of reliable sources than an editorial or opinion piece.

## Basic Sources by Reliability

Excellent list -
library.humboldt.edu/infoservices/scholorpop.htm

a. *Academic Journals* (Academic/Scholarly, Substantive) – Academic journal articles are generally written by known researchers who hold academic credentials. These articles are peer-reviewed. This means that each article included in these sources has been reviewed by a set of knowledgeable people in the field before being approved for publication.

b. *Dance Journals* (Academic/Scholarly, Professional, Substantive, or Popular) – Dance journal articles can fall into any category depending on what is included. Look at the focus of the publication, the author and editor biographies, and the types of information included to gauge how trustworthy these are on an individual basis.

c. *Journalism* (Substantive, Popular) – Journalism refers to articles written by trained journalists, such as newspaper reporters. These can range from detailed, researched in-depth pieces to fluffy personal interest stories.

d. *Books* (Academic/Scholarly, Professional, Substantive, or Popular) – Books are a huge category themselves. This includes everything from peer-reviewed edited academic books to fictional accounts of the life of a dancer. Among the non-fiction books, academically-focused or first-person biographical pieces are most likely to be valuable to historical research, but if you are looking for information on how belly dancers are portrayed in the media, fiction and popular pieces will also be very helpful to you as examples.

e. *Research Reports and White Papers* (Academic/Scholarly, Professional, or Substantive) – Research reports are based on actual data collection and can be a precursor to academic publication or take its place in professional or industry publications. Assuming that the research was well-designed and reported fairly, these are relatively good sources of data.

f. *Personal Experiences & Anecdotes/Blogs* (Academic/Scholarly, Substantive, or Popular) – As these types of items can be based entirely on the author's personal experiences or opinions, the reliability and accuracy will be limited to the author's own experiences. That does not make this data any less useful; it only means that you will need to be very careful in how information obtained from these sources is referenced. Example: If a blog post by a dancer in Cairo says that business is fabulous and there aren't enough gigs to go around, you could report this accurately by quoting this dancer's experience or inaccurately by generalizing it to say that it is a definite occurrence experienced by dancers in Cairo.

The types of data within your sources are also helpful in knowing how to best use and interpret your findings. The following is not an exhaustive list of all types of data and labels that you may find while doing your research, but it will give you an idea of what to look for as you get started. I highly recommend study in social science, historical, and statistical research if this is something that you want to pursue more fully. Remember that not all numerical data is created equally. Some items can be calculated and used as you would any integers, but other numerically coded data is actually based on a scale or category. If your data doesn't make sense if calculated, re-check your data types. (Example of data that doesn't make sense with calculations: 50 dancers take a survey and rank their favorite dance styles from 1 to 5. If you were to average these scores, you would find ranks of 1.5 or 3.9 which don't make sense in context. A better method for interpreting this data would be the percent of dancers who chose each option, such as, "15% of the 50 respondents classified their favorite style as general belly dance." Types of Data:

A. *Quantitative* – countable, numbers
   i   Numerical– Data displayed in numbers that can be counted and calculated without invalidating data. Example: A group of 5 dancers each have 15 hip scarves, so if they pool their resources, they have 65 hip scarves available.

B. *Qualitative* – verbal, feelings
   i. Nominal or Categorical – Numbers used as labels are considered nominal. Example: US Social Security Numbers, Coded dance styles, such as Egyptian = 2, Tribal = 3.
   ii. Ordinal – Numbers used as rankings are considered ordinal. These cannot be used with all types of calculations. Example: Rating 5 dance workshops from 1st to 5th in enjoyability
   iii. Anecdotes and Oral Traditions – This is a category of data that refers to free-response questions, like 'How do you feel about the changes in the dance community?' The responses from these types of questions or sources are not generally quantifiable or even categorical, so you have to use different methods to turn these into information. Text-based coding and analysis is a great tool that allows you to use multiple sources, but tag or code them to be specific topic areas. (Lichtman, 2006)
C. *Mixed Methods* - quantitative and qualitative together
   i. If you have multiple sources of data available, you may find that not all of the data is of the same type. This is where mixed methods research comes in. By using the different types of data in your examination, you are able to begin quantifying the qualitative data and providing needed context with the qualitative responses. (Angrosino, 2002)

## Things to Remember

Now you are ready to start gathering all of your sources and developing your interpretations of the data you find. There are a few final things to keep in mind. First, if you aren't sure about something, contact the source. Even if the article was published in a prestigious academic publication, sometimes something unusual will catch your eye. When this happens, do your best to research it on your own, but also feel free to turn to the professional researchers for help in understanding your data. Second, remember to use your information appropriately. Don't use tangential evidence to prop up a theory or idea that can't be supported through your findings. If your data is largely anecdotal, embrace that and do a text analysis. As long as you are open and honest about your data sources and findings, you will be making a contribution to the greater knowledge base for this dance.

Whether discussing the past or the present, ask yourself about the evidence to support your statements. If you suspect something, but do not have the data to support it, you can always say that in your research. Theorizing based on current data is one way to help find new avenues of research to explore. Always be willing to admit that you don't know something. The lack of knowledge about something specific isn't a personal failing, it is an opportunity to learn more and expand your horizons. There is also a big difference between what can be supported with evidence and what we, as individuals, believe. If the data is supporting something that is counter to your personal beliefs, do not try to make the data fit your preferences. Always be open to the idea that there may be more information out there for you to integrate into your personal belief system. Just as important, remember that the absence of evidence is not the same thing as evidence of absence. Even if something cannot be directly proven or supported by the available evidence, that does not mean that it isn't true or will never be supported by findings in the future. To help you with interpretation, try to pick up at least some basic statistics and determine how to use them. This will help you to interpret whether the sources you are using are misinterpreting their information as much as it will help you to use statistics with your own findings.

## Now...Start Researching!

This quick guide to reading like a researcher won't make you a social scientist, but it will give you a head start to evaluate the information you find on your own. Good luck and best wishes in your research! Don't forget to share and publish your findings with the dance community. By sharing our knowledge, we both deepen and broaden the understanding of the many forms of belly dance.

## References

Angrosino, Michael. *Doing cultural anthropology: Projects for ethnographic data collection*. Longrove, IL: Waveland Press, Inc., 2002. Print.

Kiecolt, K. Jill, and Laura Nathan. *Secondary analysis of survey data*. Newberry Park, California: SAGE Publications Inc., 1985. Print.

Koomey, Jon. *Turning numbers into knowledge, mastering the art of problem solving*. Oakland, CA: Analytics Press, 2008. Print.

Lichtman, Marilyn. *Qualitative research in education*. Thousand Oaks, California: SAGE Publications Inc., 2006. Print.

Pierce, Roger. *Research Methods in Politics*. Thousand Oaks, California: SAGE Publications, 2008. PDF.

"Journals - Scholarly or Popular? - HSU Library." *Journals - Scholarly or Popular? - HSU Library*. N.p., October 13, 2005. Web. 21 Nov. 2012.

"Welcome to the Purdue OWL." *The Purdue OWL: Research and Citation*. The Writing Lab and Owl at Purdue and Purdue University., 1995-2012. Web. 21 Nov. 2012.

"Gilded Serpent, Journal of Record for Middle Eastern Music, Dance, and Belly Dance." *The Gilded Serpent*. N.p., 2012. Web. 21

Best of Habibi. "Home." *The Best of Habibi*. N.p., n.d. Web. 21 Nov. 2012.

"All About Belly Dancing!" *All About Belly Dancing*, by Shira. N.p., n.d. Web. 21 Nov. 2012.

"Resources." *Shemsdance RSS*. N.p., n.d. Web. 21 Nov. 2012.

### Mahsati Janan

*Mahsati is an instructor, performer, choreographer, and workshop instructor in Asheville, NC. She began her journey in belly dance in 1996 and has studied and performed throughout the US. She specializes in classical and modern Egyptian styles, but also enjoys many other modern belly dance forms. Mahsati's educational and research background focuses on cultural traditions and anthropology.*

**A coffee break during the International Bellydance Conference of Canada 2010. Pictured left to right: Lynette Harris, Barbara Sellers-Young PhD, Lynette Harper PhD, Andrea Deagon PhD.**

# Orientalism
## Zumarrad's Completely Non-scholarly Quick & Dirty Guide

by Brigid Kelly

**What's so bad about Orientalism anyway? I love those old paintings!**

Who could not? Many of them are gorgeous! Nevertheless, Orientalism is more than just an artistic movement, which is where the confusion lies.

When we talk "Orientalism" we could be referring to one of three things: The artistic movement, or the study of Oriental languages and cultures, or the racist discourse known as Orientalism that was outlined by the Palestinian critic Edward Said in his 1978 book of the same name. Said wanted to show how the West constructed the East (the "Orient") in ways that subtly present the occupants of its lands as inferiors that must be controlled, and their lands and cultures as exciting and desirable to plunder. The three are interrelated, so what might seem innocent, like the pretty artworks and the intellectual study, can be used to feed the racism at the discourse's heart.

Orientalism presents the world as split in two: Us and Them. On the side of Us, the Western side, are concepts like reason, masculinity, modernity, Christianity. On the side of Them are irrationality, femininity, antiquity, and Islam; the rational brain versus the sensual body; human versus beast. Sometimes this discourse is flat-out obviously negative towards Them, as when the Crusaders went to battle Islam in the 11th century on the grounds that the Holy Lands needed saving from an evil non-Christian menace, or when Switzerland banned the building of new minarets in 2009. However, other times, it is much more subtle, drawing on fantasies and fears to build a picture of Arab and other Middle Eastern peoples that we take for granted. This is what Said called "latent Orientalism", and it is what's most important to us, as belly dancers.

**"The Connoisseurs" by Gyula Tornai**

Popular Western culture reflects the subtle ways Orientalism constructs (usually) Arab people in essentially two ways. Sometimes it's crazed, irrational extremists from cruel, ancient cultures. Other times it's exotic, oversexed belly dancing women who need rescuing. The image of the veiled woman is particularly fraught: Beneath the burqa may lie a richly-clad sensualist, or a fanatical killer. The problem is the way Orientalism prevents us from thinking of the woman under the veil - or in the belly dance costume - as a real person. It encourages us to dehumanise Arab people, which makes it easier to justify neutralising the threats we think they pose, even as we enjoy playing dress-up in our fantasy versions of their cultures.

**What's wrong with celebrating our womanly sensuality and femininity and fertility?**
Nothing, but there can be a problem when we locate it in fantasies of the exotic Orient without thinking about what they might mean. The existence of belly dancers, or of women who wear hijab (covering), is not why stereotypes exist. However, the double-edged image of the Arab woman as both (or either) seductive oversexed belly dancer or harem girl, or the unsettling veiled figure that could be victim or threat, also presents Them (and Us) as undifferentiated objects. When we play with being the "Sultan's favourite" or "harem slave girl", we also play into the fantasy of penetrating the harem, which lays out Arab or "other" women as sex objects for the pleasure of Western men or for the sexual or emotional salvation of Western women. We can step out of our imaginary harem and back into our real world: For Arab women, especially in the Western world, these stereotypes come along as baggage into everyday interactions, and they can be harmful and limiting.

**I would never do those tacky, tacky harem fantasy things! I am careful only to present the most authentic material, gleaned from extensive research into all things Middle Eastern. That means I'm off the hook, right?**

Not so fast! You remember how we said that students of Oriental languages and culture were and are also known as "Orientalists"? There is still a danger that in our intensive studies, we can be guilty of making generalisations and perpetuating an Us and Them way of thinking. Worse, our well-meaning attempts to pin down and preserve what is authentic about another culture can put us at risk of representing the Middle East as something properly tied to the past, not a region full of different kinds of people who are part of living, developing and changing cultures. We also risk treating things that interest us within those cultures as our own; we see belly dance as ours to rescue, and ending social inequalities or abhorrent practices as our job. By stepping in to "fix" things, there is a risk that we may take agency away from the people we're trying to help. We treat them like children. Some would also say that we risk entering the realms of the minstrel show if we imitate to the point of "Arab-face" rather than seeking a more personal, thoughtful kind of authenticity.

**Thankfully, I don't do Middle Eastern belly dance. I am a World Fusion artist! That totally lets me off the Orientalist hook!**
Unfortunately not. The images and associations of Orientalism are so pervasive that all you have to do is wiggle in a two-piece to exotic music to be coded "belly dancer" by people unfamiliar with the dance form. Furthermore, if you call what you do "belly dance", then people will, by default, associate it with Middle Eastern and North African nations. Because we're belly dancers, we feel so comfortable with the form that we can forget that, to outsiders, it has these associations. We might know that our music choices, movements and costumes signal that our dance is Tribal Fusion, but only other belly dancers will know this; so we have to remain aware of what non-inductees will imagine when they see us dancing, even if that seems unfair. At worst, doing "belly dance" for pleasure and profit while negating its cultural associations and origins puts us in line

**"Dance of the Almeh" by Jean-Léon Gérôme**

for charges of appropriation - or stealing, in ordinary language.

**Can't this Us vs. Them, modern or primitive, intellectual or sexual division be applied to just about any non-white, non-Western cultural group though, not just those from the Middle East and North Africa?**
Yes. That's one of the common criticisms levelled at Said's work.

**So, does this mean that if you're a white western person and you do anything at all that doesn't come from your own culture, you could be called a "racist colonialist appropriator"?**
Yes. As we know, however, the relationships between Western women and the world of belly dance during the past few decades are a bit more complex than that.

**They copy us, too! Why is it bad when we do it but not when they do it?**
It's largely about power. Taking elements from Western-originating dances like ballet and ballroom, as in Egyptian dance is, in part, a result of having been colonised. Colonised cultures tend to adopt whatever the colonisers present as good. Adding elements from ballet - the most revered dance form in Western culture - in the early days of Raqs Sharqi was a way of making dances more commercially appealing to both the colonisers and locals with money, who sought a more cosmopolitan way of life. Those elements came from the top down, and encompass a much wider sphere, not just the arts. In the USA and other Western countries, belly dance arrived as an exotic novelty, and even at its peaks of popularity it has always stayed that way. Americans don't, as a rule, feel an overwhelming social pull towards adding Middle Eastern "improvements" to their whole society,

because the influences have been comparatively small and narrow.

The different power dynamics and perspectives from which we as Western dancers come to belly dancing cannot be ignored, but today especially, belly dance takes place in a world of transnational interactions and porous borders. It's much harder to put things in boxes and say, "This is Turkish; this Egyptian, this American...", because we are interacting with each other all the time. Ideas, influences, and images run in multiple directions. It's complicated.

## How do I know you're not just making this up?
This article aims to be a starting point for discussion and thought. Check out these resources which have way more information:

## References

"Reclaiming Identity: Dismantling Arab Stereotypes | Homepage." *Reclaiming Identity: Dismantling Arab Stereotypes* | Homepage. N.p., n.d. Web. 21 Nov. 2012.

Bernstein, Matthew, and Gaylyn Studlar, eds. *Visions of the East: Orientalism in Film*. New Jersey: Rutgers University Press, 1997. Print.

Dox, Donnalee. "Dancing around Orientalism." *TDR The Drama Review*, vol 50 no 4. (1997). Print.

Kealiinohomoku, Joanne. "An Anthropologist Looks at Ballet as a Form of Ethnic Dance." *Moving History/Dancing Cultures.* Ed: Dils, Ann, and Ann C. Albright eds. Connecticut: Wesleyan University Press. 33-43 (2001). Print.

Said, Edward. *Orientalism*, London: Penguin, 1978.

Shaheen, Jack. *Reel Bad Arabs: How Hollywood vilifies a people.* Massachusettes: Olive Branch Press, 2001. Print.

Yegenoglu, Meyda. *Colonial Fantasies: Towards a feminist reading of orientalism*, Cambridge: Cambridge University Press, 1998. Print.

### Brigid Kelley
*Brigid ~ Zumarrad is based in Christchurch, New Zealand. She graduated MA (Distinction) in Cultural Studies from the University of Canterbury in 2008 with her masters thesis Belly dancing in New Zealand: identity, hybridity, transculture, examining the ways belly dancing intersects with concepts of a New Zealand identity.*

**Young Girl Feeding the Sacred Ibises in the Hypostyle Room at Karnak by Sir Edward John Poynter**

# The Soul of Belly Dance:
## The Most Important Thing is the Feeling

### By Alia Thabit

Traditionally, belly dance is a dance of improvisation, of on-the-fly musical interpretation, of subtle emotional timbres and intuitive interaction between dancer and musician - and that musician plays improvised music, created in the moment as an expression of the musician's feeling. Each and every performance becomes a never-before seen, never-to-be repeated art happening, uniting dancer, musician, and audience in a state of ecstatic joy. This is our calling. This is our cultural heritage. And yet we see fewer and fewer such performances as Western values, student expectations, and recorded music erode our connections to the heart and soul of our dance.

Let us unpack the riches of this artistic treasure chest, and return ourselves to this ecstatic state.

### Creating Dance in the Moment

Dance moves. We all have them. We collect them. We polish them. We display them. We shop for more. We go to workshops, buy DVDs, compare notes with our friends. We see how many we can cram into eight counts, and give ourselves extra credit for the really hard ones, the ones we had to work at. Yes, we are proud of our moves. But moves are the domain of the analytical mind. They are about thinking. To use one, we have to make a decision, we have to have debate, we have to select one from the many, over and over again. This is fine when we construct a choreography, but not in an improvisational setting. In the moment, everything is moving too fast for this. Decisions must be made on the fly. In the moment, we rely on intuition.

Musicians do not decide note by note what to play when they improvise; they just go. They trust their fingers to be there for them and that notes reflecting their feeling will come out. As dancers, we, also, must just go. We must leave our technique at the studio door and express what we feel in the moment. We must trust our bodies. What comes

**Alia improvising in the moment with D'Jinn. Pictured, back row, l-r Fung Chern Hwei, Carmine Guida, Brad McDonald, Pete List, Dancer Alia Thabit.**

out will be a glorious unity of intricate splendor, unique, ephemeral, each element individually shaped to mesh brilliantly with the whole.

We have few core moves in Oriental dance: Circles, infinities, s-curves, and straight lines, each one infinitely variable in size, speed, height, direction, force, and weight. This variability is what we mean by micro-movements. Each move can be infinitely customized to fit the music. This is why people talk about Egyptian dancers who only use four moves for their whole show, but those moves are married perfectly to their feeling for the music. They evoke the heartbreaking, joyous thrill of intimate, tender art created spontaneously before one's eyes. This is how the music and the dance are meant to interact, complement each other, and become one.

In dance, most of us have been trained to copy. We have to exactly recreate the shape, size, and force of the teacher's chosen movements. If we are in a group dance, we all have to match. Some of our newer genres, such as American Tribal Style, employ limited and highly stylized movement vocabularies. But this is not the soul of the dance. This is not the real deal. Why are we learning this way?

- Recorded music has largely replaced live music. Few of us have an ensemble waiting in our studio, ready to play at our beck and call!
- Students want a product they can take home and show their friends.
- Group dances have become ever more ascendant. They allow the teacher to include entire classes in shows, and students feel safer dancing in a group, safer being told what to do, and, audiences love them.
- People bring Western aesthetics and hierarchies into belly dance rather than understanding and valuing Eastern aesthetics.

Most of us came up in Western dance, where exact stylization is valued (yes, ballet, I'm talking to you), along with a distinct valuing of technical perfection over freedom of expression, and a sharp delineation between the dancer (to whom movement is given) and the choreographer (who makes the dance). The teacher's status as the creator of choreography supersedes that of the lowly student, who slavishly copies the creation of the higher-ranking teacher. Yet the traditional nexus of Oriental dance is improvisation to live, improvised music. Learning choreography does not help us learn to create dance in the moment as we respond to live, improvised music. In fact, it makes this more difficult.

Why? Because learning and retrieving are cerebral, analytic activities while improvisation is an intuitive embodied process. Additionally, copying choreographies discourages personal creativity, invention, and style. We need to learn technique. We need to understand how to put movements together, develop combinations. We need to understand the aesthetics of the dance, and to its cultural values. But we also need to learn how *we* respond in the moment to what we hear. And to do this, we need to practice it.

Why dance like someone else? You are you. You are special, unique, individual, precious. Nobody feels exactly what you feel. Nobody else's dance expresses your experience. Find your voice. Let the music move you, physically and emotionally. Let your feelings infuse your body, from the expression on your face to the carriage of your arms, to the swing of your hip, to the turn of your foot. Radiate the emotions that you feel from the music, from nostalgia, to sorrow, to joy.

### Dance What You Feel

Traditionally, dancers show the audience what they feel from the music. Traditionally, the music is live. Traditionally, the musicians play what they feel. The dancer feels what they play, and communicates these feelings to the audience. The moves are racks on which to display the feelings. Famous dancers from Azza Sherif to Raqia Hassan all agree: The most important thing is the feeling.

**Arabesque Orchestra Quartet:**
Oud- Bassam Bishara, dumbek- Suleiman Warwar, riqq- James Freeman, violin- Eddy Sulaiman

### Forget Your moves - Trust Your Body

Technique is the servant of expression. That double flip is awesome, and it took a long time to get it right, but it is just a container. A beautiful container, but empty, a bowl without food, a pot without a living plant. With what will you fill it? What do you want to say to the audience? What gift will you give them?

Moves are Lego blocks. We snap them together, interlocking units of Dance Construction. You can build a lot of things out of Lego, and some of them are pretty cool. But...

You can't build drama out of Lego. You can't build pathos. You can't build laughter, or tears, pleasure or pain, or any of the myriad feelings that we convey in dance. When the evening is over, no one's going to remember that double flip. But they will remember that you made them cry.

### Creating Music in the Moment
### The Takht

Traditionally, Oriental music is played by a *takht*, a small ensemble composed of classical instruments, usually *kanun, oud*, violin, *nay, riqq, daff, tabla* (aka *darbuka*), and a singer. For pictures and sound files of each of these instruments, please visit the site maqamworld.com. Each instrument has a unique timbre, so when played together, each stands out against the sonic whole. In a song, all the musicians play the same melody (*heterophony*) and rhythm (*heterorhythm*). This music may be simple in terms of structure; however, Eastern music has something extra. Each musician ornaments the musical line, playing sonic arabesques and curlicues around the established melody. Eastern musicians play what they feel in the moment, and they pride themselves on never playing a song the same way twice. So even a simple melody becomes a complex interaction of overlapping heterophonic interpretation, as each musician both ornaments, and listens and responds to, the ornamentation of the others. Therefore, in a relatively simple song, i.e. verse, chorus, verse, there is quite a lot going on.

### Microtones

In addition to the ornamentation, Eastern music simply has more notes with which to play. Think of a piano. The tones march up the keyboard in measured whole and half steps. The half step between A and B is called either A sharp (A#) or B flat (B♭). But Eastern music has notes between these notes. For example B half flat, a note between B and B♭. So those strange, off-key sounds you hear? They are not off-key; but they don't exist in Western music, so they sound strange at first.

However, it doesn't stop there. Though these are often called quarter tones, they are more accurately microtones. Why? Because Eastern musicians tweak the notes, pushing them sharper or flatter as their feeling for the note indicates. So we have not only ornamentation of the notes, and extra notes, we have ornamentation of the extra notes as their pitch is modulated to better express the musician's feeling in the moment. It was the search to represent these elusive Eastern microtones, or "blue" notes, on Western instruments that drove African-American musicians to bend guitar notes with bottlenecks and create what we now know as the blues.

## *Putting it All Together*

As dancers, these elements give us the textures we need to interpret the music. When a traditional Eastern song is played without decoration, the music is empty. When we have a half-dozen musicians adding texture, coloring the music with their interpretations, we have a rich palette of material from which to choose. And just as the musicians are free to play what they feel, dancers have equal artistic liberty. We have the freedom to pick and choose which lines to interpret, the melody or rhythm, which instrument, and what aspect of it, both with our bodies and our finger cymbals.

Just as the musicians use microtones to better express their mood, dancers have micro movements. We modulate our movement's size, shape, direction, speed, and force to better fit our mood and the music, carving calligraphic lines through time and space. Just as calligraphy has thin and thick lines, so our dance arcs have slower and faster segments, portions that are rich with tension and intensity coupled with sleek tracery. We cultivate a long, lazy line, dripping like thick, sweet, scented syrup. Like Arabic calligraphy, we resonate with the shapes and textures of the music.

Consider the textures and dynamics of the song 'Ala eh Betloumy'. As you listen, paint the music in the air with your hand. Vary speed and force to articulate the shifting quality of the sound. Close your eyes. Just feel it.

**Amina performs at the Casbah on Broadway in San Francisco's North Beach in 1970.**

Now let your body paint the sound on the air, from wide, sweeping brush strokes to elegant slender curves and cushioned accents. Try the shapes on the calligraphy link. Dance them, so that they become animate, living letters. Script messages with your body, your chest, your hips, shoulders, arms, hands. Radiate rich, precise, exquisite lines into the hearts of the audience. Love the music with your body. Rub up against it like a cat.

When musicians play for a dancer, they watch the dancer carefully. They respond to the dancer's movement, literally playing what they see, just as dancers dance what they hear. For example, while interpreting a violin taqsim we might begin trembling. The drummer notices this, and begins to play that vibration, allowing us to then amplify it. Egyptian *tabla* player Yousry Hafny maintains that his job is to watch the dancer's waist, and to play whatever she does. His job is to follow the dancer, not the other way around.

### Taqasim and Emotional Timbres

Belly dance is a profoundly elastic genre, expressing an array of emotional timbres. These timbres are built into the music. While even musicians disagree on the specifics, it is traditionally held that many of the *maqamat* (plural of *maqam*, Arabic modes, a type of musical scale), evoke specific emotional responses, from nostalgia, to sadness, to exaltation. Eastern musicians play what they feel. So every time, that song is going to be different, as it's going to be colored with today's feeling, this moment's feeling.

This is most directly expressed in the *taqsim*, (plural *taqasim*) a musician's solo improvisation. A taqsim will begin on one note, and then wind from maqam to maqam, modulating through sometimes wild, heroic leaps. Where a musician goes depends entirely upon their feelings in the moment. So the music is a container for the feelings of the musician in the same way that

**Jill Parker**

movement is a container for the feelings of the dancer.

Let's talk first about improvising to taqsim, as this is a core skill. A lot of dancers choose to interpret only the *chiftetelli* rhythm underlying the taqsim. This is a valid choice, but there is much more available. The elements that lend themselves to taqsim are the undulations and waves of the torso, along with arms and shimmies. These are so infinitely variable that you can stand in one spot and express the music with only these elements. Indeed, it is customary to take a taqsim in place rather than traveling, as a gesture of respect to the musical soloist, and to travel during periods when the whole takht plays together, a chorus, for example, or a splashy entrance. Traveling and covering space are relatively novel concepts in the dance; traditionally, a dancer was thought accomplished if she danced her entire show within the space of a bathmat.

The two main melodic characterizations are *sahr*, smooth, flowing sounds, such as the violin and wind instruments, and *naqr*, the percussive sounds, plucked instruments like the kanun, oud, and buzuq. These characteristics influence the texture of the body's response. As we are the visual representation of the music, we seek to describe the sound quality through movement.

Convention suggests specific body parts to represent specific instruments, but these are only conventions. In floorwork, we might not use these at all. Some people have noticed that the place the instrument is played often corresponds with the location in the body where it is represented. Here's a brief review. Again, these are only conventions. You can see pictures and hear these instruments at maqamworld.com.

- **Nay** (often pronounced nye) - the most spiritual of the instruments; also other winds, clarinet, horns, etc: Arms and hands/upper body.
- **Oud** - Hips. Shimmies, overlain with snakes, undulations, etc.

**Yasmina Ramzy**

- **Violin** - Shoulders and upper body into the torso and arms. Snakes, undulations etc.
- **Kanun** - Hips and upward. Shimmies, overlain with snakes, undulations, etc. Some kanunjis play rich harp-like arpeggios that cry for arm treatments and turns. Go for it!

## Naqr

The trick comes with matching the movement to the sound. For example, you have the naqr of an oud taqsim. The musician plays many notes, some close together, some farther apart. Therefore, the shimmy will echo that. Ideally, we are talking one "shim" per note, so, fast when the music is fast, tekkatekkatekkatekka, slow when when the music slows down, tek, tek...tek.... tek.... tek........

And when there is no note, there is no movement because the notes and the movement are deeply connected. When the musician pauses in the taqsim (the pause is called *qafla*; plural *qaflat*), we coast to a stop, gently, softly, fading out the movement as the echo of the tone dies away, easing into it again as the notes recommence, or coasting through the qafla into the next phrase.

So that is the percussive aspect of the oud taqsim. On top of that we have a melodic layer. Oud has a rich, buttery, warm tone; it tends to center in the hips and lower torso. So here we also articulate the pitch, volume, and speed of the melody line through infinities, circles, and undulations. Variations in size, force, speed, height etc, represent the variations in the melody line. The faster the picking, the smaller the move - or you can do longer, bigger, slower arcs with or without a shimmy or a little pulse, wafting over the fast parts. Though traditionally, taqasim are taken on a spot, you might travel or change your location, especially if the taqsim is long. All this you can layer over the shimmies, or just represent the melody.

Does this make sense? Just as the dancer listens to and interprets the music, musicians watch the dancer and play what they see, so there is a magical interaction between the two. It helps immensely to listen to many taqasim. Dr. George Sawa recommends listening to one musician's taqasim to get a feeling for how they phrase their improvisations. Rather than attempting to predict what the musician will do, relax into the music and let it move you. Studies of anticipating randomly projected points of light have shown that feeling the coming moment is more accurate than attempting to predict it. Practice allowing yourself to wait for the music.

Try this out with this beautiful taqsim from Farid al Atrach. Close your eyes and let the music move you. Let yourself be a leaf in the wind, a twig on a stream, wafted and shaped by the sound.

### Sahr

Now let's look at the nay. Its characteristic is sahr, smooth and flowing, spiritual. We cast our focus upward, and highlight the upper body: Shoulders, arms, hands. We roll the shoulders back, smoothly as bicycle pedals, allowing that wave to radiate up and out of the arms.

Even in arms and hands, the energy rises upward from the *dantien* below the navel. So all moves originate there, and radiate outward, while the push/pull of contraction and expansion constantly recycles the energy inward, shoulders pulling down, arms yearning

**Alhazar of Spain**

away. When the arms are filled with isometric energy, they carve strong, graceful lines, providing stability and an elegant frame.

The shoulder moves the upper arm; the wave radiates through the elbow to the forearm. The wrist leads the hands. The wrist is the head of a fish, the fingers its brightly-colored tail, waving along behind. The hands criss-cross the midline, the eyes glance from side to side, cast their gaze down, then up through modest lashes, then away. The arms extend for turns, open wide, then draw the energy inward. Everything directed outward is recycled inward.

Long sweeps express long notes, or slow, slow, shoulders, the shape and size of their rolling, the shoulder snakes, determined by the quality of the sound. A rising pitch may bring up the arms, curlicues become hand flowers, chest circles, or whatever form your body feels. Take your time. Feel the music. Coast along it. Let it caress you and dance with you, like a curl of scent wafting through your dreams.

Now close your eyes and let this truly lovely Taqsim Nay Kurd into your heart. Ah!

## Joy
### Tarab

The goal of Eastern music is to enter an exalted state. This state, *tarab*, translates, insofar is it can be translated, to "musical ecstasy." Tarab affects not only the musicians; this state is shared with the audience. Eastern audiences have an investment in the evening, as they are part of this state. They encourage the musicians, call out, engage with them, appreciating elegant modulations, a well-turned taqsim, etc. The best of these audience members are called *samiyyah*, educated listeners. In the early days of recording, musicians brought their samiyyah with them to the recording studio, as engagement with the audience was such an integral part of the music-making process.

**John Compton at Tribal Fest**

### Ecstasy and Dance

As dancers, we also reach this state of musical ecstasy. Many of us have felt it. We know it. We may not know how to name it, or how to reliably attain it, but we know it is there. And here we come to solid evidence of the sacred nature of this dance. Because this is not just our imagination. This it is not merely a charming folk dance of wide geographic range. It is a *Sufi* dance. And Sufis, Eastern mystics widely known for their whirling practice, use the dance to to go within, to enter into an exalted state, to become closer to the Divine.

Dunya Dianne McPherson, American Sufi master, Juilliard graduate, and classically-trained ballerina, was also a professional belly dancer. She came to belly dance through Sufi dance, as transmitted by her teacher, Adnan Sarhan. At first, she was fascinated by the subtle internal movements

Adnan expressed as he entered a trance state, the same undulations, infinities, and vibrations we know so well. As her understanding deepened, she realized that Adnan's movements were those of belly dance - differently focused.

So we enter into this dance with an intention to attain an ecstatic state. This is not your average folk dance.

Traditionally, Oriental dance and music are performed in fairly close quarters. Amplification is a relatively new technology, and for many of the rural areas of the world electricity came late. So people sat close, and the dance accommodates this. We still dance close to the audience, in cafes and living rooms, at weddings and celebrations of all kinds. We engage our audiences. We make eye contact. We flirt. We visit. We converse. All these are traditional activities. The desire to elevate the dance, to give it respect, often comes at the cost of traditional values. Putting this dance on a larger stage, further from the audience, valuing technique over expression, choreography, recorded music, and theater stages all conspire to make this a colder, more distant dance.

Instead, let us delve more deeply into the soul of an ancient art form that has existed longer than any of our sophisticated artificial constructs. Let us value the dance for what it is.

This dance is deeper than any box, deeper than any paradigm, deeper than any of us. It existed

**Najia dances on the weekly Naji Baba TV show in 1974.
Back row, left to right are an unknown dancer, Taka, and Johara.**

before us, and it will continue long after we are gone. The core movements, our circles, infinities, s-curves, arcs and accents, are timeless, universal, profoundly organic. Buddhists say that should the *dharma* (teachings) disappear from the world, one person could stumble upon a bit of bone, and in contemplating that bone, find all the teachings reveal themselves. So it is with belly dance. This languid joy that connects us to the music, to each other, to our beauty, to our power, to the divine, exists for all of us to access any time, any place, any where.

The next time you dance, cast your cellular memory back. Connect with this lineage of dancers, the people who have danced before you. Feel their stories, their loves, their cares. Welcome them. Love them. Allow them expression through your body. Feel their infinite power and beauty. Feel your infinite power and beauty. Know yourself as the present manifestation of thousands of dancers, through thousands of years, all of whom are within you at this very moment, loving your courageous transformation.

This dance heals and empowers. It inspires creativity and joy.

It is a wild, free dance. It has resisted patriarchy, fundamentalism, naming, and shaming. It lives, it evolves, it survives. It is our gateway to another world. It is our strength, our heart, our soul. We, who dance this dance, know it is sacred. We know it is a devotional dance. Why tame it and water it down, make it live by foreign rules? Educate audiences and students as to the core values of the traditional dance.

Another world is possible.

Thank you for being part of it.

## References

"Maqam World." *Arabic Musical Instruments.* N.p., 2001. Web. 21 Nov. 2012.

*Ala eh Betloumy.* June 9, 2012. Youtube.

"Arabic Calligraphy." - *The Origin Of Every Things [ Storm Your Brain ].* N.p., n.d. Web. 21 Nov. 2012.

*Bint il Sultaan* by Akhmet Adawaya. Feb. 9, 2012. Youtube.

*Farid al Atrach Live oud.* June 8, 2008. Youtube.

*Nay Taqsim Kurd.* Sept. 11, 2010. Youtube.

Author's note: This article uses the term Oriental in its vintage sense, to encompass the many lands of the Near and Middle East; additionally, Eastern and Oriental are used synonymously, and belly dance will be occasionally referred to as Eastern or Oriental dance.

### Alia Thabet

*Alia is an Arab-American and a Vermont Juried Artist, who draws from four decades of technique, history, regional and folkloric styles, props, theatre, fusion, costuming, music, choreography, improvisation, and performance. She highlights creativity and expression grounded in tradition, uniting dancers, musicians, and audience in a radiant oasis of warmth and delight.*

**Axelle,**
**in St-Eustache, Québec, Canada**

# Section 2
# Dancing through the Stages of Your Life

The essays in this section address a range of age-related issues in dance, beginning with a look at the distinctive knowledge needed to teach children. The psychological complexity of the student-teacher relationship is paired with several essays on the stages a teacher passes through. We take a personal journey through the one writer's discovery of belly dance and her development into a professional. Another provides an accounting of the ins-and-outs of becoming a professional dancer. One retired professional performer examines her own passage into becoming a professional teacher. Another explores the paradox of her crone years when she can look back with great perspective, but also look forward as belly dance evolves.

People of all ages practice belly dance - some discovering it as children, some as teens and some who are entering their senior years. But all of them begin as novices. To read more about how belly dancers deal with issues around stages of life visit GildedSerpent.com

# Teaching Children to Belly Dance
## Joys and Pitfalls

*by Martha Duran*

Kids love and expect to be led, and when motivated, they will soak up whatever new knowledge is made available to them. For countless little girls and boys each year in Mexico, familiarity with an art becomes an important knowledge base, and since kids love to be active, taking a dance class is often a logical step.

If you choose to become a dance teacher, your life will be full of lively experiences. Most likely, your days will have flexibility and an easy schedule. It is a job that can double as a daily workout, and offers an opportunity to be creative endlessly. However, the best gift of all will surely be the joy of teaching children.

With their fearless personalities and willingness to try anything, you'll find yourself working to keep up with kids; introducing the world to them through dance can be easy and hard work at the same time. Teaching an art form springing from different cultures such as those of the Middle East gives you a chance to pass forward an art rather than just another history class!

Back in 1992-3, I started teaching the Egyptian style of Raqs Sharqi, taking advantage of the popularity of Disney's movie "Aladdin". Children

**Martha's Students at Danceme Academy in Mexicali Mexico.
Group from left to right, top row--Annel, Claudia, Nallely, Mariela, Diana, Paola, Diana.
Second row, left to right--Mariel, Karely, Claudia.
Third row, left to right -- Karla , Mariana Paola.**

were interested in that part of the world: How they danced, dressed, and talked during that time. It was easy to plan a lesson that would not lose the interest of my students. However, after a while, it was only my love for dancing that kept me going because belly dance was not popular in Mexico for a while. It was a discipline that was ignored and had little popular support. Although well known artists worldwide (such as Michael Jackson and Madonna) used it in their choreographies, videos and concerts, it wasn't an obvious influence; so it wasn't a big help to attract students to the classes for several years. I kept teaching belly dance class in a "combo" class, and some students took it along with Jazz, others with Ballet and Tap, but no one wanted a "just a belly dance class" where one might teach anything beyond simplified Raqs Sharqi...

Dancers enjoyed the opportunity of seeing how the steps and movements interpreted the music and learning to move just like a belly dancer. However, it wasn't dancing like their favorite top-chart singers danced! All that changed back in the year 2000 when a popular Colombian singer named Shakira introduced the fourth single on her album "Laundry Service". Ojos Asi had that tabla beat that makes every dancer want to move, and Shakira introduced in her presentations a dance with a short drum solo halfway through the song. That 20 seconds changed the life of every single belly dance teacher in the Americas! Students were breaking down classroom doors to sign up to learn how to move and shake just like Shakira. That's when being a belly dance instructor in Mexico became a triple threat, and we belly dance teachers became more popular in our communities. We enroll more and more students all the time, but also, we have both good and lousy competition...

> Indira Gandhi said, "My grandfather once told me that there are two kinds of people: Those who work and those who take the credit. He told me to try to be in the first group; there was less competition there".

**Pepper Alexandria assists Sophia Harris with holding both her 1st place ribbon and Mohini, the albino boa constrictor.**

Many dance teachers had found their classrooms empty because of belly dance gaining popularity in Mexico. They started searching how to get into the current dance craze fast so they could bring back their students. Many of them took a sample class, bought a video, and read a few articles about belly dance on the Internet. That limited information gave them enough credentials to open a belly dance class in their own schools, because that was where the money was for them.

Students from ages as young as 3 came into my classroom asking for belly dance classes and stuck with it. They completed the whole dance program that I had developed to give students an opportunity to learn by region, by traditions, and prop after prop. Step-by-step, they all learned everything from fundamental Raqs Sharqi to a complete folkloric range of Arabic style Oriental dances from Egypt to Lebanon. It was easy to include historical cultural facts about etiquette and stylization. In the end, however, children came to their dance classes to dance, and that is a concept that all dance teachers must keep in mind.

> "The truest expression of a people is in its dance and its music. Bodies never lie." - dancer and choreographer, Agnes de Mille

However, teaching children how to dance can also be difficult. Some kids are in dance classes only because their parents have dropped them off. Many families treat such extra-curricular activities as a daycare service rather than an enrichment opportunity; so, learning an ethnic dance style and its manner was difficult for that kind of student. The children weren't very motivated about dancing and their parents didn't want to invest in authentic costume pieces at all. Some children were too shy or didn't get any encouragement to participate fully, leaving me with the awkward challenge of attempting to force a youngster into doing something that just did not matter to them.

Sometimes, parents can also be a challenge themselves, scrutinizing everything from your prices to your costume and music selections. My job was wonderful and rewarding, but definitely, there were some tough days along the way!

Teaching children how to dance is usually an easy task, provided that I am organized. Kids can sense nerves and unpreparedness, so I devote some time each weekend to prepare my lesson plans on providing a structured, orderly environment while they are in my classroom. All dance classes start with a warm-up, dance combinations and technique, but children also need some combinations that move across the floor. They need time to hear the history of dance, absorb new insights, work through problems, develop social skills, and practice self-control. So, although it may seem like they are wasting time with blocks, puppets, drums, scarves, trays, dolls, and pretend-play props, they know most definitely what they have learned the week before.

**Children learn to balance a tray of candles.**

If you are teaching belly dance to young ones, spend some time introducing them to "center floor" and the dance steps that can be done there; allow them time to freestyle with a catchy tune. Each dance genre offers different ways in which to be creative, so don't be afraid to try new things. Teach or observe a dance class in your chosen style to glean new ideas.

Providing a dance syllabus is often neglected. The syllabus helps young

**Chok Guzel of Korea competes at Belly Dancer of the Universe**

opposite: Two feet to one foot. Surprisingly, this can be a fascinating subject for young people.

" What we learn with pleasure, we never forget." - Alfred Mercier

Teaching children how to dance is one of the most rewarding jobs within the art community. At times, teaching Oriental dance to children can be challenging; although, as a teacher, you are making a difference in your students, and one of them may grow up to be an extremely successful dancer someday. You are also introducing them to the fact that there are people with different traditions out in the world who can expand their horizons.

### Martha Duran

*Martha, a dancer since age two, has been the director of Danceme Academy for the last 14 years. Considered the first belly dance teacher in Mexicali, she received her masters degree in Communications in 2002, a degree in Arts and Education in 2004 and a degree in Oriental Dance Education in 2010.*

dancers understand the meaning of the Arabic songs lyrics because it gives them an image of what the step should be and what they are trying to communicate with their movements. Dance theory is important also, as well as how this dance is influenced by dance forms. The dancer must understand that for an *assemblé* you spring off one foot and land on two, while a *sissone* is the exact

# A Dancer's Journey
## From Beginner to Semi-Pro

### by Elianae Stone

I have found my time as a Belly dancer to be a magical experience. The art form has opened such a vast, colorful world for me; one that I never knew existed about a decade ago. I think there are many parallels that we experience as dancers, and that there are many highs, lows, and poignant moments along the way that have been woven into a rich tapestry of shared beauty and learning. I have grown and learned so much about myself and the lives of women in my journey, and hope that in the phases that I have experienced, you will see yourself and love your journey. I feel that Danse Orientale is a dance of pure beauty and grace.

### The Beginning

**My first studio shoot in 2007, Also my first "Tribal-Fusion" foray. As a young dancer I was enamored with all styles, and trying to find my way.**

I saw my first Belly dancer at the Ohio Renaissance Festival. Her name was Laylia, and she portrayed a wonderful "gypsy" with live drumming, swords, full skirts, flowers, and a foxtail attached to her bum! I know now that she is an example of a Rennfaire Fusion/Tribal Belly dancer. However, at the time, I did not know about additional different styles. I had grown up in the classical ballet dance form, and thought I'd like to try something different. I was tired of the strictness and uniformity of ballet and thought Belly dance would be fun as well as freeing. I was participating in yoga regularly at the time, and pictured Belly dance to be an Earth-Goddess, bare-footed, mellow, kind of venture.

In the local paper I saw an advertisement for a Belly dance studio called Habeeba's Dance of the Arts. It was the only studio advertised extensively at the time in the Columbus area, and was marketed as the longest-running studio in the Midwest. I thought it would be a good place to start. After my first few classes, I was hooked! These dancers looked different than Laylia, but our classes taught us so many things. I adored the idea that Belly dancers were free to use props. We learned how to use veils and finger cymbals. I got into wearing the hip scarves, chiffon skirts, and choli tops to class. I used to apply exotic makeup and jewelry, and brushed my hair out so it could swing freely in class. Within a few months, we were learning shimmies. This is the ultimate Belly dance move I believe all beginners pine to learn. Some ladies were already getting their first beginner's bedlah (matching skirt, bra and belt set). It was an exciting time!

The first big show I remember seeing was the Bellydance Superstars, and it introduced me to the world of glitter and make-believe that those in the Belly dancing community experience. There was no going back now! I saw vendors with sparkling jewelry and costumes for sale; there were dancers everywhere in all forms of regalia, and I saw my first fake eyelashes, wigs, stiletto heels, etc. These dancers were so exotic and fascinating! I saw the Bellydance Superstars when they were on their "Raqs Carnivale" tour, and felt privileged to see Jillina, Petite Jamila, and Sharon Kihara, who did Tribal Fusion. I loved Tribal Fusion, which I had never seen until that time. I always thought of the dance form as one big lump. I didn't realize that there were so many variations. This is when I began to see divisions between Tribal and Cabaret. The Tribal girls hung out back of the hotel, smoking cigarettes and wearing top

**First solo performance 2009 Viva Valezz fundraiser.**

**Soloing in 2008**

hats, feathers, and silk flowers, while the Cabaret girls sipped Cosmos and compared jewelry or their nails and spray tans in the bar.

## The Performer

After about a year or so, I decided that I was ready to take the next step into performing. I was very lucky at Habeeba's studio because the instructors had established many local performance opportunities for their students. There were many festivals in which I could participate. Habeeba also arranged monthly haflas (Middle-Eastern style party) as well.

I purchased my first bedlah, with all the requisite skirts, accessories, and trims. I discovered that I loved performing, and danced my first solo at the hafla. I learned that, as a soloist, I could develop my own style, and I worked on trying to choreograph movements for myself. It was challenging at first, but a process that helped me to grow.

I even dabbled in Tribal style for a bit, although I wasn't sure which style I liked best. I realized that my school had been training me in the American Cabaret style, and discovered dancers and teachers in the community who worked in other styles. I liked Cabaret because I felt it gave me a strong foundation. I liked the traditional class format, and I found that a lot of my previous ballet skills were useful in that style.

## Teacher and Soloist

After several years of being a performer at Habeeba's, I was invited to take the next step and become a dance instructor. I had always enjoyed helping others, and was delighted that some of my skills and friendly nature might be of benefit to my dance sisters. I joined the instructors troupe at the studio, had my picture put on the teacher wall, and got my first troupe costumes. Being an instructor at the studio was an exciting honor for me, but a lot more work than many of the starry-eyed students realized.

I put in long hours on the dance floor, seeing chipper students come and go while I gulped down water, toweled off, ate handfuls of nuts for stamina, and put up my limp, sweaty hair, trying not to look gross. I wanted to project that aura of mystery, beauty, and excitement that I so loved when I began the dance.

I shared in the students' enthusiasm when they got a tricky move down, or when they got their first costume.

At this time, I realized that doing a lot of the same routines I'd done for years wasn't as exciting as it had been, and even local shows weren't as much of a rush as they had once seemed. When you're caught up in the thrill, excitement, and love of Belly dance, it is shocking when you realize some of your audience members are less than interested. I became weary of seeing people walk out on shows or check their cell phones while I danced. I wanted to do more, to become

better and be taken more seriously, so I decided that my next move was to compete!

## Competitive and Gigging Dancer

Competitive dance was an eye-opener for me. I enjoyed the thrill and pressure of having to prepare for the competitions, and I witnessed dancers taking the art form to a whole new level. I also experienced a huge blow to my ego. I thought I was doing well, being a teacher and local figure, but some of these women had exceptional skills, bodies to die for, looked like models, and costumes in the four-figure price range! I became aware of a whole new level of professionalism. I had begun my foray into paid gigs, which was a huge thrill for me. However, I saw how many other women in town wanted these opportunities as well, and how competitive professional dancing was. I discovered the meaning of undercutting, and

**"That's me dancing for one of my first private birthday parties."**

found that some women lost friendships over these issues. Suddenly, I had to market myself, and this new concept raised all kinds of insecurities. Many of the dancers I had trained were also ready to spread their wings, and I had to compete for gigs against them. As a paid dancer, looks mattered, and I was dismissed at times for being too fat, old, or blond. These types of remarks hurt.

I had been taught that belly dancing is for all women, and that one should be proud of her body, no matter her age, shape or size. In competitive dance and paid gigs, this proved not to be true!

Additionally, I began to dislike dancing for the general public. Although they were mesmerized and appreciative of my costuming and the exotic music, many just wanted a party girl. Their biggest thrill of the night was tucking dollar bills into my belt or getting drunken Uncle Bill to get up and dance with me. I disliked the angry, evil stares of women who seemed to think I was a loose woman just shaking my attributes for attention. I became disillusioned with the dance.

## Semi-Pro On Her Own

I wanted to venture out into the world, study with other teachers, and find my place. I had only studied at one school so now I started taking workshops from traveling instructors and teachers of different forms of Oriental dance. All of this change came at a difficult time for me. I was growing into an adult woman, and had enjoyed a fast progression through the dance, but now I'd hit a plateau. My body had changed. I was spending more money on my dancer's lifestyle than I was making, and in order to advance to the holy grail of dancing professionally, I was going to have to spend more hours in the studio and work harder than I had before. I still had a day job, a relationship, and I began to wonder where I was going. Friends and family who knew me before I started belly dancing told me I'd had a good run, but also told me that belly dancing wasn't everything. They thought I was obsessed with my dancing and that my internal conflicts with my body image and dance capabilities had brought me down. Nevertheless, I had invested so much into the dance that it had become part of me. I wasn't ever going to leave.

## Where to Go?

I think many dancers reach this stage and I know I am not alone. Oriental dance is a glorious, soul-inspiring art form. I do believe that I have something to offer the dance community. As performers and teachers, we need to take a realistic look at our dreams and goals. I will probably not be a professional Belly dancer, touring the world and headlining sold-out shows, but I can still be grateful for all that I have accomplished. I can appreciate the joy that each new experience brings into my life. I can love myself and take stock of the talents I do possess.

I still dream of teaching again, and doing workshops that feature my gifts. I am still a work in progress. I think 90% of all Belly dancers are semi-professionals like me. We can do so much to educate the public about what a unique, complete form of dance this is. We can work to better the working conditions for ourselves and others. I may seem idealistic, but my advice to you is: Never give up, and enjoy your dance journey!

### Elianae

*Elianae has performed in the "Nutcracker" and various professional productions. In 2004, she studied the Art of Oriental Dance at Habeeba's Dance of the Arts where she is currently an instructor. She performs with the Troupe and as a soloist and has won many awards.*

**Habeeba's Instructors for the 2010 Ohio State fair. Author on the far right.**

# The Teacher-Student Relationship
## A Psychological Point of View

### by Izzah, PhD

The teacher-student relationship: When I first wrote on that subject in 2008, I was fascinated by the topic as I was then a dance student. About one year later, I decided to become a dance teacher! Well, I didn't really "decide", as I was pushed by my teachers to "fly with my own wings". I was also pulled by a really strong desire to dance, create choreography, discover my style and share my passion. Despite all the doubts and fears I felt at the beginning of my journey, I never regretted it.

But let me begin with how all of this reflection started. First, I must say I have an hypothesis: To better understand the relationship between a student and a teacher, we have to understand the psychological dynamic behind the very first relation we develop; the parent-child attachment relationship.

### Attachment

Attachment theory (John Bowlby, 1907-1990) describes how infants become attached to their parents so they can develop on an emotional and social level. When infants start to walk, they use their parents as a secure base for exploring, returning to the parent when needed. Infants will seek to stay near their parent, and they feel anxiety when the parent is away. It is Mary Ainsworth, a psychologist in the 1960's, who developed the concept of secure and insecure attachments. Today, psychologists recognized how attachment styles influence us all of our life, in our friendships and romantic relationships. I believe that attachment can also have an impact in a long term teacher-student relationship.

### Attachment Relationship in the Dance Class

Catherine Yelnik (2003) did her studies on how a school class influences a teacher. For me, her conclusions apply to dance classes as well. She said, "The teacher-student relationship is educational and intergenerational, very similar to families". In her opinion, "Education means to restrict, to impose, to manage, to assess and to sometimes take disciplinary actions" in both the teacher-student and parent-child relationship. She adds that it is in a secure relationship that the student will be ready to accept comments and advice on their performances and grow as performers (or, as dancers).

Being a learner inevitably comes with insecurities because the learner feels dependent on the teacher. Having a secure and warm relationship with the teacher enables the student to feel capable of going beyond the limits she imposes on herself. It takes trust to follow the direction shown by a teacher, which means teachers inherit an important responsibility. The teacher, like a parent, is responsible to give good direction to the student. The Association départementale Danse et musique de Maine-et-Loire (France, 2007) explains this idea well. They state the dance teacher has a great responsibility because teaching dance helps students discover and construct their bodies in a physical and social space, a bit like the construction of the personality.

## Dysfunctional Teacher-Student Relationships

Dysfunctional relationships… they happen everywhere, in dance studios as in families. We all know what I call the "sect phenomena": Teachers who prevent their students from leaving by any way possible. They present the outside world (meaning any other teachers) as dangerous or incompetent. They can also make the student believe she is not good enough, in order to unconsciously prevent her from becoming a professional (therefore becoming competition for her teacher). Those "dysfunctional parents" can act in various ways but they share one characteristic: If you leave them, you are condemned and banned. Sadly, this is a story I have heard too often.

Dysfunctional teacher-student relationships exist partly because nobody teaches the teachers how to teach! The teacher's financial concerns or personal insecurities can add to the problem. I also feel that narcissism can be a problem in teachers who are frustrated because they wanted to be a star but didn't achieve that. A student may also feel guilty about her skills in relation to her teacher and refuse to participate in a workshop or competition because she fears her teacher will feel sad or incompetent.

On another level, we can have another type of dysfunctional relationship: The cold and distant teacher. Some teachers are simply cold and cannot develop the secure relationship a lot of students need. There is also the reverse problem of teachers who are too friendly with their students. This is like the situation of parents who want to be friends with their kids. Friendship relationships are characterized by equality, so how can you hope to direct students and tell them what to do and not to do if you don't have the authority to lead and supervise them?

It would be so simple to say that students just have to choose the right teachers! But if, as a child, you developed a certain kind of relationship with a parent, you might continue to seek the very same kind of relationship as an adult because you are on known ground, even if it is a toxic territory. In every relationship, we can decide whether

to grow as a person. It might be easier to grow in a secure relationship, but perhaps you need to grow out of an insecure relationship. We all know people who grew up in bizarre families and become mature and loving. Sadly, we also know people whose families drove them to self-destructive behaviours.

As a teacher, I now understand how complex the teacher-student relationship is. We need trust to grow, and the teacher needs also to know when to let students follow their own path, just like a parent who has to know when they are needed, and when to take a step back. This takes sensitivity. Psychologists call this being in the "zone of proximal development| (ZPD)".

### The Zone of Proximal Development (ZPD)

Vygotsky (1896-1934) was a Russian psychologist who developed the ZPD concept. This zone consists of the gap between the current level of the student (what she is capable of doing) and the student's potential level, which we can hopefully see when she is under her teacher's guidance. When you are teaching in the ZPD, you are helping embryonic dance behaviours to emerge until the student understands and uses them by themselves. Teaching in the ZPD means to teach just a little bit beyond what the student can already do.

As parents, we encourage our babies to crawl, then to pull themselves up and stand, then to walk with the help of furniture, until they can finally walk alone! They look funny at first, but at that point walking becomes a behaviour that is in their own "repertoire" and they can do it on their own. Consider beginner students as baby dancers. In every baby dancer we meet, we must try to adapt our teaching to their ZPD so they can develop. There is no recipe here; we have to look, listen, and show them the way, and don't forget that the student-teacher relationship is always central to transmitting knowledge. The sensitive teacher knows how to listen and can analyse the student's body language: How many bad postures might be linked to emotional knots, lack of confidence or self-esteem? In those situations, students really need supportive teachers.

Being a student also means that the student must accept being observed and listen to the teacher's remarks. Lack of self-esteem can prevent the student from staying open to learning. The

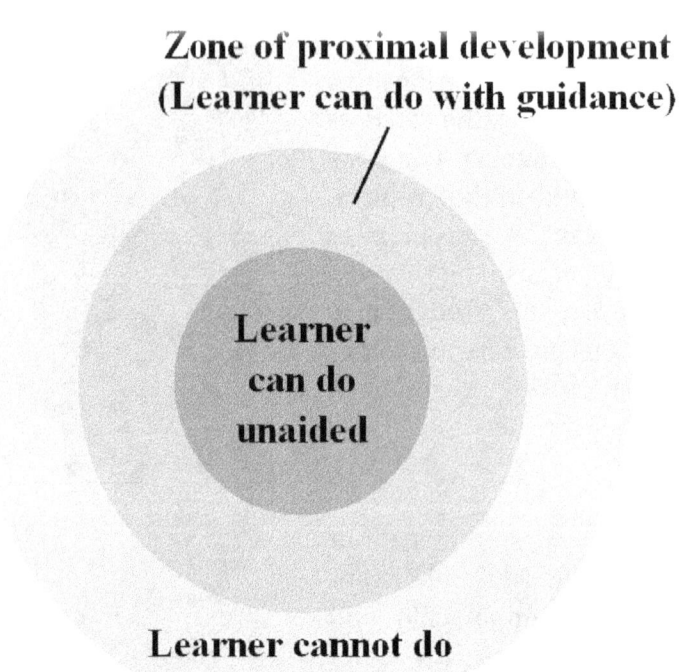

teacher must have the sensitivity to diagnose that kind of problem without putting down or hurting students who look unmotivated or uninterested. Self-esteem is essential to experiment with new things and try to achieve dreams.

## The Road to Autonomy

At the beginning of the relationship, the student often loves and admires her teacher, a bit like kids viewing their parents as the greatest and strongest in the world. Idealizing the teacher is a normal phase in student-teacher relationships. The teacher may also project a lot of hopes onto her students. Will they like me? Will they perform nicely? Will I be proud of them? Teachers often seek approval from their students, because how their students perform confirms their knowledge and competence.

Then the "teenage" years occur. This is a necessary step to maturity. In the student's mind, the teacher falls off her pedestal, and the fall can be hard if the student really idealized the teacher. In that stage, the teacher can feel abandoned and rejected, like some teenager's parents, and the student might learn some hard lessons through misadventures. (For example, "Wow, I am a star, this restaurant's owner told me to do this free audition..."). The teacher must remain solid and confident and accept that their job is almost done, but not quite finished. They must accept that others have influence on their "baby" and be there when the teen comes back home and needs some advice. As the student grows slowly into "adulthood" as an experienced dancer, the student-teacher relationship becomes less marked by authority and the student can even surpass the master. At the end, the teacher can watch with satisfaction as the butterfly emerges and flies toward its destiny.

## References

"Le métier de professeur de danse". Association Départementale Danse et Musique de Maine-et-Loire. February 2007. Internet article.

Yelnik, Catherine. "Face au groupe-classe". Thesis. University of Paris, 2003.

### Izzah

*Izzah is a Canadian belly dancer and psychologist. Izzah considers herself as a student who teaches, and a teacher who will never stop learning. She can't wait to connect with you and help you on your journey of discovering the belly dancer you were born to be!*

Artwork by Leela Corman

"Sula studied with Bert that first year for a minimum of 6 hour per week. By 1966 she was dancing at several clubs in and around Northern California, including the Baghdad in San Francisco, Zorba's in Sacramento and San Jose, Arabian Nights in Fresno, and more in the East Bay. In 1967 she opened the Belly Dance Navel Academy in Walnut Creek, teaching 4 classes per week. She later changed her studios name to "Sula's Belly Dance World", and it is still in business today at the original location under the name "Belly Dance!", run by a former student of Sula's, Leea Aziz." from Monica Berini's article on Sula on GildedSerpent.com

# Turning Pro
## From Hobbyist to Star to Teacher

*by Lauren Boldt*
*with commentary by Jillina*

It's over. You've been bitten. No longer satisfied with a weekly belly dance class at the "Y", you are now traveling across town for a more challenging class, back-to-back Intermediate and Advanced levels, twice-a-week. You practice hand waves when driving, shimmies at the sink, shoulder circles in the shower, and you break out compulsively into a giant hip circle at the grocery store as you grab something off the bottom shelf. It's obvious, you are desperately in need of a new creative dance outlet. It is time to take your obsession to the next level: It is time to go pro.

Being a professional belly dancer can be great. There is good money to be made and adventures to be had if you are willing, dedicated, and disciplined in your craft. In this article, I am going to reference some tips and tricks that I have learned as well as some lessons and anecdotes from my mentor, Jillina, that she acquired during her climb up the belly dance career ladder. Both Jillina and I hope that this serves as a reference for young dancers hoping to break into the scene as well as seasoned professionals expecting to "up" their game. It is important, depending on how much of your living that you need to earn from belly dance, that you diversify your income streams. I will go over two of the basic "jobs" belly dancers have: Teaching and performing on a local level, and also, I will cover breaking into the workshop and festival circuit.

## Getting the Gigs

Okay, you have been a student for a number of years. You have performed with your student group at your teacher's annual or perhaps monthly hafla. You feel confident in front of a crowd, and you think you are ready for a new challenge, but how do you know for sure? The best thing you can do is ask your teacher if he or she feels that you are ready to begin performing professionally or not. If your teacher is a competent teacher she will be honest and guide you in the right direction. There may be some habits you need to break, or a few more things you need to learn before you are ready to be in front of a paying audience.

Jillina says, "When I began belly dancing, I enrolled in a performance level class taught by Diane Webber. Each week, we were required to bring a costume, zills, veil, and arrive in appropriate hair-do and makeup to perform for our class and teacher. What a way to get over stage fright! It's either sink or swim when your teacher and classmates are watching you and tallying up criticisms. What a great learning experience! If any little thing was off, or sub-par, we heard about it, and learned how to fix it. This experience instilled in me a level of professionalism that advanced me to where I am today, and I am so grateful that my teacher had the guts to be so brutally honest and, at the same time, incredibly nurturing to all of our careers."

Once you know that your craft is at a professional level, and you are ready to break into the scene, wait! There is a strategy to consider here, and it is best to think before you pound the pavement, handing out business cards.

## Networking

Get to know your new colleagues. Haflas and open stages are a natural avenue to showcase your dance and your personality as well as to meet potential business contacts. Be sure that your performance piece is polished and perfected. Find out "who is who" and who is dancing where. Introduce yourself; let the other dancers know that you have been a student for X number of years and that you are interested in finding some gigs. You will be available to cover or enter into the rotation. While there are still a few clubs that feature resident dancers, most venues are booking from a group of approved dancers that rotate from week to week. Many times, a dancer is in charge of this rotation. (Perhaps, she will be able to recommend you to the club owner or manager who is in charge). Therefore, it is important to make a good impression on them.

This process takes time and dancers will want to get to know you before they send you out on gigs. In between your showcases, it is important to continue to train. Ask your teacher for advice or direction; you may need to visit a ballet class or two to improve your turns, grace, and upper body. You may need some yoga training to improve balance and breath. Whatever it might be, remain humble and open so that you are able to continue to grow and develop as a dancer.

Jillina's Comment: "Many dancers audition for my company, and while I see potential in them, they aren't quite ready for the level of our repertoire. My advice to them is to continue training, take ballet, jazz, or yoga (or whatever it is that they are lacking from their traditional routine) and I invite them to re-audition in a few months. It is important to me that my company dancers represent a high level of art and skill at our performances, but I also recognize each dancer's ability to grow and develop. I am so happy when I am able to cast a dancer who has been working diligently and is ready for her opportunity to dance!".

## Ring! Ring!...Cash Customer!
The phone rings, and you are needed to cover a gig. When you are asked to do the gig, you need to ask your client or colleague these things:

- What is the address for the gig?
- How many sets and what is the show time?
- What is the ethnicity of the audience?
- What is the occasion of the gig?
- CD, iPod or live music?
- Who's gig is it? If you are working for a dance company, you may be required to hand out only cards for the company that sent you. If you are covering a gig for a friend, she may or may not mind if you hand out your card to audience members or venue staff. Just be sure you clear the air before you go to the gig. Don't bite the hand that feeds you.
- What is the rate?
- Do you have to share tips with the management or band? Knowing these things before the gig will save you from confusion afterward.

Hopefully you are given more than 30 minutes notice and haven't just slipped into a relaxing bubble bath, but even if you have, its okay because you are prepared! Remember the five "Ps": Prior preparation prevents poor performance.

Here is a checklist you should use to be sure you are ready for the gig:

- **Makeup** - You have practiced your stage makeup and had a mentor critique and guide you. Be sure you practice the techniques for stage makeup, because very few of us are born with the ability to apply a smooth line of liquid eyeliner and false eyelashes. Practice before the gig so you are ready.

- **Hair** - Your hair needs to be big, healthy, clean, and shiny. If your hair is curly, go curly, or straight go straight, just don't go with bed head or helmet head. Arrive with hair and makeup completely done.
- **Costume** - Your costume needs to fit without the use of safety pins that can damage your expensive costume, or even fail. Do not be the dancer whose top popped open! If you are able to do 10 jumping jacks and keep everything in place, you should be good to go. If you can't do 10 jumping jacks without your knockers knocking around too much, go back to the drawing board. If you can't do 10 jumping jacks, go back to the gym anyway. Pack your costumes and props in a small sophisticated suitcase or bag and wear something nice, but conservative, to the venue. It seems obvious, but I have seen a dancer who showed up at a formal restaurant in jeans, carrying her costumes in a garbage bag! Showing too much skin before the show is not recommended. If the audience or staff is going to see you before your grand entrance, let it be in something professional and sophisticated; not too tight and not too bare. Build some mystery for the show, don't give the goods away too soon.
- **Music** - Find out the ethnicity of your audience. This is so important! Be sure that your play list has music that your audience will enjoy, appreciate, and relate to. It's a smart idea to run your music by your teacher or mentor and be sure you have different play lists prepared for different audiences so you are ready to perform for anyone. Bring all your play lists with you in case you show up to what you thought was an Arab audience, but turns out...oops! they are Persian. We all want to make it rain. The amount of precipitation is hugely influenced by the level of thought you put into your song choices.
- **Timing** - Be at the venue at least 15-20 minutes before showtime.
- **Warm-up** - Pack a yoga mat so you are able to warm-up back stage. This is so important, not only to prevent injury, but to ensure the best and most enjoyable experience for you and your audience.
- **Behavior at the gig** - Don't date, fraternize, franchise or fertilize with staff or customers. If you want to be a professional dancer, be a professional. If you want to be a socialite, be a socialite, just don't mix the two, the results are rarely pretty.

"I always tell my dancers to be polite and friendly, but tell staff or clients that they have to run to another gig across town after the show. It's an easy way to dismiss unwanted invitations without hurting egos and keeps up the appearance that they are busy and in demand", says Jillina.

## Pounding the Pavement

When the time is right, and you want to begin booking your own shows, here are somethings to keep in mind:

- **Rates** - Ask your colleagues and teachers what their rates are for nightclub or restaurant performances, weddings, and other private events. You are going to want to keep your prices at that range, at least. While we are eager when booking our first gigs, we may be tempted to low-ball a lot of prices in order to get the gig. Don't do it. Not only does this hurt everyone in the community by forcing them to compete with a cheaper price, you will soon find that in order to stay fresh and competitive, you will be investing a lot of your earnings into new costumes and more training. While you may think that you can make up for the difference through volume, there are only so many shows you can do in a night before you end up looking like the dancing dead. Dropping your rates is a downward spiral, don't get sucked into it! You are a professional dancer now, your training and experience is extensive; your costumes are expensive; you are a rare and unique gem. If the client is wanting to hire a dancer to perform at a party for 25 dollars, then they need to hire a 25 dollar dancer, not a 250 dollar dancer.

- **Marketing Materials** - Carefully consider the photo you choose for business cards and websites. They should be recent and representative of your look. Marketing materials should showcase your personality first, and highlight your physique second. Be sure that your photo is eye catching and memorable. I recommend having at least two photo shoots a year to keep your materials fresh and up to date.

At some point you will want to invest in a demo video. There is a lot of easy to use and inexpensive software available for video editing today, but if you are unsure about your skills, hire a professional. Your video does not need to be longer than 2 minutes and be sure that your contact info appears at the end of your video. A website and social networking presence are great materials to use for booking shows. Be sure that they are easy to navigate and easy to find. Also, look into running an ad in your local Middle Eastern newspaper (for whichever ethnic group you want to work); this can be a great way, especially during the holidays, to get your group seen by new potential clients.

## *Teaching*

Teaching is an art and a responsibility. Not all talented performers are skillful teachers, most people find they are more successful in one than the other, but many belly dancers find teaching and performing equally rewarding and equally necessary for their careers to remain viable.

How do you know if you are ready to teach? You might realize it because your friends and colleagues demand it, but a certain level of preparation needs to happen before the school bell rings. Many dancers offer teacher training sessions where you learn how to design a curriculum and

**When Lynette used this photo to advertise as a dancer in the Arab Yellow Pages, the only inquiries she received were from Arab men in the middle of the night not about a gig. This made her husband very upset and Lynette confused!**

how to present and build upon the basics. If you can't find any teacher training sessions near you, there is nothing wrong with approaching other successful teachers and asking to train with them privately.

"I started teaching when I needed some of my friends to cover a gig for me, and they insisted that they would only cover the gig if I started teaching them classes. I had never thought of myself as a teacher until this point, my focus had always been on learning and perfecting my craft. Today teaching makes up about 80% of my income from dancing but more than that, I find it is a beautifully rewarding way to share my passion with dancers in my community and around the world." says Jillina.

Here are some general rules to go by when you begin teaching:

- Have a plan of what you will teach. There is nothing wrong with jotting down some combinations that you want to do or having a breakdown of the class schedule. Glancing quickly at notes during the class is a lot better than staring at yourself in the mirror, trying to come up with a plan on the fly.

- Prepare your music. Don't waste time hunting for tracks in your 160 gig iPod, create a play list for your class that will flow through your topics that you plan to cover. If you plan your play list right, it will also help remind you when you were going to drill undulations vs. shimmies or stretches vs. across the floor.

- If possible, create handouts with some information on your topic. I would say this is a standard requirement for workshops and class series, optional for drop-in classes. Handouts are a great resource for your students to reference when they are practicing between classes. We all want to have amazing students, so make your knowledge available to them.

- Do your research. Our dance form has a geographical origin and within the styles that fall under the wide umbrella of "belly dance" many distinct ethnic groups are represented. Do yourself and students a favor by giving them a geographical reference for the styles you teach and the songs that you play in your class.

- Remember, students are there to have an experience with you. Try to connect with them. As the teacher, you set the tone for the room. Be enthusiastic, positive, open-minded, and prepared. Your students will become loyal and excited to escape along with you into the magical world of belly dance.

"Sincerely respect every one's motivation for joining your class. You may have professionals, hobbyists, people who come for a workout, dancers who come just to take photos with you, and dancers who show up in full costume for class. Everyone has her own reason for dancing; so don't judge it. Just enjoy the beauty of what the art of belly dance

**Yuvone, Sunny, Issa, and Tequila are tribal style dancers who competed and trained for 8 days in Jillina's Bellydance Evolution in Taipai, Taiwan.**

brings to people whether it is joy, healing, income, passion, education, self confidence - embrace it all!" says Jillina.

## Taking Over the World

You might be finding the pond you are in is shrinking, and in today's world with the benefits of the Internet and social networking, it would not be uncommon for you to develop fans and connections in different parts of the country and the world. The world can be a big and crowded place, but there are somethings you can do to navigate, manage, and claim your piece of the pie.

"When I started my international career, a big thing for me was producing the first instructional videos that I did with IAMED. This was at a time when there were relatively few products on the market; so I was fortunate to benefit from a lack of competition on the video shelf. At the same time, these videos were an opportunity for people all over the world to not only see my style, but also to get to know my personality. I believe this helped to increase demand for my workshops. Today, while there are many more products on the market, there are also many opportunities to self-produce and promote instructional and performance videos. With the Internet, you are able to distribute your product internationally for free or minimal cost. To be sure you stand out from the crowd, be certain your material is thoughtful and creative and your personality stands out as sincere, personal, and fun." says Jillina.

You can also look at your new international market as the same, only larger, as your local market. Visit festivals and sign up to dance on the open stage. Be sure you introduce yourself to the organizers of the event, and thank them for the opportunity to perform. Even if you weren't able to find them at the event, send an email with a link to your performance on their stage on YouTube. Take workshops with instructors you admire, and do your best to learn.

Look at opportunities as investments, and these investments as opportunities. You are going to have to take a weekend off work to travel and attend these festivals. Be sure you are prepared so that your 3.5 minutes on stage isn't wasted. Be sure to visit regional as well as national and international festivals if possible. There is nothing wrong with starting regionally and slowly increasing your market range.

Jillina says: "Most of all, continue to learn. Truly, one thing I believe is that you cannot remain stagnant in your dancing. You are either getting better, or you will be left behind. Constantly seek out new opportunities to learn, cross-train with other styles, continue to sharpen the saw on your principal style. The time you spend at home between gigs and travels should be spent investing in your potential."

When that opportunity comes knocking, be prepared with an agreement ready to go. Get an idea for workshop prices and rates. Ask your peers and teachers what you should charge for workshops. Some sponsors prefer working on a flat rate, some like to work on a percentage. If a sponsor wants to pay you by the hour, use a sliding scale based on the number of students that attend your workshop. If the sponsor wants to pay you a percentage of the net profit, keep in mind that expenses such as airfare and lodging will be taken out of your piece of the pie. If the sponsor offers you her guest room to keep costs low, especially when you are just starting out, you might want to take her up on the offer.

## Your Agreement Should -

- State how many workshops you will teach, what topics and the length of each workshop.
- If you will be performing in the gala show, be sure the contract states how many minutes your performance will be in how many sets.
- Clarify how you will be paid (whether its a flat hourly rate or percentage). Clarify what and when you will be paid (whether its in US dollars

or local currency, bank transfer, Paypal or cold, hard cash).

- Specify your technical needs for your workshop and performance. This means if you need a CD player or iPod connection for sound, a 15 foot stage and follow spot, or a translator for your workshops.
- Specify your hospitality needs such as, a light snack between workshops or a dressing room with your name on it, and a chilled bottle of Perrier between shows. Breakfast is standard in many contracts, while dinner may be optional.

Keep in mind, especially when starting out, that a huge list of luxury requirements in your contract might be viewed as discouraging by a sponsor who is hiring you. If you are "Jane Bellydancer" and require a specific brand of orange juice and a bottle of Dom Perignon waiting for you as you check in at the Four Seasons, you are likely to not get the gig. At the same time, it is important to be clear about what you need to perform. If you are offered a contract to teach in a foreign country, you need to be sure that you will be in a safe hotel and will have a translator or assistant available to help you get to and from venues and to and from the chow hall. Most sponsors want to be hospitable and want to be sure that you enjoy your time with them; we are all belly dancers after all. Just be sure that your contract is clear, fair, and professional, and you will likely form a lasting relationship with your sponsors.

No matter what level of fame and success you achieve in belly dance, the most important thing to remember is your passion and that your love for the dance and fellow dancers comes first. As a dancer you are serving the community, bringing joy, opening hearts and minds, allowing people to escape the ho-hum of everyday life and enjoy something beautiful. As a teacher you are transforming everyday people into dancers, teaching them to enjoy music, movement and the wonderful feelings we get when our bodies know how to move well. You are giving women (and men) an opportunity and an outlet to express themselves, to be proud of their bodies, to enjoy moving to music and to connect with culture.

"Take pride in your work and keep in mind your teaching can make a big impact on young dancers. Be diligent in your research so that you are not only a good choreographer but also a good educator. You may be influencing a whole new generation of dancers and this is a huge responsibility not to be taken lightly.

The last piece of advice is to be true to who you are as an artist. Whether you love Folkloric dance, Egyptian, or Tribal, follow where your heart takes you, and whatever inspires you. However, take the time to familiarize yourself with the history, movements, and terminology of the other belly dance styles so that you can be a well rounded and knowledgeable teacher in the art of belly dance." - Jillina

***Jillina and Lauren***
*Jillina and Lauren both live in Los Angeles and have worked together in Jillina's company: The Sahlala Dancers, The Bellydance Superstars and Jillina's latest project: Bellydance Evolution. Jillina has produced and starred in a dozen instructional videos. Lauren received a Bachelors in Professional Music from Berklee College of Music.*

AUTHENTIC MIDDLE EASTERN entertainment is featured nightly at the Fez supper club on Vermont at Sunset. Headling the popular nitery's new entertainment policy is Damascus-born belly dancer Antoinette Awayshak. The orchestra features Shuckri Barham on the Oud, Lou Shelby on the Tambourine, Lemi Pascha on the Kanoon, Majid Harb on the Durbuckee and Najeeb Khoury on the Oud.

# A Boomerang Career
## Life & Dance in the Land Down-Under

### by Amera

### Becoming a Performer

I lived for my life as a professional Belly dance performer! It was how I made my living; for 2 decades beginning in the 1980s, I worked my way from newly opened Middle Eastern nightclubs in Sydney, Australia, to some of the best hotels and nightclubs in the Middle East. When Rozeta Ahaleyas took me under her mentoring wing and groomed me to become a professional belly dancer, there were no belly dance classes in Sydney. It was a profession and not a hobby for the handful of belly dancers that worked in nightclubs in Sydney. Our working week was the better part of 4 days with 8 to 10 shows a night. It was not unusual to arrive home in time to watch the sunrise at the end of a night of work.

### Classes

Some of the dancers started group classes for women during the week at evening colleges, church halls, and women's gatherings. Some dancers did it just to teach and others wanted to train new performers, as there weren't enough dancers to satisfy the amount of work available! In the early days, classes were not targeted primarily for their exercise value. That came much later when dancing for fitness became popular.

In the beginning, we didn't have a syllabus. We made up names for moves, developed our own techniques and asked our bodies what felt comfortable, but more importantly, we did what the music told us to do. In those days, dressing up and looking the part of the exotic Middle Eastern woman in class, was a big part of coming to class. These days it's Lycra and hip scarves!

### Amera's Palace and Performances Overseas

When I left school after struggling to commit to an education at Fashion Design College, I eventually decided that we needed a place to be able to buy dance supplies, so "Amera's Palace Belly Dance Boutique" was born in 1987.

The nightclubs in which I danced on the weekends were closed during the weekdays, so my stage became my platform for teaching, but that didn't last long. The call of the Middle East nightclub scene was too strong for me. I wanted to live the experience and find out what it was really about!

In the late 1980s and early 1990s, with a suitcase-full of costumes, a one way air ticket, and $100 in my pocket, I boarded a plane to Beirut and arrived around the end of their recent civil war; a foreign dancer among the nouveau Lebanese dancers. I met a popular Lebanese agent that led me to contracts in 5-star hotels around the Middle East and beyond. It was ground-breaking territory for a girl from Australia, catapulting me into the Middle East dance scene at a fast pace. This was the world in the pre-Internet era. Contracts came to me by Telex machine, and fax machine; a new invention then!

### Fast-forward to 2000

Years of high-level performing, and the inevitable fact of my growing older, took a toll on my body. Where did a full time professional Belly dancer go from here? The obvious choice seemed to be to become a full-time belly dance teacher.

I was lucky that the business in which I had started with nothing in 1987, had been left in the capable hands of Leonie Sukan and had grown into an iconic place! I was able to slip back into the boutique side of things. I had new and alluring contacts for costumers and suppliers from Egypt. I set out to make Amera's Palace into a one-stop hub for all the budding belly dancers coming from the many belly dance schools established while I was on my journey overseas.

Studying belly dance was at its peak in Australia in the early 2000s. Some students wanted to be professional performers, and some wanted to be teachers, starting classes in their own suburbs. Mainstream women wanted to try belly dance and some freely gave themselves the titles "belly dance teacher" and/or "belly dancer". It was always an eyebrow-raiser when you told someone at your day job that you enrolled in belly dance classes. Now, in 2012, these same people come back to the day job and declare that they do pole-dancing or burlesque without the suspicions; so most eyebrows have been laid to rest by now!

### Retired Performer and Beginner Teacher

Now I was a retired professional belly dance performer, so I decided my market was to teach the dance; an easy transformation, right? Initially, I found it somewhat difficult. Eventually, other belly dancers flocked to my workshops and classes to learn the new dances from the Middle East. I was the first to teach Khaleegy dancing in Austrailia, which I learned from my years of Arabian Gulf contracts.

In Egypt, I had also learned Malaya/Eskanderany and other folkloric styles that I was the first to teach in Sydney. These Middle Eastern dances from Egypt like "Eskanderany" (Egyptian term meaning Alexandrian) are character dances and easy for people to learn. Additionally, I was the first to teach the modern Egyptian style in Sydney that I had learned from my classes with Raqia

Hassan; I found it easy to choreograph this style to Arabic pop songs.

How do you teach someone to dance to music that is foreign to their ears? How do you teach them to feel and to lose themselves and become one with the music? What a challenge was ahead for me! I hoped to be a teacher who was skilled enough to pass on this knowledge to my students. I was always confident on a stage in front of thousands as a professional dancer; so why did a room full of students make me feel less self-assured?

I started to think of myself as a dancer from the "old school", because most of the new dancers who came on the scene more recently were fusing styles, not using Arabic music, and bringing multiple props into their dance. I love watching innovation and styles that some say is the future of the belly dance, but it just wasn't my pedigree! I came from an era that wanted to connect to the audience from its root level, to talk to their souls, to make them experience Tarab (passion in music), let them feel what I'm saying with my dance, and share a quick glimpse into my soul. I wanted to share the moment that I connect to the music.

I started to question my dance repertoire: What steps did I dance? How did I move from that move to the next? How did my movements take place, particularly: Sequences of the melody - or rhythmic beat? I really didn't know. I danced and my body was "just there". I surrendered to the singer or an inner knowledge of a particular piece of music. How did I intuit the music? My body tried to connect with my logical thinking, and I

was afraid I was going to lose what came to me naturally!

Things I found challenging when I transformed from professional belly dance performer to a belly dance teacher:

- Loosing myself to the music; I have students in the room who are watching, and they will ask me, "What did you just do? Break it down!". I had never danced to the same music the same way the second time around; if you asked me to repeat a performance with the same steps, I guarantee that I would change what I had done a minute before!
- Trying to convey my feeling to the student: How can I teach someone to exhibit emotion? My emotional journey with the music will always be different from yours; that's guaranteed!
- Concerning choreography, a process new to me initially: My method was to "hear and just dance". I had learned to dance my beginning steps in a "follow me" fashion, and I had never notated my dance for my own stage. I had always chosen and had music written for me (or existing music, re-arranged for me). How do I choreograph music to suit myself or for someone I hardly know?
- While looking at a group of people, I thought: All of these people are so individual! How do I give them some of what I perform and make it their own?

To me it's a group of people standing at a shelf in a supermarket with rows and rows of the same ingredient on the shelf. They will buy that ingredient, take it home, put it in their own recipe, and make it their own. I'm just like an ingredient on the shelf: Take what I give you, make it your own, and make your dance unique.

I have succumbed to teaching choreography! It works the best in a group setting, but students don't use choreography as a frame-work in belly dance and add their own flavor. Too many students take the choreography and dance it from start to finish without adding any of their own personality into it!

I remember taking my first Egyptian private class with Ibrahim Akef in Egypt 1994. He told me "Stand at the back of me, and follow me" then he turned around and said "OK! Now Dance!". He was most proud when you took some of his direction and not his own personal reflection of the music and meaning: He gave me a framework and steps for a majensi (entrance dance) but if I didn't add my own flow, nuances, and emotion, he would start screaming: "No! No! No!". Professional Dancers are entertainers who must feed off an audience's chemistry. When there is no audience, it is difficult to dance; so the student has to come next to me and learn from me."

How does one progress from stage to classroom? My answer came to me after seemingly endless streams of students, workshops, and meeting the most amazing people who have accepted "the call to Belly Dance" into their lives. I found my answer by spending time with them, watching their growth. I see them discover that inexplicable thing that belly dancers are... I am grateful to all the wonderful women that came and still come to me, allowing me to teach and pass my knowledge on to them. I watch them now: Beautiful, graceful, popular and strong performers, and realize that I owe them my gratitude.

**Amera Eid**
*Amera Eid is a well known Australian belly dancer of Egyptian and European background. She began her rise to fame in 1990, soon reaching international stardom. Amera returned to Australia, continuing as a professional belly dancer and managing her own belly dance boutique and school. She currently focuses on teaching, hosting international workshops, and producing belly dance albums.*

## It Ain't Easy Being the Crone
### by Shelley Muzzy ~ Yasmela

The move from student to dancer to teacher is logical. It follows a pattern that has been set down for learning any craft or art. We all start as novices, beginners, and move in a path from A to Z. At Z, we are considered masters. We work, we teach and we retire, but as I have discovered, that path is not linear, nor is it logical, especially when applied to belly dance.

I can't seem to get this compelling dance and music out of my life. I stepped into a dance studio on Presidio Street in San Francisco in 1972 and when Jamila Salimpour took her place in the center of a huge circle of women, I was hooked. What began as curiosity became a lifelong passion. It was also the beginning of my education about the music, dance and history of the Middle East, North Africa and Central Asia. I obtained a BA in History and Research, and organized a formal belly dance program at the University, all in order to indulge my obsession.

I consider myself a "retired" dancer. Or maybe I am just tired. I quit performing and took myself off the stage in the late 1980's. In 1996, when my eldest daughter launched her dance studio, I returned to teaching. Things had changed while I was busy living life. The clubs in which most dancing took place when I began classes in the '70's had disappeared. There was less live music around but more dancers. Video tapes of dancers abounded. You didn't even need a live teacher, and then there was the internet! I was confused when new students asked me what I taught.

"I teach belly dancing."

"No, I mean, what style do you teach? Cabaret or tribal?"

"I didn't know there was a difference. I teach basic technique and at the end of the class I introduce some folk styles."

What was this whole tribal thing? Which tribe? What country? I loved the exotic costumes I had seen on the dancers who called themselves Tribal, but their dance confused me. The steps looked vaguely familiar, but the arms were different and there was no floor work. It looked very serious, and someone told me it was all based on "cues", not choreography.

On the other hand, cabaret dancers didn't play finger cymbals or do floor work! I was an Edsel in a BMW world. I was obsolete, old fashioned, out of step. I heard my style described as not only old, but wrong. Apparently all the women I had danced with or seen in the clubs 20 years ago had been doing it wrong and didn't know it. Now it was all Egyptian and lots of shimmies. I have to admit, the first time I saw an Egyptian dancer in bicycle shorts and a sports bra I was horrified. The new dancers I saw looked suspiciously like they had taken several years of ballet. After spending years learning to relax and center over my heels, everyone was pulling up and centering over their toes. I felt like Rip Van Winkle. Or had I been beamed up into another time dimension?

Despite my confusion, I persevered. I studied some videos, went to see some of the new dancers coming up through the ranks, created some choreographies and combinations, and voila! I was teaching again. My classes were full and I enjoyed teaching more now that I was "out of the game", not competing for jobs with my students, not focused on my career. I had something to give and a real desire to impart some of the truths I discovered on my dance journey; truth about technique, musicality, humility and responsibility.

Do I sound bitter? Angry? Yup, you bet I do. There are times when I feel neglected and forgotten. I don't perform and so I seldom am asked to do workshops or come and teach outside of my own community. Lately I gave up regular classes altogether. I still have a competitive spirit. Of course, I deny this, but let's face it, who doesn't want to stand on stage and be worshipped? I can say I am altruistic about the dance, that what I do has no ego in it, but that is a lie. Like everyone, I want to feel loved, heard, important. I want all those years of dance classes, of scrambling to get the gig, to be on stage, to mean something, and not just to myself, but to others as well. I can't go back and change the dance I learned. I can't know everything new that comes along. I don't want to be the dancer who uses a trowel and spackle to put on her makeup, who wears a neck to ankle body stocking and pads her sagging ass to shore it up and look perky again. I get tired of having to wear long sleeves to disguise my batwings, and honestly ladies, I may understand my dance better now than I did at 30, but I am an older woman. No amount of praise and compassion will make me look great in a bedlah. When I started classes, Jamila had just retired from the stage, and I thought she was wonderful. I didn't need to see her dance to know she had a lot to teach me. Wise women know it's better to leave them wanting more and bask in the remembered glory of your dancing, than to take the stage and remove all doubt that you are past your prime. The bonus of doing this is that your mystique, your beauty and proficiency grow with each passing year. I am a much better dancer in other people's memories. But who among us really wants to leave?

What conclusions can I draw for you? None. I am still sorting all of this out. What is my role? I don't know. I want to be involved in our community in some way. Thank god I studied writing and English at university. I can still write scathing opinions, but when that heavenly music starts, something makes me wave my arms around and shake my shoulder a little and cast a coy eye at the furniture. This behavior doesn't look as cute as it did when I was young, but it is in my blood. I don't care about a lot of the things that inspire hot debate among younger dancers, like, what was the first original belly dance move, or, should we call it belly dance, or when did it all start. I know when it started for me, and how it felt on stage, surrounded by my wonderful band and my fellow dancers. I know how much I want to take young dancers in hand and show them how it's done, and I know how hard it is to be marginalized, dismissed and forgotten for the flavor of the day.

But don't worry, you're right behind me, because that is the way life works. So I do know some things you don't know, but I ain't tellin'.

*Shelley Muzzy ~ Yasmela*
*Shelley serves as an editor and advisor for the Gilded Serpent. She was the founder of the Bou-Saada Dance Troupe and has been dancing and teaching since 1972. Shelley holds a BA in History and Research from Fairhaven College/Western Washington University with a concentration on the Middle East and North Africa.*

**Above: Zelina started dancing after having three children and has now been performing for over 3 decades. She is currently planning her 8th trip to Cairo. She enjoys showing the world that you can perform this dance your whole life.**

**Previous page: Shelley, the author on left, Her troupe Bou-Saada on the right.**

Lynette Harper and Rahma Haddad, granddaughters of 1st cousins from Lebanon, share the joy of dance, in Vancouver in the early 80's. Joy becomes ecstasy as Lynette Harper, seen here above, on left at 56 and Rahma Haddad at 64, dance the finale of "Bekaa Valley Girls" a narrative exploring their entwined histories; Vancouver's Dance Centre, 2010.

**The Simoom by Ludwig Hans Fischer**

# Section 3
# HISTORY

Since the earliest days of GildedSerpent.com, there has been an ongoing dialog about the origins and history of Middle Eastern belly dance. Numerous articles have been written by independent scholars and academics contributing to our growing body of historical knowledge.

The following essays reflect the most current themes in today's research across a broad spectrum of disciplines. Contributing authors include historians, journalists, feminists, cultural anthropologists and dance ethnographers. History is not an immutable topic, but rather reflects newly unearthed data and reanalysis of long standing facts.

Enjoy this collection of essays and many more in the Gilded Serpent archives- GildedSerpent.com

## "Harem Girls"
### Dance in Historical Harems, Early 1700s-Early 1900s

**by Andrea Deagon PhD**

In the last years of the 18th century, Charles Nicolas Sigismond Sonnini de Manencourt, already a renowned explorer and collector of oddities, traveled through Egypt at the behest of the French government, and reported back the remarkable depravity he found there. Although, as a foreign man, he had never been admitted to a harem, he had little trouble speaking with impassioned authority about this dreadful failing of Islamic life, a place "where beauty languishes, prey to many vices". "These women visit each other frequently. Their conversations are not always noted for their decency and modesty. The total lack of any education or morals, the laziness and the wealth in which they spend their days; the relentless constraint under which they are held ...all of this helps to direct their fiery imagination, their desires, their conversation towards one end...". He meant sex, of course. Their frustrated passion, Sonnini assured his readers, led women of the harem to various acts of degeneracy too shameful to name.

Sonnini's account, like many other early descriptions of harems by Western travelers, presented men with a titillating fantasy: Rooms full of sensuous, sex-starved women, all for the pleasure of a single man! A hidden display of naked beauties, bathing, smoking opium and massaging one another! How shameful! How disgusting! How pleasant to contemplate!

As the 19th century progressed, the visual arts whetted the appetite for this particular sexual fantasy. Odalisques (the term we use for these fantasy harem women, derived from the Turkish word for a female attendant, odalik) and harem scenes became a popular subject. Exhibited at the prestigious Paris Salon, a juried exposition of the best paintings of the year, or in other elite venues, many of these delicious visions were then reproduced in popular magazines and circulated widely. You could think of them as a form of high-class, artistically impeccable pin-ups, coming from magazines that you could claim to be reading "for the articles."

**The Turkish Bath
by Jean Igres**

What lovely visions they were! Odalisques reclined half-naked on divans, looking sultry. (Often a little vacant too; perhaps it was the opium they were smoking as sometimes depicted). They received massages from darker-skinned servants while their casually discarded clothing lay heaped on the floor. (How sweet it would have been to see them take it off!) They indulged in naked music making, though the most decorous of them could be seen clothed in exotic splendor, lounging in the kind of luxuriant surroundings a harem would surely contain. A few even read books. However, mostly they arranged themselves in seductive poses. One of the most famous harem paintings is Jean-Auguste-Dominique Ingres' "The Turkish Bath", 1862. Its round frame gives the viewer a sense of looking through a keyhole at the dozens of naked women lounging in the baths. Across the room, there's even a dancer, up on her tippy-toes like a ballerina, or perhaps an ancient Greek sculpture. In any case, anyone who wanted to see naked dancing, which was not as readily available in the 19th century as it is today, would have found at least a tickle of pleasure from this vision of Turkish excess.

It goes without saying that none of these painters had been anywhere near the harems they illustrated. These paintings are so clearly sexual fantasies that I'm not completely convinced that their audiences thought, in their heart of hearts, that they were really accurate depictions of what went on in the average Arab home when the men were away. With very few exceptions, in these paintings the men were most definitely away! Harem scenes were women-only, with no Arab studs to detract from the Western viewer's voyeuristic insertion of himself into the scene. The prospect of naked lounging could also have titillated the sexual imaginings of women trained by corsets to rigid posture and breathless self-restraint, who might have delighted in lounging, at least in their imaginations, in circumstances like these.

These Orientalist paintings are, of course, the artistic precursors to the "harem dance-off" of later days. However, they weren't like this in the beginning: They were more properly the vigorous mid-life of this satisfying fantasy. The beginnings of the classic harem fantasy developed in the 16th and 17th centuries, when Western travelers and traders first made extensive contact with the Ottoman Empire. The Empire arose in Turkey but had expanded far into the Middle East and even probed its grasping fingers into Europe (as the Europeans might have conceived it). Unlike the other Middle Eastern countries, Egypt and Algeria in particular, where belly dance was witnessed and described later, Turkey was never colonized by Europeans, and perhaps that was why it was so important to demonize the Turks by exposing their supposed degeneracy. Our Western prurient images were not solely based on the readings of the Ottoman court. Sonnini's evocatively erotic condemnation of harems, for example, resulted from his Egyptian travels, but the Ottoman Imperial Harem has provided

**The Pasha and his Harem by Le'Paulle**

the most influential image of a powerful Sultan surrounded by sexually eager concubines; so I'm going to start picking at the seams of this particular fantasy.

One of the most sensational accounts of the Ottoman court to make it to Europe, Histoire Genéral du Serrail, was written by M. Baudier, who had traveled to Turkey to establish trade relations with sources of Eastern luxury goods. The 1626 publication of his account of his adventures there features woodcuts purporting to show the goings-on in the Sultan's harem. The enormously-turbaned Sultan (he even wore it to bed, apparently) is portrayed surrounded by his many concubines in pleasurable activities. In one of the scenes, they are dancing for him, although it looks more like playing "Ring-Around-the-Rosy" than belly dancing. He looks pleased with himself, the lone man amidst the nearly identical women who entertain him and, it appears, give him sponge baths too. Over time, the stories of the Sultan's degeneracies only grew more outrageous, as he evolved into the exemplar of a morally weak and petty despot supported by a nation of helpless slaves who lacked the initiative to seek or even conceive of freedom. (How nice that we Europeans were so different!)

Yet there was some truth behind the fervid fantasy. There really was an Ottoman Sultan, who actually did have a huge number of concubines, and who might have been despotic. In reality, there were eunuchs guarding the women's quarters, and the women of the Imperial Harem, at least the elite among them, didn't leave it. Truly, there were bitter rivalries in harems, and subtle, yet violent, power plays; although these were about whose son was in line to positions of power rather than who got to be the Sultan's love toy. The harem actually contained fair-skinned European women "pleasuring their dusky captors." There were women whose special duty in the harem was to dance for the Sultan, and there were surely occasions in which dance skills brought the Sultan's attention to a particularly promising future concubine.

**Hamida Banu Begam, 'Maryam Makani' (1527–1604) was a wife of the second Mughal Emperor, Humayun**

All the same, our Sultan-centered harem fantasies said more about our inability to understand the complexities and power dynamics of foreign royal courts than it did about the actual nature of life within the harem, which was quite different from the hotbed of luxuriant, opium-laced languor and oozing sexuality that we enjoyed envisioning. In fact, as the historian Leslie P. Pierce observed: "the Imperial Harem was really more like a convent than the sexy holding tank of Western fantasy."

Perhaps "bureaucracy" might be a better description as another Islamic court showed. The 16th century memoir of Gulbadan Banu Begum, daughter of the Babur, the first King of the Moghuls (a group originating in Turkistan that conquered much of the Indian subcontinent), describes the Moghul harem in some detail, and rank and order were far more important than who slept with whom in its daily functions.

The Ottoman Imperial Harem, too, was a well-ordered place, and its founding principle was not the imprisoning of sexually desirable women, but the more general mandate that the elite of the Sultan's household and court were protected from the mundane world by a concentric circle of attendants and assistants, with increasingly fewer admitted the closer one got to the royal family.

Bearing in mind that the Sultanate changed over the long period of its dominance (from the 14th century through the early 20th), this is how it worked in a nutshell:

Over time, there were several palaces. They had a men's side and a women's side. The men's side was organized in concentric rings around the Sultan. The juvenile pages and eunuchs who were allowed in his inner domain were not "men" in the fullest sense, being too young or lacking some of the genital features that supposedly defined manhood. In concentric circles around this inner sanctum, there were various levels of officials and attendants, with the men of each successive layer allowed a little less further into the Sultan's domain.

Then there was the women's side. From fairly early on, the women of the harem were all slaves, because it was considered politically foolish for the Sultan to marry into a Turkish aristocratic family that might challenge his power. Like the pages on the men's side, women of the harem were chosen for their physical perfection and potential talents. (At the time of their purchase, you could legitimately call them "harem girls"). A strict hierarchy reigned within the harem: At its top was the Sultan's mother, with the princesses and upper-echelon managers following. Indeed, the Sultan did have many concubines, and it was probably their beauty and the sparkle of their personalities that attracted him, but did they exert any actual influence over him? Rarely. Early accounts of palace finances show us that the average concubine's luxury allowance was substantially below that of some of the other harem women. What bumped up a concubine's stipend, and possibly put her in a position to influence the Sultan, was bearing him a son. Too bad for the harem "dance-off"! It turns out that maternity, rather than sexual succulence, is what gave a concubine her clout.

Once brought into the harem, girls were steered into separate and specific career tracks, according to their talents and beauty. Those who were considered excellent enough to be potential concubines were educated in all the social graces and held to a strict standard of behavior which, according to one insider, meant no dancing, at least where anyone could see it. Reasonably enough, although disappointingly for those enamored of Orientalist harem scenes, in the Sultan's court, as in its European equivalents, elegant behavior and manners were considered more desirable amongst the courtiers closest to the center of power than a propensity for opium-fogged naked lounging.

From among the not-quite-as-promising (yet, still undoubtedly pleasing) harem women, those with the appropriate talents were chosen for training in music and dance or other courtly capabilities that would enable them to entertain the Sultan, his concubines, and his daughters. Promising pages on the men's side received this sort of training as well. Other girls, who were more talented in administration than other arts, grew up to be high-ranking bureaucrats, with considerable power within the harem, and possibly second-hand influence outside of it. Essentially, however, the majority of the girls of the harem were servants, whether they were the "scrub the floor" kind or the "attend the mistress while looking attractive" kind.

Contrary to the image of the frustrated harem girl aging in sexless obscurity, many of the harem occupants did eventually leave for marriage in the outside world. In fact, those who had been selected for education in court manners, as long as they did not actually become the Sultan's concubines, often were married to former pages who had graduated to less privileged, but longer-lasting, positions in the state bureaucracy.

This is a bit of a letdown - if imprisoned, erotically postured women are your cup of tea, and the sex-starved harem "where even the cucumbers are served sliced" exerts a pull on your imagination - and if, indeed, that's where it pulls. However, this was the real context in which harem belly dance was performed, and it was probably performed with a refinement and style very different from the one performed publicly that was described by those Western visitors who didn't make it into the Imperial Harem – which is to say, all of them.

Since most of the evidence for the training of dancers and their roles in the Imperial Harem comes from later periods, I'll address that subject later in this article, but for now, I'll focus on the year 1717, when we get the first true description of belly dance in a harem. A woman wrote it of course.

**Lady Mary Wortley Montagu with her son Edward Wortley Montagu and attendants by Jean Baptiste Vanmour**

## The Perpetual Masquerade

Today is best known for her role in introducing the Western world to inoculation against smallpox, after she had seen it practiced by women in Turkish harems and taken the radical step of inoculating her own children. She is appreciated in academic circles for her literary talents, which included a knack for satiric poetry, and culminated in her influential account of her experiences in the Ottoman court. In her own time, she was known for her wit and intelligence (she had taught herself Latin at an early age), her petite, graceful, dark-eyed beauty that presumably, made up for her excessive education and, rather scandalously, for her romance-novel escape from an unwanted marriage to the improbably named Clodsworthy Skeffington, by her elopement with a suitor her father had rejected previously. Her husband and partner in the scandal, Edward Wortley Montagu, took her (at age 26) to Turkey a few years later when he was sent to the Ottoman court as ambassador.

She never made it into the Imperial Palace – either side of it. Rumors that her second son was the love child of Achmet II were completely fanciful, as there is no indication that she ever even saw the Sultan.

In any case, she was already pregnant when she got to Turkey. Lady Mary managed to interview a woman who had lived in the harem for many years. This elegant lady exploded a number of popularly held Western myths, but also told her that "Sometimes the Sultan diverts himself in the Company of all his Ladies, who stand in a circle around him," and she confessed that they were "ready to dye with Jealousie and envy of the happy. She that he distinguished by any appearance of preference." Lady Mary concluded, with equal measures of insight and naivete, that "this was no different from the fawning on Kings observable in European courts".

She also visited a hammam, or bath house, and was quite impressed with the elegance of the naked women therein. Not quite daring to join them – even an elopement had cost her several years of ostracism from London society, so what might public nudity do? She offered the stays beneath her gown as an excuse for her reticence. The sympathetic Turkish women assumed they were a sort of extended chastity-belt forced upon her by a cruel husband.

Nudity was all right in the hammam, but in day-to-day dealings, the low and expansive décolletage of European fashion offended the sensibilities of Turkish women, so it was Lady Mary's diplomatic duty to have Turkish clothing made for herself. When these garments arrived, she was in ecstasy over their beauty, and raved to her sister about her rose damask drawers brocaded with silver flowers, her gauzy blouse with "the shape and color of the bosom very well to be distinguished through it," her form-fitting anteri, an outer garment of gold damask with long falling sleeves, her caftan of the same rose damask as her drawers, and her diamond-clasped belt. If her later portraits are any indication, she splurged on a number of such outfits.

However, adventurous spirit that she was, she soon realized that it was not primarily exotic delight, nor diplomacy, nor even comfort, that dressing "a la Turque" offered. It was freedom. In her comparatively streamlined Turkish clothing, wrapped in a face-veil and the all-encompassing outer wrap, the ferigee, she could become completely anonymous. She could, therefore, go anywhere. Who was to know? "This perpetual masquerade," she said, "gives [Turkish women] entire Liberty of following their Inclinations without danger of Discovery." Where Turkish women, she saw, might be able to carry on extra-marital affairs without constraint, she herself was more interested in exploration. Alone, mercifully eluding the 24 footmen who solemnly accompanied her even to quiet lunches with the French ambassador's wife, she explored Adrianople, indistinguishable from other women just as anonymous as she. Nowhere else had she encountered such exhilarating freedom. "Upon the whole," she wrote to her sister, "I look upon the Turkish Women as the only free people in the Empire."

She had been in Adrianople, where the Sultan kept his summer court, for only two months when she received a surprise invitation to dinner from the wife of the Sultan's Grand Vizier. It was quite a coup, as this was "an Entertainment that was never given before to any Christian." Comfortable as she was in her Turkish clothing, she suspected that one reason for this prestigious invitation was that the Lady wanted to see the oddity of European pomp and circumstance, and she determined to play the role of the English ambassador's wife to the hilt. The most ornate – and indeed ridiculous – clothing she had was the outfit she had been obliged to wear when she and Edward had stopped at the Viennese court, which she had described to her sister as "more monstrous and contrary to all common sense and reason than it is possible for you to imagine." The enormous skirt was so stiff with whalebone petticoats that Viennese women had to negotiate a ballroom like bumper cars, but while the lower body virtually disappeared beneath the surreal skirt, the bodice was laced very tight, and pressed the breasts into apple-like protrusions in an impressive show of décolletage. To complete the bizarre effect, one's hair had to be teased up into an edifice Lady Mary had described as leaving one's head "too large to go into a moderate Tub."

Strapped into her bodice, hampered by expansive yards of stiffened skirt, and burdened by the sheer weight of the costume, she could barely move without the assistance of an attendant to carry her substantial train. Of course, sitting with her feet tucked up on a divan (as the delightful young Turkish noblewoman whom she met later that night would do) would have been completely impossible. However - anything for diplomacy! Once strapped into this "machine," she ditched her entourage and, with only her interpreter and train-carrier, she escaped into the streets.

The dinner was a dead bore. The Grand Vizier's wife was an older woman, devoted to religion and good works. After a painfully protracted meal, an entertainment of music and dancing was offered, but it was hardly "Arabian Nights". A group of women, chosen from the array of attendants who were the lady's only extravagance, played music and danced, "which they did with their Guitars in their hands." Their hostess apologized for their lack of skill; undoubtedly due to her religious devotion, she took "no care to accomplish them in that art."

Having put in several tedious hours, Lady Mary was ready to go straight home, as anyone in a dress like hers would be. However, her Greek interpreter urged her to pay a visit to another important lady, the wife of the Kahya, an influential officer in the Sultan's court. Lady Mary protested, but in the end, luckily for her and for us, she went. Here, in the harem that Fatima, the Kahya's wife, had lovingly designed for her own pleasure, Lady Mary finally found the Arabian Nights glamour for which she had hoped.

Moving from outside through the layers that led inward to the mistress's domain, she was first admitted by a pair of black eunuchs, then escorted to a receiving line of beautiful young attendants. Passed by them into the harem's succulent center, she found herself in a pavilion shaded with ornamental trees and blossoming with the heady scents of honeysuckle and jasmine. The rush of a free-flowing fountain permeated the air. Awaiting her on the raised, room-length platform that the Turks called a "sofa", the lady Fatima reclined on three layers of Persian carpets with her young daughters seated at her feet.

**Lady Mary Wortley Montagu**

"Her beauty," Lady Mary wonderingly told her sister some time later, "effac'd every thing." Exposed to this new brand of beauty, in the sensual yet relaxing environment of the harem that brought it out so strikingly, she realized that what she had always thought of as beauty was pale and without character. While she was still taking in this sudden confusion of paradigms, Fatima had risen to take her hand. Her smooth, flawless complexion, her dark eyes, the perfect proportions of her body, her enchanting smile, and above all, the welcoming grace with which she greeted her guest and offered her hospitality, were exquisite in a way that Lady Mary had never before imagined, and the vision left her uncharacteristically tongue-tied.

Everything here was breathtaking, from the dreamily beautiful surroundings to the attendant maidens, to Fatima and her adolescent daughters. Yet, despite this harem's enclosed, perfumed, be-fountained beauty, and despite the sofa-lounging, the long loose tresses of dark hair, and the many richly-dressed maidens who now discreetly brought her refreshments, Lady Mary was perfectly aware that this harem was nothing like the masculine fantasy that shared some of the same trappings. It was not a metaphorical chocolate-box of feminine beauty, awaiting the enlivening presence of the sexually masterful lord. It was that fantasy's direct opposite, a pleasure garden of sensuality in a wholly feminine world. All its beauty was chosen, enjoyed, and exemplified by women, for their own pleasure, with their own particular grace.

Caught in the enchantment, Lady Mary could now relax (to the extent her dress allowed her) and bask in Fatima's magnetic charm, but there was more entertainment to come! The next morning, still breathless and energized from the previous night's deluge of experience, Lady Mary wrote it out in a letter to her sister back in the dismal grays of Scotland.

Fatima had signaled her attendants to begin the entertainment.

As Lady Mary tells it:

> "Four of them immediately begun to play some soft airs on Instruments between a Lute and a Guitar while the others danc'd by turns. This Dance was very different from what I had seen before. Nothing could be more artfull or more proper to raise certain Ideas, the Tunes so soft, the motions so Languishing, accompany'd by pauses and dying eyes, halfe falling back and then recovering themselves in so artful a Manner that I am very positive the coldest and most rigid Prude upon Earth could not have look'd upon them without thinking of something not to be spoke of." (351)

Perhaps it was not to be spoke of, but she had found a way of speaking of it. In this brief passage, Lady Mary describes many of the hallmarks of the best of Oriental dance today. The dancers were all soloists, and presumably, each had her unique charms, but the dance also had a cumulative effect, as each fresh expression added to the heady sensuality that so moved Lady Mary. The rapture of the dance was based on its artistry and elegance. The dancing unfolds with subtle rhythms and variations: Rising and falling, pauses and expressive glances. The dancers, with their "languishing and dying eyes," exude the kind of emotional expression that is so vital to belly dance.

Lady Mary does not describe the techniques of the dance; she only implies them, but there are enough features described here, and enough confirmation from other accounts, for us to become pretty sure that this is "belly dance" in an elite manifestation, and whatever else it involved, there must have been some hip and torso movements. (Nonetheless, that potential emblem of vulgarity didn't rate a mention). For Lady Mary, the impact of the dance came from its emotional and sensual evocation of the excitement-within-relaxation that is so central to woman-centered eroticism.

Although Lady Mary would never have put it in these terms, she does describe the transformative power that so many modern belly dancers seek through the dance. This dance had the power to bring a tremor of delicious ecstasy even to those prudes who had tried to excise it from their lives. Here, with this dance, and in this company, the

**A New Attraction in the Harem
by Frederick Goodall**

juice would flow back into even the driest and most shriveled soul.

Yet, the thing that seemed to move Lady Mary most was the fact that it had this momentous effect in a wholly feminine environment. It evoked the delights of sex, but detached them from masculine possessiveness and dominance. This harem dance was indeed, as so many modern belly dancers claim still, "by women, for women." The sexuality of the dance was not thrusting and direct but ambient; a mist that enhanced every other aspect of life. In spite of her ridiculous clothing and the burden of her identity as an English aristocrat, Lady Mary was deeply moved by this perfect, man-less experience of sensual delight.

Nearly giddy from the pleasures of this place of womanly beauty, Lady Mary finally took her leave. She had encountered a world in which extremes of sensual feeling could be expressed and shared without repercussion, where the sensuality, even sexuality, of the dance flowered in an environment that proved it was a women's pleasure rather than a man's right or his possession. The dance of Fatima's attendants embodied literal freedom.

Of course, Lady Mary had no harem to which she would return. Among her peers, she continued to wear her stays, if not her court dress, and she lived mostly in the mixed European company in which inter-gender head games played a significant role. When she left Turkey less than a year later, she left behind reluctantly, the very different experience of a sensual, intelligent, and gracious world that flourished without men. At home, she commissioned her portrait painted in Turkish clothing that still she sometimes wore. In England, which offered her the seeming freedoms of veil-less travel and free passage in the world of men, she must have continued to miss this great adventure, and regretted losing the very different freedom that, as a guest in another world, she had enjoyed so briefly.

## Ladies Dancing

It is clear from Lady Mary's account that an elite woman like Fatima would never break into a dance herself to entertain even the loftiest guest. Quite properly, she would have her slaves do it. Nevertheless, elite women did dance, and they took it seriously - both as a social grace and as a source of pleasure.

The memoir of the Turkish aristocrat Melek Hanum, published in 1872 with the title "Thirty Years in the Harem", hints at the many roles dancing could play in the lives of her peers.

Melek Hanum was the daughter of a half-Armenian mother and a French father, raised in Constantinople, where she fell in love and married a friend of Lord Byron. Five years and two children later, they parted ways, leaving Melek Hanum living comfortably in Paris. Invited to all the official functions of the Turkish embassy there, she met a Turkish nobleman, Kibrizli Mehmet-Pasha. He asked her to marry him, but she refused; she didn't want to go back to harem life. He asked her again, and once again, she refused. He begged pitifully – at least as she tells it – and finally, not without anxiety, she relented. Melek Hanum criticizes harem life harshly as full of manipulation and intrigue, but as it turns out, she was both equipped and inclined to scheme with the best. Her harem life allowed her free rein for the intrigues that – however much she plays them down – were the foundation of her relationship with the world.

It was one intrigue too many that finally brought her down: While her husband was away pursuing his official duties, their only son, his heir, became very ill and lay close to dying. Melek Hanum realized that if he died, she might lose her position as the favored – indeed, the only – wife of a very important man. He might take another wife, and she would be reduced to second best. The solution? She should be ready to cut her losses if her first son died, and produce a replacement son for her absent husband. The difficulty was that she wasn't pregnant. However, that obstacle could be handled, if only the timing were right. A little less than nine months after her husband's departure, she secured an infant, and emerged from her feigned confinement as the mother of a new heir. (She doesn't mention what happened to the old one).

Unfortunately for her, her infant substitution left her open to blackmail and manipulations by the women whom she had chosen to help her. When one of them died under mysterious circumstances, she was arrested for the murder and thrown into prison. The whole sordid affair came out, causing her husband to reject her. She was left destitute. All the same, after wrangling her release, she managed to flee with her older daughter and eventually make her way to Paris, where she wrote an account of her adventures.

It's difficult to like Melek Hanum, or in fact, anyone she mentions in her memoir. She wasn't very likable, and apparently, her friends weren't either. Her bitterness seeps out on every page of her memoir. She positively revels in painting a picture of Turkey, her former friends, and especially her former husband, as scurrilous, sinful, and crass. You emerge from reading her memoir with the feeling that you've just spent hours on the phone reluctantly hearing-out the rantings of one partner in a bitter divorce, and you can't help wondering how the other one would have described the incidents in question. In the end, you wonder if the memoir isn't, as its New York Times reviewer said in 1872, "four-fifths romance and one-fifth fact".

However, Melek-Hanum is far more believable (and enjoyable) when she describes the texture of women's life in elite harems than when she tears down her former friends, and one thing that appears in her narrative is the way belly dance permeates elite women's lives. She describes scenes that are similar to Lady Mary's narrative, such as the harem in which "some young slaves danced, accompanying themselves with zaganets (castanets of copper) while others sang."

Also, she describes dancing among elite women. Like all social graces, it was important for reasons other than enjoyment alone. In Melek Hanum's social circle, it was a way in which women who have never met each other could break the ice, size one another up, and test the potential for future friendships and alliances. Social dancing was also thread in the texture of elite women's lives. Describing her several-months stay in the harem of a family friend, she says, "We passed the time very pleasantly together, in conversation, dancing, music, and telling stories." It's one of the things elite women – the equivalent of modern "ladies who lunch" – do.

**The Bath
by Jean-Leon Gerome**

## In the Palace

A more intriguing variety of dancing takes place when Nazib-Khanum, the young adopted daughter of the Sultan's elderly sister, invites her to the palace.

"She made me seat myself in an immense room, and then Essemah-Sultan, the sister of the Sultan Mahmud, a lady of already considerable age, joined us. She was accompanied by several young ladies, one-half of whom were dressed in male attire, and took her seat on a large gilded chair. Some of them began to dance, and the princess invited me to follow their example. I was dressed in a magnificent costume, and mingled with the other young women."

While the slave attendants begin the dance – half of them in drag, no less – apparently, it is appropriate for aristocratic young women to join them, especially at the behest of the presiding matriarch. Nazib-Khanum contented herself with playing a "kind of guitar."

To add to the intrigue of this particular occasion, the Sultan himself made an unexpected appearance, and while Melek prepared to slip away, the Sultan's elderly sister assured her, "His Highness will be much pleased to see you thus." In the following interlude, Sultan Mahmud became quite enamored of the delightful Nazib-Khanum, and asked his sister if he could have her for a concubine. His sister refused, explaining that he would "keep to his new wife for three or four days, and then, she would have to pass the rest of her life in the corner of the palace". The Sultan took this rebuff without noticeable distress, and went off to dinner. Not only did Nazib-Khanum escape the honor of becoming the Sultan's concubine, she eluded propriety altogether and later eloped with a Greek scoundrel.

## At the Wedding

A more public occasion for dance arose at the wedding of her young former slave. When the girl grows into a little too much beauty, Melek Hanum marries her off quickly while her possibly-tempted husband is away.

At the elaborate wedding ceremony:

> "Two of the principle assistants began to dance: They stood facing each other at a certain distance, then they swayed themselves forward and backward successively, following the time marked by the music. This dance allows no movement of the legs; the feet scarcely stir. The performers balance themselves on their haunches, inclining their heads right or left, make graceful gestures with their arms, and assume attitudes most charming and most impassioned; every thing breathes in them, while dancing, an ardent yet restrained voluptuousness."

In its "ardent yet restrained voluptuousness," this seems to be the kind of dancing Lady Mary describes, the kind of dance that expresses feminine beauty and sensuality - not only in the body - but in the rhythm and flow and emotional intensity it evokes. It is not performed by soloists, but by two women dancing together. Given the public occasion, the performers' focus on one another creates a safer context for the expression of this sensuality than would solo performances. Melek Hanum says only little about technique, except that the feet didn't move much and that movements of the arms and inclinations of the body played a role, but it's hard to imagine sensuality emerging through the dance unless the hips and torso move in counterbalance to the graceful arm movements. This dance was probably very different from the danse du ventre presented at the World's Fair, and if it contained the restrained elegance Melek-Hanum describes, perhaps it was far more acceptable to the audiences of 1893 America. It might either fascinate a modern audience or bore them to tears.

Nevertheless, in the elaborate display of this wedding, it played a key role, and it was not only the assistants who danced: "The dancing was kept up until all, old and young, the wives of the cadi (judge) and naib (first interpreter of the law), the imim (priest), and of other officers, civil and military, of every rank, had successively taken part in it." In a world where elite women were usually private, interior creatures, the wedding ritual requires dancing by the wife of virtually every member of the establishment from the military to the clergy. The display of these women's dancing, or perhaps more importantly, the fact of their dancing, was necessary within the wedding ritual to confirm the marriage and begin it with the appropriate degree of respect, acknowledgement, luck, and fertility that women can bestow.

The dancing was not over yet. After the public celebration:

**Unknown sitter, Cabinet Card.
A style of photography used between 1875-1900.**

"The husband goes up stairs and seats himself on a chair, while his wife, accompanied by two old female slaves, each carrying a candle, presents herself before him, and all three dance; they withdraw, change the bride's dress, and return to renew the dance. This performance is repeated until all the robes in the trousseau have been put on. The husband then takes his wife by the hand and enters the bed-chamber with her."

The candle-lit dance of the new bride before her husband is obviously a very sensual act. I don't know many husbands who would watch it without thinking pretty eagerly of the consummation to follow, and I can imagine the men who got this entertainment becoming just a little impatient with the succession of outfits and finding their eyes wandering to the bedroom door. However, the two old women diffuse the overt sensuality of the bride's dance, or at least, they remind the husband that there is a whole women's world to which his wife belongs. By showing her trousseau, the bride is able to establish her own identity, her own worth; she is more than just a body. She is a wealthy woman herself (even if she is only a dangerously pretty slave girl married off to an older widower, as in the wedding Melek Hanum describes). Until he has seen her trousseau, with all its tokens of wealth, family support, and feminine identity, the groom has to stay in that chair! When all of this has been established firmly, the old women retreat, and the sexual promise of the dance can be fulfilled.

Why do the old women also dance? Wouldn't it be enough for them to simply be there? So perhaps there is something more going on here, with the juxtaposition of the promise of the virgin bride and the old women at the opposite end of life, still dancing after all these years. I wonder how they felt as they retreated to the next room to re-fold and pack away the beautiful clothes, leaving the bride to the pleasures – or perhaps, the terrors – of maidenhood lost?

## The Slave Girls

In the 18th and 19th centuries, Europeans knew that Turks had slaves, and held it as a sign of their moral inferiority. Yet, visitors to Turkey were surprised, and often were offended by the liberties that slaves took, daring even (for example) to greet upper class visitors and shake their hands. In the class-conscious world of Lady Mary's Europe, or in European countries even through the 20th century, it was obvious that a slave shouldn't take liberties that even the yeomen of the European working class would not be allowed.

However, as sources from the 16th to 19th centuries tell us, slavery in Turkey was quite a different thing from that found in the slave-owning society we know best, the pre-Civil War American South. In contrast to the dehumanized and abused Africans here, slaves in Turkey had legal rights. A woman could not be sold as a concubine without her consent, or sold away from her children. The children of slave women and their masters were free, and bearing children to a master usually

**Turbaned Oriental
by Gabriel Ray Morcillo**

resulted in the mother's freedom as well. Some slave women were treated with great affection by elite mistresses, raised with all the social graces, and could hope for a favorable marriage when they were not far out of their teens.

On the other hand, any system of slavery allows for horrible abuses. Some male slaves were castrated, since eunuchs were considered necessary both in administrative roles and as harem servants. From childhood on, other male slaves spent their lives in the military, facing un-chosen dangers in an army that was constantly at war. Female domestic servants faced a life of hard work with little compensation. Even the attractive, genteelly-raised female attendants of capricious mistresses could be beaten or otherwise maltreated without repercussion. Attendants had no set "working hours" and could be worked to the point of exhaustion. Slaves who were sexually attractive to a master could find themselves caught between the enchanting hope of motherhood and freedom, and the appalling fear of retribution from a displeased mistress. Even the most fortunate of concubines could find herself embroiled in tensions as she made her way within a household in which she had little power. All of these difficult situations are recorded in our sources, making it clear that life of a slave in a contentious harem had the potential to be very unpleasant indeed.

Yet, even within a system that allowed such abuses, the most attractive and talented of Turkish slaves, male or female, could hope to achieve high status, positions of power, and eventually freedom and even wealth, and these fortunate few might be treated as family members, feeling comfortable shaking the hand of a Western visitor when introduced.

Female slaves came from two main sources. One we are all too familiar with: Sub-Saharan Africans, captured in war or in raids, were sold to traders who took them North and East to be sold as servants or potential concubines. Invariably, Orientalist paintings show women of African origin as servants of lighter-skinned women, but this was not always the case, and African slaves could rise to positions of power as concubines, wives, and administrators.

The second source of female slaves was from an area of the Caucasus that is part of the Russian Federation today, and was then the kingdom of Circassia. These Circassian maidens, typically fair-skinned and sometimes fair-haired, achieved something of a reputation among Europeans, for whom they represented the titillating fantasy and appalling insult of white women who were sexually subjugated to dark, domineering Turks. In the late 19th century, P. T. Barnum, of circus fame, introduced "Circassian Beauties" to the displays included in his "museums" that were forerunners of circus sideshows. These "Circassians" were attractive, fair-skinned actresses who sported bizarre "afros" (lengthy kinky hair texture) that were unlike any hairstyle found in Circassia, but impressive enough to become a staple of the dime-museum and sideshows for decades.

In any case, the dead-end poverty of Circassian farmers might lead them to sell their "extra" daughters to Turkish purchasers, in the hopes that slavery to a rich master or mistress would be the first step up to a better life than they could hope to attain at home. For most of them, it probably didn't really work out that way, but for some, it certainly did. After a period of service, and having been instructed in the social graces, the most fortunate and most attractive of these young women were given their freedom in an arranged marriage that probably did offer them far more comfort than their native farming village would have provided.

Lady Mary, in describing Turkish customs, says that men do not surround themselves with concubines, and that the one man she knows of who does so is "spoke of as a Libertine ... and his Wife won't see him." Lady Mary may or may not have been naïve about the fate of attractive slave women owned by men, but additional sources confirm her statement elsewhere that a woman's slave was her own and not to be commandeered by a husband with a none-too-distantly roving eye.

From early on, some aristocratic and middle-class women made a home-business of training slaves to be lovely attendants with all the social graces. "This trade," says a disapproving Frederick Millingen, writing in 1871, "is, thus, carried on by the greatest ladies of Constantinople, many of whom have become rich through it... A girl of ten or twelve, bought for two hundred pounds, can be sold at the age of sixteen or seventeen for a thousand." The modern equivalents would be something like $20,000 for the purchase and $100,000 for the sale. Writing at about the same time, Melek Hanum comments more specifically on the training of the slaves: "Their mistress makes them dress becomingly, teaches them to conduct themselves properly, and to speak the Turkish language. Their attention is bestowed on the cultivation of the particular talent by which they are to distinguish themselves; such as music, dancing, hair-dressing, etc."

Besides showing us that dancing rates about the same as hair-dressing as an accomplishment, these accounts raise some interesting questions. Aristocratic women raised slave girls to the social graces they themselves had been taught, and music and dance were among these. Fatima, certainly, had women who were particularly accomplished at dancing among her attendants. So, who taught them? To what extent did aristocratic ladies, themselves, play a part in the education of these young girls in music and dance? Was it all left to other slaves? Who taught the great ladies' daughters their social accomplishments? Was that, too, left to slaves? Were aristocratic women, who enjoyed music and dancing themselves after all, more direct guides for both their own daughters and the young women whom they took under their wings or did it depend on one's relative wealth and the size of the household? These are intriguing questions, given the close relationships some women developed with their slaves, but not ones the evidence allows us to answer.

Going a step further, was this sort of entertainment offered to the men of the household also? Among other accomplishments and attributes, could dance have been a way in which an ambitious slave – one who was not confident that her mistress would settle her into a good marriage when she reached her mid-twenties and lost her charm as an attendant – made her play for motherhood and freedom? Maybe, in some households and for some women, the "harem seduction" of our imaginative histories had at least some seed of truth behind it. However, this, too, is somewhere our evidence doesn't go.

In any case, the music and dance that Fatima enjoyed, provided by her own well-trained attendants, seems to have had its parallel in less exalted households, whether elite or middle class. Aristocratic women danced for their own pleasure, and trained or had trained their attendants to perform for them or for the other women who visited them. One wonders if, amongst these women, the quality of her slaves' music and dance accomplishments, when they performed for her friends, reflected on her own elegance and abilities, and if well-trained entertainers were a sign of status amongst women who valued elegance in every form.

## Musicians and Dancers of the Imperial Harem

Belly dance, in the sense of solo-improvised dance featuring hip and hand movements, was probably a feature of the dances of the elite performers of courts throughout the Arab world, and as we shall see, in the 19th century certainly, it was an element of the dances of the Ottoman Imperial Harem, but there, as in other courts, it was only one of many dances which elite dancers were expected to do.

The Arab author Al Mas'udi's "The Meadows of Gold", dated to about 957 CE, describes the qualities of good male and female dancers. They include things such as:

"grace and charm ... a good innate sense of rhythm, and to seek joyful creativity in his/her dance."

Also to be desired are:

"coquetry and flirtation, good nature, ability to sway the sides of the body, narrowness of waist, sprightliness and agility...patience in enduring the process to reach a long goal, graciousness of feet, suppleness of fingers and mastery over fingers movements in the various types of dances such as the camel and horse dances, suppleness of joints, speed of motion during turns, suppleness of sides of the body...[and] knowledge and mastery over a large repertoire of all types of dances."

The musicologist George Sawa points out that the suppleness and swaying of the sides of the body imply something like belly dance.

On the other hand, there is also a large repertoire of dances to be learned, so belly dance, in whatever form, is only a part of what an elite dancer should be able to do. So in the court dancers Al Mas'udi describes – and probably in elite dancers of all sorts in the Middle East – what we have is not exactly "harem belly dancers." It is dancers for whom a form of belly dance was only part of a large repertoire of dances for which they underwent significant training: A "process to reach a long goal."

The result made them not only pleasant to have around at banquets, but a form of human riches that could reflect a king's benevolence. In 1526, the first Moghul king, Babur, sent gifts to his relatives and other elite subjects consisting of "one special dancing-girl of the dancing-girls of Sultan Ibrahim...with one gold plate full of jewels – ruby and pearl, carnelian and diamond, emerald and turquoise, topaz and cat's eyes ..." along with a quantity of other sumptuous goods.

Apparently, these material items were appropriately counterbalanced by a human delight, and the dancing-girls provided it. It's hard to imagine the uncertainties of these dancers' lives over their past few traumatic years. They had been raised in the court of the last king of the Punjab's Islamic Lodi dynasty, Ibrahim, whose reign had been spent in fighting off the Afghans and Moghuls. When he was finally killed in battle, the women of his court – at least, the lower-status ones like dancers – became spoils of war, co-opted by Babur for his own household. After their long journey from Delhi to the Moghul court in Agar, they faced a potentially uneasy integration with the musicians and dancers of Babur's court, but at least they were together. Yet, before long, as

**Almina. daughter of Asher Wertheimer by John Singer Sargent**

expendable commodities, they were dispatched, one-by-one, to distant points of Babur's sizeable Empire. Their beauty and skills, in one way, ranked them as equal to jewels, but they, themselves, were totally ruled by the whims of their current master. One wonders how easily these dancers, defined as valuable gifts yet unable to direct their own fates, adjusted to their new homes in another foreign harem, and how things turned out for them in the end.

The dancers of the Qatar court in Iran were probably more secure. There, in the mid-19th century, Muhammad Shah supported many "dancing girls, those lavishly decorated women who typified the luxurious living of the monarchy" who are illustrated so enchantingly in any number of Persian miniature paintings. Some of the Persian dance styles, elegant performances that emphasize delicate hand and arm movement complemented by "suppleness of the sides of the body," have survived in some form to the present day.

The kind of varied dance expertise described by Al Mas'udi, probably achieved by the hybrid culture supporting the Moghul dancers, still surviving from the 19th century Persian courts, is exactly what we find in the Ottoman Imperial Harem. The most complete account of the training and roles of harem musicians and dancers is very late, and we can't be sure how much of it translates into earlier periods (presumably not its Tchaikovsky and pianos) but it's the best we have from which to work.

Leyla Saz Hanimefendi was the daughter of the chief physician of the Imperial court through the reigns of several Sultans, and one of the few outsiders (male or female) who was allowed into the exclusive society of the Sultan's harem. In a memoir that she wrote in 1920-1921, she gave her recollections of harem life from the 1860s and '70s. Just as Melek Hanum's vitriolic account has to be taken with a grain of salt, so does Leila Saz's glowing narrative, in which no conflict exists and no one can do any wrong. However, where she describes institutions and training, she may be more believable than when she describes a harem environment wholly composed of sweetness and light.

As Leyla Saz Hanimefendi knew it, the harem (or as she refers to it, the serail) was, as the Sultan's harem had presumably been for the three previous centuries of Ottoman rule, a place of refinement and accomplishment. Its elite women, whether daughters or courtiers, were given daily music lessons in Western and Turkish music by male teachers, who were accompanied into the harem by watchful eunuchs. The women who attended the music lessons veiled themselves lightly, with a gauzy cloth attached to a headdress and covering the features, and Leila Saz assures us that there was no impropriety with even the most handsome of the male instructors. In previous generations though, it's likely that female instructors within the harem were the norm.

In Leila Saz's time, there were any number of pianos scattered throughout the harem, and women were encouraged to practice as long as the Sultan was not around to be disturbed by their wrong notes. Particularly talented students were chosen to form a women's orchestra that played both Western and Turkish music, and there was a parallel orchestra on the men's side of the divide.

The women who had exhibited particular talent at dancing were given further training, again by male instructors. Presumably, the early training that revealed their talent was managed by female teachers. They attended their lessons unveiled, and learned both Turkish and Western dances. Some of the Turkish dances were not exactly belly dance: For example, the "Dance of the Rabbit", which apparently involved bounding vigorously around the dance floor while dressed in white pantaloons. Leila Saz does not mention whether dancers and musicians specialized in either Western or Eastern forms, but as I read it, they did not. Both dance and musical training required substantial dedication and study

– although not to the exclusion of other duties. As Leila Saz comments, "Dancers were in normal services and performed diverse functions just like all the others."

Leila Saz describes at some length a typical performance of the serail's dance troupe for Sultan Abdul Mecid. One of its features is a tour around the room by a corps of young women playing zils, each of whom might – as the individual spirit moves them, it appears – "fold herself back on her calves, placing one knee on the floor while inclining her upper body backwards or toward one side," a movement found in modern belly dances as well as in other kinds of Turkish and Iranian dancing.

Nonetheless, "belly dance" is clearly a sore spot:

> "Among the dances executed by the köçekler (a dance troupe comprised of boys who were brought in from outside) was also to be found what the westerners call a belly dance. This dance was hardly favored in Turkey and certainly a dance in the Imperial Serail never takes the provocative, lascivious or indecent form which the westerners imagine it to have and which can be seen performed in their own countries by dancers more or less Oriental. The actual belly dance is really a dance of Arabic origin."

Even today, that last line is still used in Turkey, where the dance has apparently flourished at all levels of society for hundreds of years - if not more. Still, you have to acknowledge that the dances of the Imperial Harem were most likely quite distant from those that Western travelers in Egypt and Turkey describe in more common venues.

One interesting facet of the dance troupe Leila Saz describes is the variety of dances it performs – not only Turkish and imported Western dances, but dances from all the subjects of the Ottoman Empire. In the modern era, as the dance scholar Anthony Shay observes, "State-supported folkloric companies in many nations adapt regional dances to their own refined tastes in order to display national solidarity." So in a way, the dancers of the serail were the first "national dance company," displaying the unity of their Sultan's empire though adapting (or appropriating) the dances of its varied people.

**Turkish Dancing Kocek
19th century**

Leila Saz tells us, "The dancers had a costume which consisted of a double skirt in a single color, a little shorter than the waist, opened at the front, with sleeves in the form of a bolero. The satin or taffeta skirt was straight cut but very wide, with a weighted hem so that it spun out in turns but settled quickly into its line, and a similar knee-length skirt was worn over it. A belt with two buckles made of gold braid surrounded the waist but since it was a little too long, it hung down in front." However, it was purely ornamental, as the form-fitting upper garment did not need cinching. This cut would have complemented whirling and turning, and a group of dancers performing these moves in sync would have been quite impressive. Its top, close-fitting to below the waist, also complemented subtle movements of the torso.

While the dance specialists of the Serail apparently formed a capable and versatile troupe, they

**The Dance of the Bee in the Harem
by Vincenzo Marinelli**

were also exposed to the most elite of the dancers who performed in the outside world, in the form of troupes of koçeks, (boy dancers) who came to perform for the Sultan, while the women watched from beyond the broad latticework that divided their part of the performance hall from the men's. They also saw the Western dance troupes that were brought to entertain the Sultan and his household. They were taught by instructors brought in from outside, as well as by harem residents who had achieved a high level of expertise. Their dancing, belly or otherwise, would have had the advantage of influence from many different sources.

While Leila Saz heaps scorn on belly dance as seen in the outside world, her insistence that it can be performed with no impropriety, suggests that in the harem, it was performed with an eye to elegance and beauty also. As a firmly integrated element of Turkish social dancing, even among the women of elite though non-royal harems, it's easy to imagine that harem women often did it for their own pleasure. The music available in the harem, as taught to and played by the women whose talent marked them out, would have been rich and nuanced, and presumably, their dance would have reflected these qualities. The dancers would have been attuned to the ways of presenting themselves as uniquely beautifully and seamlessly elegant. The personality of the performer, as well as any skills she might have as a dancer, were meant to shine in her elegant performance. So however hackneyed the idea of harem slaves trying to win a Sultan's favors by vigorous belly dancing, clearly a particularly accomplished and personable dancer might have won his notice, - or accomplished dancing might simply have been the icing on a concubine's delicious cake!

## Harem Fantasy Revisited

The pelvis-rocking harem dance-off obviously has no place in this court, but belly dance and eroticism are quite capable of walking hand-in-hand through the luxurious corridors of the Serrail. Leila Saz narrates this story that was circulating in the harem:

"One evening after dinner, the Sultan chose to make a visit to one of his favourites and in order to surprise her he asked the beznedar (female chamberlain) who was on duty, not to warn her. After having crossed the hall and while approaching the door, he heard some melodious sounds which were coming from the room of the lady whom he was going to honour with his presence.

'Well,' said the Sultan, 'it seems that we are having some music, so much the better!'

After waiting a few instants, he had the door opened without having himself announced by the girl of the service who stood there, and entered the room while lifting the curtain and saying:

'Would you kindly admit to your gracious company he who has chanced to arrive so unexpectedly and guided only by his good fortune toward this most agreeable encounter?'

The young favourite had invited one of her companions and both of them were playing some music and dancing quite intimately. The unexpected appearance of the Sultan caused them a joyous surprise which was quickly followed by a certain unease. In those days, it was considered improper for ladies of station to succumb to the pleasure of the dance. The Sultan seeing that the ladies were disconcerted, hastened to put them at their ease.

'I have not come to interrupt your pleasure; please permit me to stay here in a corner so that I may watch and listen to you. I beg you to continue your pastimes and not deprive me of the pleasure of participating in your divertissements.'

The ice was broken. The doors were closed again and there followed a very gay and most agreeable evening in complete privacy. The Sultan was enchanted and presented the ladies, as a remembrance of the encounter, some magnificent jewels which he had brought by a bazdenar; he also made presents to the kalfas (chief servants) and withdrew while begging them to let him know when they intended to have a similar meeting in the future."

This is about as delectable a belly dance harem fantasy as anyone could wish, beginning with a little girl-on-girl eroticism, the forbidden pleasure of engaging in sensual dance, and the startled guilt – quickly converted to happiness – the Sultan's chance arrival brings, as the young concubines respond with delight to the gracious, complimentary, and later, very generous Sultan. The pleasure of the young women, playing music and dancing for each other, shows the same woman-centered delight in dance that appears in the dancing Lady Mary describes in Fatima's feminine domain. The Sultan enters the scene as a delightful adjunct to this feminine diversion. He almost seems to be the culmination of their fantasy, rather than the author of his own. Whether Leila Saz puts the stamp of her own perspective on it or accurately reproduces the tale as it circulated in the harem at this time, the authors of this particular story are female.

The "dance for me, slaves" mentality of the Orientalist harem fantasy is nowhere to be found. The women are dancing for their own pleasure, and the Sultan's presence is an unexpected extra. Rather than competing with one another for their frustrated passions to be assuaged, they are busy assuaging them, themselves (whether Sappho-like or chastely), and this mutual pleasure almost magically summons forth the potential for even greater delight. The Sultan, far from being a cruel and demanding despot, is a courtly gentleman who glosses over his own very real power and graciously asks permission to be included in the women's festivities. He is thoughtful enough to be concerned at the embarrassment the young women might feel, and wants to make them comfortable, as clearly, this will make everyone happier.

The message is that it's not only acceptable but emminently desirable to escape propriety into the pleasures of dance, and that even greater pleasures may come to the woman who does so. This story resonates with the fantasies of the East shared by the woman-centered world of modern Western belly dance within its evocation of the atmosphere of shared female enjoyment, its promise of greater delights magically called forth by indulging one's own pleasure, and its creation of the Sultan as the most thoughtful, considerate, and desirable of lovers. Maybe it was even true.

## *A Few Words About Sources:*

Historical Harems and Dancers: Primary Sources: Melek-Hanum, Thirty Years in the Harem (available through Project Gutenburg); Leyla Saz Hanimefendi, The Imperial Harem of the Sultans: Daily Life at the Ciragan Palace during the 19th Century: Memoirs of Leyla (Saz) Hanimefendi (Peva Publications 1994); al-Mas'udi, The Meadows of Gold ("The Oration of the Geographer Ibn Khurdadhba in front of the Caliph al Mu'tamid") (ca. 957), translated by George Sawa, first presented and discussed at the International Belly Dance Conference of Canada, 2008; available online at www.georgedimitrisawa.com/arabic_articles.html#qualities .

Historical Harems and Dancers: Secondary Sources: Leslie P. Pierce, The Imperial Harem: Women and Sovereignty in the Ottoman Empire (Oxford University Press, 1993 (harem structure and economy) Several works by Anthony Shay cast light on professional entertainers; The Male Dancer in the Middle East and Central Asia (Dance Research Journal 38 (2006) 137-162 is a good place to start. The quote from Sonnini was taken from Judy Mabro, Veiled half-truths: Western travellers' perceptions of Middle Eastern women (New York: I.B. Tauris, 1996, an invaluable collection of primary sources. My section on Qajar music and dance is largely based on Robyn Friend's article, "The Exquisite Art of Persian Classical Dance," originally published in Habibi, is available online at www.thebestofhabibi.com , and the quotes from S. J. Falk's Qajar Paintings are found there.

On Slavery: Leslie Pierce deals with this topic at length; see also Ehud R. Toledano, "Late Ottoman Empire: Concepts of Slavery (1930's-1880's) (Poetics Today, 14.3: 477-506) for an academic perspective; for an 1870 denouncement, Frederick Mulligan, "The Circassian Slave and the Sultan's Harem," Journal of the Anthropological Society of London 8 (1870-71): cix-ccx; 1890-1910 accounts in Western newspapers describe Ottoman slavery with varying degrees of amazement and moral disapproval. Melek-Hanum provides interesting perspective on this as well.

Lady Mary Wortley-Montagu: The main source for this section is The Complete Letters of Lady Mary Wortley Montagu, ed. Robert Halsband, Oxford University Press, 1965-67), in which Lady Mary speaks for herself, with the editor providing helpful biographical notes.

### *Andrea Deagon PhD*

*Andrea received her PhD in 1984 from Duke University and is currently on the Classical Studies and Women's Studies faculty at UNC-Wilmington. This piece is an excerpt from a book in progress, Belly Dance: An Intimate History, the lively tale of belly dance across the ages, revealed through the lives and words of the dancers, audiences, lovers, aficionados, entrepreneurs, and adventurers who lived it.*

**Harem Life in Constantinople
by John Frederick Lewis**

# The American Belly Dancer in Early Burlesque and Vaudeville Theatre

## by Catherine Mary Scheelar

After the 1893 Chicago World's Fair closed, the dances that were originally introduced as part of a cultural exhibit found a place with performers in the many traveling circuses and carnivals as the *hootchie-kootchie* or *cootch* dance. By 1905 there were forty-six carnivals traveling the rails and over forty larger three-ring circuses, ensuring that the dispersed American public had access to big city entertainment (Bogdan 1988: 59). These were further transformed into a standard in popular turn-of-the-century burlesque theaters, where men also often comically performed the 'Little Egypt' persona in drag (Sellers-Young 1992). As female public performance was still taboo, most dancers came from the lowest rungs of American society and amplified the erotic aspects to gain employment as the exotic persona gained popularity with the American public (Immerso 2002: 74). Virginia Keft-Kennedy uses Bhaktin's notion of the grotesque to explore historical perceptions of belly dance in the West as bodies which, through twisting, undulating and writhing, deviate from the ideal by transgressing culturally accepted physical limits (2005: 283-284). As women without corsets who moved freely in front of men not their husbands, these performers embodied social transgressions through public dancing which challenged appropriate female behaviour by alluding to both self-sufficiency and sensuality (Keft-Kennedy 2005: 288). These performances reinforced the popular perception of a link between striptease and belly dance (Sellers-Young 1992: 142, Shay 2008: 140-144).

While popular to observe, most Americans who viewed the early dances on the midway from afar did not display a desire to learn and perform the authentic dances themselves. Rather, the Westernized versions of exotic dances widely performed throughout Europe and the United States by American pioneers of modern dance more easily resonated culturally and aesthetically with audiences, as supported by the high culture domains of ballet, opera, and haute-couture fashion (Shay 2008: 9).

### High Culture: Ballet, Opera, and Early Modern Dance

While *cootch* and burlesque dancers often incorporated elements of the movement vocabulary of the original fair dancers, the higher-class European ballet and opera began layering the aesthetics and storylines of various real and imagined Oriental cultures over their own movement vocabularies (Windmuller 2011). Sergei Diaghilev's *Ballet Russes* performed six Oriental ballets in Paris

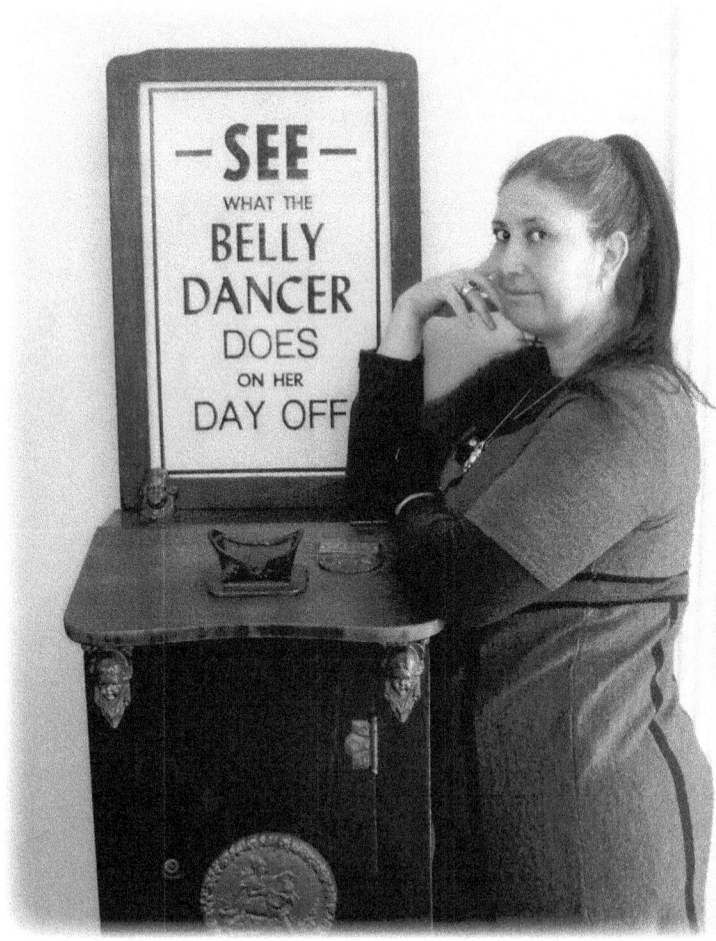

**Monica Berini**

between 1909-1912, and first toured America in 1916. Costumes designed by Russian painter and designer Leon Bakst influenced the costuming of future *Raqs Sharqi* belly dancers, both Western and Eastern (Windmuller 2011: 12; Edwards 2000: 227). Orientalized fashion as depicted by highly streamlined and athletic ballet dancers blurred gender boundaries in contrast to rigid Victorian fashions which concealed the body and emphasized the differences between male and female; on the ballet stage "men in fancy dress draped themselves in pearl necklaces; women in harem pants revealed that they had two legs" (Edwards 2000: 228). This theatrical aesthetic overlapped with Orientalist fashion already popular amongst elite Westerners. The Orient has, after all, symbolized opulence to the West for millennia. Luxury items such as pearls, silk, gold, inlaid metalwork, carpet weaving, perfumes, and spices have long come from the expansive East.

In the early 1900s French haute couture fashion designers such as Paul Poiret and Jeanne Hallée supplied women of means with fashion inspired by the East: Beaded bags with fringe and tassels, knee-length dresses worn over flowing harem pants gathered at the ankles (styled after Turkish trousers and called bloomers after suffragist Amelia Bloomer) with metallic threads and jewel-toned fabrics which hung light and loose on the body (Edwards 2000: 227). [2] Creative (and wealthy) women might add a small feminine turban to their outfit and drape it with strings of pearls and glass beads, to wear to fashionable Orientalist parties (Shay 2008: 8, Bentley 2003: 41-42). This looser, uncorseted form of Orientalist dress became popular with both the New Woman and later went on to influence 1920s Flapper fashions.

Another figure that became quite popular as a representation of the exotic feminine was the biblical character of Salomé; in 1896 Oscar Wilde produced a popular play about Salomé and her lovers, as did Richard Strauss in his 1905 opera (Karayanni 2008: 117). Whereas the Bible portrays Salomé as a docile girl, Wilde's portrayal of this Middle Eastern woman is one that challenges Victorian era gender norms by exhibiting excess, power, exotic and erotic movement, and ruthlessness. Here and in turn of the century films such as 1903's *The Vision Salomé* she dances the

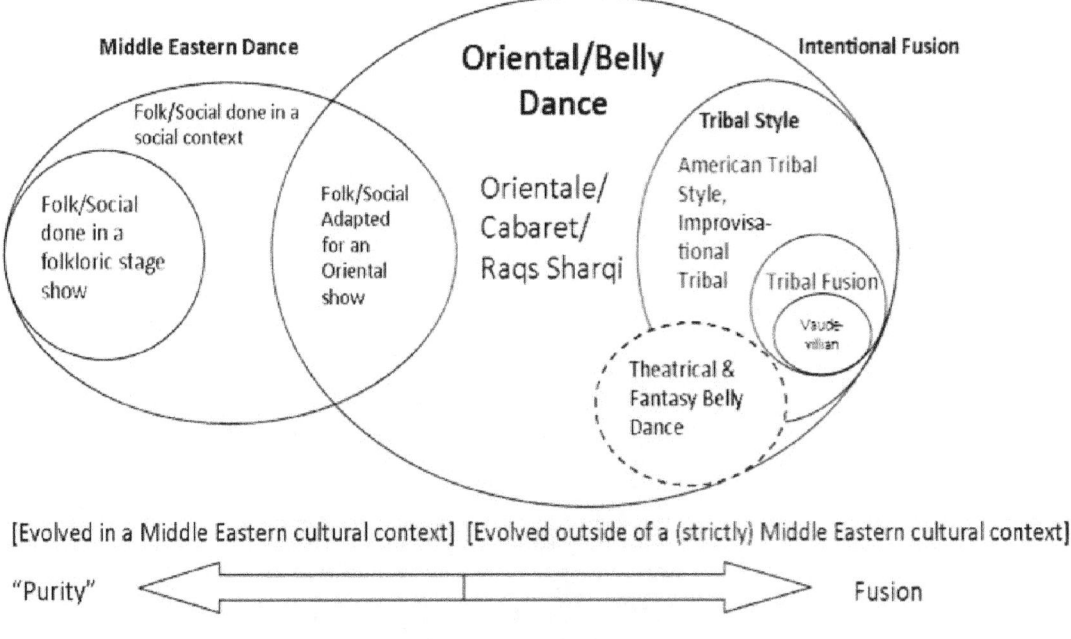

Figure 3. A Synchronic Look at Current American Belly Dance Genres.[22]

hypnotic and unveiling *Dance of the Seven Veils* (which Wilde was believed to have invented himself) and has St. John the Baptist decapitated on a whim (Karayanni 2008: 105). These productions spurred a cultural phenomenon that came to be known as *Salomania* in Great Britain and the United States as the figure became especially popular with young women experimenting with changing gender identity and social norms (Shay 2008: 8, Studlar 1997: 15).

Along with the American ethnic-inspired *art dance* performances of the 1910s, this craze was led by pioneers such as Dutch circus performer and dancer Margaretha Zelle also known as Mata Hari (1876 – 1917), Canadian Maud Allan (1873-1956), and Americans Isadora Duncan (1878-1927) and Ruth St. Denis (1879-1968). Most of these performers never formally studied dance and relied on orientalist images and writings for their dance inspirations (Desmond 1991: 30-32). They were not cultural anthropologists concerned with accuracy but rather performers with artistic and theatrical skills who interpreted the Orient according to certain mystical themes to delight their audiences in order to make a living (Buonaventura 1983: 86, Shay 2008: 14). St. Denis herself got her start in the lower class vaudeville circuit alongside magicians and trained animals before her dances made their way into higher class theatres (Haynes-Clark 2005: 36).

La Meri (1898-1988) was one of the few such dancers noted for her involvement in researching and recreating existing Eastern dance cultures (Shay 2008: 10, Karayanni 2008: 209). However, like others La Meri used Western music in place of authentic Eastern music, as "this has proven to be good theatre, for the average audience is not conditioned to the sound of Oriental music and often resent it to the point of staying away from the theatre" (Shay 2008: 72). Also beginning as a vaudeville entertainer before performing in upper class theaters, she described herself as a performer of ethnological or ethnic dance which she differentiated from folk dance as being a form of art dance for the Western stage. Along with tying their art to questionable notions of ethnicity, early modern dancers often spiritualized their performances so as not to be seen as prostitutes but rather as artists (Shay 2008: 14).

### Low Culture: Burlesque & Vaudeville

Dance historian Toni Bentley notes that the Salomé character's famous *Dance of the Seven Veils* manipulates more than just veils; her dance also highlighted the modern woman's power to reveal and to conceal, to both create desire and to control her availability (Bentley 2002: 31):

> In such a world of oriental chaos, women might imagine themselves to be more than harem dancing girls. They might become the *Eternal Salomé* acting out all the forbidden adjectives associated with antique exoticism, but also with the New Women in search for meaningful transformation in the modern world. (Studlar 1997: 125)

While the Little Egypt character had immediately gained favour with the lower classes, as *Salomania* grew in the upper classes the burlesque and vaudeville revues began staging their own Salomé performances which centered on interpretations of Oscar Wilde's famous play. Some burlesque dancers such as

Millie DeLeon (1873-1922) even made a mockery of other dancer's artistic aspirations and claims of uniqueness, as well as the press' distinctions between low and high Salomé performances. After repeatedly being arrested for public indecency for performances which exaggerated and ridiculed the cultural fad of displaying an exotic female Other, she ironically chided her multiplying contemporaries by claiming that they were unjustly imitating her pure, artistic Salomé dance (Munro-Miller 2010: 125).

While burlesque's transgressive power can be used to challenge normative female roles and behaviours, burlesque is essentially a cultural phenomenon wherein the low mass culture makes fun of the pretensions of the high culture and in doing so inverts the class hierarchy (Allen 1991).

It is defined as "that species of literary composition, or of dramatic representation, which aims at exciting laughter by caricature of the manner or spirit of serious works or by ludicrous treatment of their subjects" (Oxford English Dictionary Online). Nineteenth century American burlesque theatre was derived from the British form which appealed to the working-class as it exaggerated and mocked respected and well-known high cultural forms in brief comic bits that relied on kitschy costumes, puns, double entendre, cross-dressing, and racial, gender, and ethnic stereotypes (Munro-Miller 2010:30).

The burlesque show was a sequence of bits without any narrative structure which became increasingly associated with popular culture and a working-class male audience. While it did act as a site for partially nude females in exotic costumes teeming with artifice, the striptease did not become commonplace in American burlesque until the 1930s as the public display of the female body became increasingly commonplace both on and off the stage (Munro-Miller 2010: 153). American vaudeville on the other hand appealed to an audience in between the upper and lower class, and tried to appeal to women and children of all ages as well as men.

This performance genre included acts from elite forms as well as popular forms such as musicians, dancers, comedians, trained animals, magicians, female and male impersonators, acrobats, and jugglers. When a focused display of the female body did occur in vaudeville it was often tied to high culture aspirations as they tended to downplay the erotic aspects in order to appeal to a more sophisticated audience (Munro-Miller 2010: 112).

As early twentieth century America urbanity evolved into a culture of display, American artists and filmmakers strove to represent the emerging consumer culture and spectacle of urban life. In drawing inspiration from the vaudeville stage and early motion picture houses, they captured many images of the Salomé dancer (Munro-Miller

**Theda Bara plays as Cleopatra**

2010: 14). The exotic archetype of a changing woman in an increasingly public culture, Salomé was the prototype for the veiled and beaded sexually aggressive Vamp (sexual vampire) of early 20th century theatre and film. The Vamp was often portrayed by American actress Theodosia Goodman, who cultivated a mysterious persona both on and off screen as Theda Bara (an anagram of the words Arab Death) who sported kohl-rimmed eyes and Oriental fashions in films such as *Cleopatra* (1917) and *Salomé* (1918) (Studlar 1997: 115-116). So common were Orientalist films at the time that rebellious flapper girls called themselves *shebas* and their boyfriends *sheiks* after the 1921 films *Queen of Sheba* and *The Sheik* (Studlar 1997: 102).

Much of the popular entertainment of these eras such as silent films and music hall performances both suggested and reinforced the popular view of an expansive, mythical Orient as a liminal space of leisure, luxury, and sensuality. Most interestingly, many modern Tribal Fusion belly dancers exploit the imagery of European colonialist art and the costuming of early Salomés and sideshow cootch dancers alike. What was once risqué in the greater Western culture - such as burlesque theatre, public exhibition of the female body, the jazz music and dance movement, the women's lib movement - and belly dance's roles in those histories - is referenced in order to invigorate the current global belly dance subculture.

---

[1] www.museemechanique.org

[2] These styles would go on to influence 21st century Vaudevillian Tribal Fusion wear.

## References

Adams, Katherine H. and Michael L. Keene and L. Michael and Jennifer C. Koella. *Seeing the American Woman, 1880-1920: The Social Impact of the Visual Media Explosion.* Jefferson, NC: McFarland & Company, Inc., 2012. Print.

Allen, Robert C. *Horrible Prettiness: Burlesque and American Culture.* USA: The University of North Carolina Press, 1991. Print.

Bogdan, Robert. *Freak Show: Presenting Human Oddities for Amusement and Profit.* Chicago: University of Chicago Press, 1988. Print.

Buonaventura, Wendy. *Belly Dancing: The Serpent and the Sphinx.* London: Virago Press. Celik, Zeynep and Kinney, Leila. 1990. "Ethnography and Exhibitionism at the Expositions Universelles" in *Assemblage 13.* 1983. Print.

Desmond, Jane. "Embodying Difference: Issues in Dance and Cultural Studies" in *Cultural* Critique 26: 33-63. USA: University of Minnesota Press, 1994. Print.

Edwards, Heather. *Noble Dreams, Wicked Pleasures: Orientalism in America, 1870 – 1930.* Princeton, NJ: Princeton University Press, 2000. Print.

Haynes-Clark, Jennifer Lynn. *American Belly Dance and the Invention of the New Exotic: Orientalism, Feminism, and Popular Culture.* Portland State University, Master's thesis. 2010. Print.

Immerso, Michael. *Coney Island: The People's Playground.* New Jersey: Rutgers University Press, 2002. Print.

Karayanni, Stavros Stavrou. *Dancing fear & desire: Race, sexuality and imperial politics in Middle Eastern dance.* Saint-Lazare, Quebec: Gibson Library Connections, 2008. Print.

Keft-Kennedy, Virginia. " 'How does she do that?' Belly Dancing and the Horror of a Flexible Woman," in *Women's Studies: An Interdisciplinary Journal*, 34: 279-300, 2005. Print.

Munro-Miller, Jennifer. *In the Flesh: The Representation of Burlesque Theatre in American Art and Visual Culture.* Diss. University of Southern California, 2010. Print.

"Burlesque." Oxford English Dictionary. December 21, 2011. Web.

Sellers-Young, Barbara. "Raks El Sharki: Transculturation of a Folk Form" in *Journal of Popular Culture* 26, no. 2 (Fall 1992): 141-152. 1992. Print.

Shay, Anthony. *Dancing Across Borders: The American Fascination with Exotic Dance Forms.* US: McFarland & Company, Inc., 2008. Print.

Sterner, Gabriele. *Art Nouveau; an Art of Transition from Individualism to Mass Society.* New York: Barron's Educational Series, Inc., 1982. Print.

Studlar, Gaylyn.'Out-Salomeing Salomé: Dance, the New Woman, and Fan Magazine Orientalism" in *Visions of the East: Orientalism in Film* (Matthew Bernstein & Gaylyn Studlar, Eds). Rutgers University Press, ON: Toronto, 1997. Print.

Windmuller, Kristen. "Dancing the Other: Early Twentieth Century Parisian Stereotypes of Middle Eastern Dance", Review Version 12/11. Print.

**Catherine Mary Scheelar**
*Catherine is a social science researcher out of Edmonton, Canada. This article was adapted from her Master of Arts thesis in Anthropology entitled "The Use of Nostalgia in Genre Formation in Tribal Fusion Dance", on the proliferation of the Vaudevillian Aesthetic in Tribal Fusion.*

**Mira Betz**

# Belly Dance as Performance
## Historical Phenomenon or Logical Evolution?

**by Iana**

Any spectator will be impressed by the variety of belly dance styles that are offered today: Belly dance with the veils, swords, fans, candelabrum, Isis wings, tambourine, fire or snake etc. Other off-shoots such as fusions of belly dance with Tango, Spanish dance, Samba, Hip-hop or Acrobatics may also be considered. Easily, one can find an alternative to please any possible audience all around the world. It would be difficult to find any other dance style that has so many types as belly dance possesses. Why has this phenomenon happened? Is it because of the belly dancer's wish to impress the public? Additionally, why belly dance exactly? Is it because of the modern fashion of belly dancing, or rather, a natural course of its development?

On one hand, a spectacular show will make any audience happy! Actually, people always come, expecting to enjoy a great show, and they will be grateful to performers for any successful innovations. For most of them, it doesn't matter how traditional your ideas about the dance style are (or are not) if you give them unforgettable emotion. On the other hand, some dancers might criticize such notions, worrying about losing the original art of belly dance. However, there is a big question remaining: What is "original" in belly dancing, and what is "authentic or classical" belly dance? These terms mean the same; however, how different are they from today's modern "show" belly dance?

**Katalin Schafer**

It is generally believed that, in ancient times, there were lots of different tribes in the Middle East that had their own particular dance styles. A few of them enjoyed dancing not only as an entertainment, but as a professional activity as well. The main role in such communities was played by women (who, by the way, were the first professional dancers in the Middle East). They earned much more money than their menfolk, and that gave them a freedom within their families as well as some independence in society. However, they were not belly dancers per se. More commonly, they presented the dance styles of their own tribes or communities, dancing in the streets or as invited dancers in the homes of the rich. Today, we perform their dances as the folkloric Middle-Eastern dances.

The main goal of dance performances was earning money; so dancers tried to entertain the public as well as possible. That is why we were able to find memories and notes - for instance - when the dancers who performed one of the most popular social dances in Egypt and some other Middle Eastern countries, "beledi", were adding elements of show business to their performances. They could dance with a glass of water or a sword balanced upon their heads or they joined together in small groups and performed pantomimes to transform their performance into a little theatrical show. All of these factors added together demonstrated two different types of dancing:

- Dancing for yourself (when you enjoy simply dancing for yourself).
- Dancing for the public (when you allow other people to enjoy seeing your dance).

Another important tendency influencing the belly dance, took place in the nineteenth century in the West. A popular fashion in the East during that period was tagged with the name "Orientalism". In general, the term "Orientalism" refers to the fantasy of western people concerning the east and describes the influence of the east on the western culture. The first source of information about foreign countries was mutual trades: Goods and services by merchandisers. Let's remember that during a long period in history, in the mind of western people, India and Egypt were associated with one large east area that was extremely far from them. Generally, the most famous products from the east were sweets, spices, gold jewelry, and fine fabrics. Also, stories of the sellers and traders were quite often far from reality and these stories were embellished by exaggerated ideas that intrigued listeners. As a result, in the minds of western people, the mysterious women under the veils were covered with jewelry; the closed harems were fully decorated by carpets, light chiffon, other exotic fabrics, etc.

A Secret or a Mystery Always Creates Legends and Fantasies! Additionally, people were influenced by western artists who took their inspiration from travelers' notes and embodied their own fantasies within their paintings. With the exception of a notable few, most of them never visited any eastern country and never saw the real eastern dancers whom they depicted in their paintings.

The end of the nineteenth century and the beginning of the twentieth century became an era of foreign contracts for the dancers from Egypt, Turkey, Lebanon and other Middle-Eastern countries. Dancers and musicians came to Europe and America to participate in different expositions in which the main attractions were in the midway tents and the Middle Eastern exhibits; for instance, the Great Columbia Exposition in

**The Snake Charmer by Jean Leon Gerome**

1893 Chicago. The dancers were usually promoted by their western agents who knew intuitively how to interest a potential western audience. By itself, the Middle-Eastern dance was a shock to conservative Victorian western people of that time because of its hip movements. What is more, many of the dancers wore light-weight shirts that made the abdomen almost visible, or perhaps, they even danced with bared bellies! To emphasize the exotic novelty, the agents announced the performances as "The Dance of Belly". It is speculated that that is how the term "belly dance" came into existence - due to promotional goals of the dancers' agents.

The dance itself started other changes also. After the first shock and amazement, the favorable impression of the western public became unreliable. Their aesthetic principals and images of beauty and femininity (based on ideas from the ballet that were more familiar to them) were in conflict with the show they thought "suggestive". Moreover, their fantasies and expectations concerning the eastern show were crushed. Conversely, the performers were impressed by the new western culture and felt that competition with western dancers (who tried to copy them without any serious knowledge about Middle-Eastern culture or dance) added a lot from western fantasies about the east.

This embodiment of vision made them competitive as well as quite successful and popular.

That's why, as had happened in past times, the eastern dancers began changing their traditional performance style, incorporating it with the goals of entertaining the public, meeting most public expectations, and earning money. Eastern dancers had performed quite often with different circus groups; so it was not difficult to anticipate what the crowd wished to see.

They had heard about western dance cultures, and they had posed for the photographers and graphic artists who expressed clearly how they would like the eastern dancer to be seen in their paintings and photographs. The period might have signified the beginning of the art of belly dance as the eastern dance show especially for western audiences and its significant separation from beledi or any other folkloric dance style.

As it was mentioned above, this process was also influenced by competition with western dancers who performed in the Oriental style. Some of them created great shows, but unfortunately, a lot of them also harmed the reputation of belly dancing. For example, a Syrian dancer, Farida Mazar known as "Little Egypt", suffered because hundreds of her clones performed inappropriate and vulgar dances using her name. The so-called belly dancers had discredited the status of belly dancing for American audiences, during the entire next century! Another example took place in 1896, when a film was produced titled "Passion Dance" (a.k.a. "La Danse du Ventre") in which an

American dancer, Dolorita, imitated the movements of belly dance in a revealing costume. It was one of the first censored films in the history of cinematography.

Inevitably, there were other examples of western dancers who became successful in this field. One of them was Ruth St. Denis. Before Ruth started her dance career, she had taken no eastern dance classes at all; her knowledge of eastern dances was limited to once having watched a dance troupe from India. She, like iconic Isadora Duncan, used her own feelings to create an embodiment of movement. Ruth took her inspiration from published images about the east. For example, the impetus to her spectacular production "Egypt" was an advertisement for cigarettes that had a Pharaoh queen on its cover. The importance of her show was not in the traditionalism of Middle Eastern dances that she presented, but rather in their theatrical nature, claiming that the dance (belly dance) could be, in reality, a serious art-form!

Thinking of folk dance as an art form was extremely unusual for those times. However, she presented Middle Eastern dances as American audience wished to see them. The same thing was true for the infamous Mata Hari. Despite the fact that Mata claimed to have never had any dance classes, she made her debut in a dance of "suggestive Oriental tones" at the salon of Madame Kireevsky on March 13 of 1905.

Toni Bentley in her book "Sisters of Salome" describes the evening's interior that created the mysterious and exciting atmosphere of the Oriental show presented to a western audience:

> "The eight ridged columns topped with classic nude beauties that encircled the rotunda were draped with garlands of white flowers. Jasmine and Sandalwood incense wafted through the air while flickering candles lit a floor strewn with rose petals. The musicians began the first sad tones of an Eastern rite... and Mata Hari was born."

The twentieth century was a period when a lot of people from the west visited the Middle Eastern countries, and the entertaining atmosphere there was also developing rapidly. Many restaurants, cabarets and casinos were first opened around that time. The most famous was Badia Masabni's "Opera-Casino" opened in 1926. Badia Masabni was not only an actress and a dancer; she was a skillful entrepreneur. She was the first to realize that a western audience, who could produce for her a considerable income, was interested not in the authentic Middle Eastern dances but in the Oriental show, which met their fantasies and expectations. She made theatrical changes in the dance style, and in fact, she became "a mother of modern Oriental dance". Until the twentieth century, eastern dancers used to perform mostly in place, using surprisingly little space.

Thankfully, one of Madam Masabni's innovations for the Oriental dance was the enrichment of moving space. One's arms began to participate actively in dancing: Wavy, serpentine movements, bizarre weaves, fascinating wrist work...Badia Masabni's pupils began to adopt western dance trends into their dances. As a result, the eastern dance style became lighter, its center of gravity moved from the hips to the upper part of the body. Some ballet-style movements had successfully become a part of Oriental dance and nowadays nobody could even imagine that they are related to ballet elements, rather than Oriental; for example, the Arabesque leg lift or Flic-Flac. Partly, these changes happened because:

- Casino programs consisted of other dances from the entire world - not from Middle Eastern dances only.
- The same dancers must have had training in different dance styles that influenced their bodies, postures, and awareness in general.

This new belly dance style was given the name "Raqs Sharqi" and was referred to sometimes as the "classical belly dance" (due to its elegant appearance).

By the way, the dance with veils became an important part of Raqs Sharqi exactly in that period! Before that, dance with a veil was not very popular and, certainly was not traditional for the Middle Eastern dance.

Sweeping changes in the style were caused by the popularity of Badia Masabni's pupils who, until now, remain the ideals for Oriental dance artists. Samia Gamal, Naema Akef, and Taheya Carioca are the legends of the Middle Eastern dance culture. Even today we admire them, and many dancers attempt to copy their styles. These famous dancers started billing their performances as a "show". The development of cinematography and the crazy popularity of Hollywood in the twentieth century made an important impact on them as well as the other dancers of that time. The eastern dancers, who could be seen often in film as actresses, tried to use the latest Hollywood trends: Gorgeous make-up and hairstyles, rich costumes and many spectacular show elements became essential parts of their performances both in the films and on the stage.

Unfortunately, numerous beginning dancers nowadays misinterpret the term "classical belly dance", thinking that it means authentic, original belly dancing. In fact, the form has existed less than one hundred years and describes quite a new belly dance style that we call "Raqs Sharqi" (Dance of the East). The question of authenticity in belly dance is still an open theory, causing fanciful discussions. In spite of the fact that the term "belly dance" is not ancient and became widely

**Oriental Dancer by Eduard Frederic Wilhelm Richter**

spread only several centuries ago, nevertheless, we could say that its origins are deep in history because this dance is built on the intermixing of different folkloric dances.

Historically, belly dance has always focused upon its audience. As a form separate from the folkloric style of dance, it was formed beneath the influence of western culture and, as such, it was developed as a showy dance art.

The noun "show" does not imply that the only goal of dancers is (or should be) to entertain spectators. Unfortunately, a lot of people think about "shows" only in a negative sense, associating them with the term "show-business"; in other words, a business rather than a true art. However, what happens if we change the word "show" to its synonym - performance? It has the same essence but a completely different attitude. Furthermore, show (concerning any dance performance) could possibly mean "adaptation to be presented for others".

I remember the statement of Mahmoud Reda, founder of the National Egyptian Troupe, during a panel discussion about foreign influence upon belly dance at IBCC 2012. He said that he did not like it when his troupe was referred to as "a traditional folklore troupe", explaining that he only used the folkloric dance material to create his folklore stage-show.

From this perspective, everything that is on stage is the show for others to experience. If a dancer doesn't want to present his art to others and to receive their feedback, simply, he will not dance on stage. However, if he performs on the stage, his dance will become inherently different from what he dances socially - at a discotheque, for instance. Let us always remember that there are two types of dancing:

- dancing for yourself (when you enjoy dancing for your own amusement and fitness) and
- performing a dance before the public (when you share your dance specifically for the enjoyment of others).

## References

Buonaventura, Wendy. *Serpent of the Nile: Women and dance in the Arab world*. Northampton: Interlink Books, 2010. Print.

Carlton, Donna. *Looking for Little Egypt*. Bloomington: IDD Books, 1994. Print.

Corn, Wanda M. *Women building history: Public art at the 1893 Columbian Exposition*. Berkeley: University of California Press, 2011. Print.

Darwish, Mustafa and Rafik el-Sabban and Yasser Alwan. *The golden years of Egyptian film: Cinema Cairo, 1936-1967, Cairo*. New York: American University in Cairo Press, 2008. Print.

St. Denis, Ruth. *Ruth St. Denis, an unfinished life: An autobiography*. Brooklyn: Dance Horizons, 1969. Print.

Flaubert, Gustav. *Flaubert in Egypt : A sensibility on tour*. Trans. Francis Steegmuller. Boston: Little, Brown, 1972. Print.

Hammond, Andrew. *Pop culture Arab world!: Media, arts, and lifestyle*. Santa Barbara: ABC-CLIO, 2005. Print.

Lane, Edward William. *An account of the manners and customs of the modern Egyptians*. New York: Dover Publications, 1973. Print.

Ohanian, Armen. *La danseuse de Shamakha*. Paris: J. Cape, 1918. Print.

Sadoul, Georges. *The cinema in the Arab countries: Anthology prepared for UNESCO*. Beirut: Interarab Centre of Cinema and Television, 1966. Print.

Said, Edward W. *Orientalism*. New York: Vintage Books, 1979. Print.

Anthony Shay and Barbara Sellers-Young. *Belly dance: Orientalism, transnationalism, and harem *fantasy*. Costa Mesa, Calif: Mazda Publishers, 2005. Print.

Viola Shafik. *Popular Egyptian cinema: Gender, class, and nation, Cairo, Egypt*. New York: The American University in Cairo Press, 2007. Print.

Yuriko Yamanaka and Tetsuo Nishio. *The Arabian nights and orientalism: Perspectives from East & West*. London; New York, I.B. Tauris, 2006. Print.

### *Iana*

*Iana has been practicing belly dance since 2004 and performed with "Ishtar Dance Co" (Ukraine) from 2007-2009. In the end of 2011, Iana moved to Canada and joined Arabesque Dance Co and Orchestra. At IBCC 2012 she presented a lecture "The historical connections between Belly Dance and Ballet", and performed a piece with Triple Isis Wings.*

**Jane Chung How of Taiwan**

**Kathy poses with a Gilded Serpent, Maloos.**

**Tahya Carioca**

**Naemet Mokhtar**

**Naima Akef**

**Soheir Zaki**

**Fifi Abdo**

**Nagwa Fouad**

**Badia Masabni**

**Samia Gamal**

**Mahmoud Reda & Farida Fahmy**

**Artwork by Leela Corman, Stats by Sausan**

### Naima Akef
*Premier Star of the Egyptian Musical Cinema*
10/7/29 - 4/12/66

1. Birth Name: Na'eema Akef.
2. Birthplace: Tanta, Egypt.
3. Was born to a circus family and began training at age 4.
4. Began her dance career at age 14.
5. 1949 - First film: Al Eich wal Malh (Bread and Salt).
6. Married film producer Hussein Fawzi.
7. Worked closely with Mahmoud Reda.
8. 1957 - Performed in an international youth festival and was nominated best dancer.
9. Photograph hangs on the wall of Bolshoi Museum in Moscow.
10. 1964 - Gave birth to a son.
11. At age 37, died of Cancer.

### Naemet Mokhtar
*The Symphony of Belly Dance*
Circa Early - Late 1900s

1. Birth Name: Naemet Mokhtar.
2. Birthplace: Alexandria, Egypt.
3. Was born to an affluent musical family.
4. Was trained to sing by Oum Zaitoun and to dance by Nebaweya Salem.
5. 1951 - First film: Fataat Al Sirk (Daughter of the Circus).
6. Singer, Kareem Mahmoud, discovered her.
7. Quote: "I never felt guilty about working as a dancer. People think that success comes easy, but the fact is that I worked hard to be a successful dancer at a time when the field was full of dance stars."
8. Married three times.
9. Has one son.
10. Produced and starred in many films well into the 1970s.

### Tahya Carioca
*Queen of Oriental Cabaret Dance*
2/22/1919 - 9/20/1999

1. Birth Name: Badawiya Mohamed Karim Ali Sayed.
2. Birthplace: Manzala, Egypt.
3. Was given her last name Karioka from the movie: Flying down to Rio.
4. 1935 - First film: Dr. Farahat.
5. 1942 - Most important film: Lu-bat Al-Sit (The Lady's Play).
6. 1952 - Stopped dancing after the revolusion.
7. 1972 - One of last films: Kali Belak Min Zuzu (Take Care of Zuzu).
8. Was married 14 times.
9. No surviving offspring.
10. Appeared in over 300 films, plays and television soap operas.

### Nagwa Fouad
*The Princess of Cairo*
1943 - Present

1. Birth Name: Awatef Mommed Al Agamy.
2. Birthplace: Alexandria, Egypt.
3. Was raised by her stepmother in Jaffa.
4. Began performing at Age 15.
5. 1960s - Debuted in popular stage show: Adwaa Al-Madina (City Lights).
6. 1966 - Appeared on the cover of Al-Kawakeb Egyptian movie magazine.
7. 1976 - Qamar Arba'tashar (Moon of the 14th) musical composed especially for her by Mohamed Abd El Wahab.
8. Married four times.
9. 1970s- Highest paid dancer in the Arab world.
10. 1974/75 - Performed for Henry Kissinger
11. 1978 - Performed for Pres. Jimmy Carter.

### Fifi Abdo
*The Filly*
April 26, 1953 to Present

1. Birth Name: Atiyat Abdul Fattah Ibrahim.
2. Birthplace: Cairo, Egypt.
3. Father was a policeman.
4. Is one of 11 children including half-siblings.
5. Began her dance career at age 13.
6. Never attended school and is self taught.
7. 1993-1996 - Earned approximately 1.1 million euros.
8. Recevied over $10,000 per performance.
9. Owns over 5,000 costumes, several Mercedes Benz, and 2 apartments on the Nile.
10. Married 5 times.
11. 1985 - Married for the last time.
12. Has 3 daughters; one is adopted.
13. 2004 - Retired from dancing.
14. Is considered to be the best of the "Big Three" which includes Dina and Lucy.

### Sohair Zaki
*The Om Kalsoum of Dance*
1944 - Present

1. Birth Name: Suhair Zaki.
2. Birthplace: Mansoura, Egypt.
3. 1953 - Moved to Alexandria, Egypt.
4. Began performing at 11 years old.
5. 1959 - Appeared on television.
6. 1960s - Received awards from Shah of Iran, the Tunisian president, and Gamal Abd El Nasser, the second president of Egypt.
7. 1960s - Began appearing in film.
8. 1970s - First to perform to Om Kalsoum songs.
9. Often referred to as "Bint el Balad" or "Daughter of the Country".
10. Shik, Shak, Shok was written for her by Hasssan abou el Seaoud.
11. 2001 - Officially retired.
12. Married once and has one son.

### Mahmoud Reda & Farida Fahmy
*The Original Reda Dance Troupe*
Founded 1959

1. Birth Name: The Reda Band.
2. Birthplace: Cairo, Egypt.
3. Initially made up of 15 dancers.
4. Presented over 300 shows.
5. Reda & Fahmy were its principal dancers.
6. Made four world tours to 58 countries.
7. Performed at Carnegie Hall, USA; Albert Hall, UK; Congress Hall, Germany; Stanislavsky & Gorky Theaters, USSR; Olympia, France; and the United Nations, New York and Geneva.
8. 1961 - Featured in Igazah Nisf as-sinah (Mid Term Vacation).
9. 1965 - Featured in Gharam fe Al-Karnak (Love in Karnak)
10. 1961 - Incorporated into the Government.

### Samia Gamal
*National Dancer of Egypt*
3/5/1924 - 12/1/1994

1. Birth Name: Zainab Ibrahim Mahfuz.
2. Birthplace: Wana al Qiss, Egypt.
3. First film: Min Fat Adimo (He Who Has No Past Has No Future); was a box office flop.
4. 1942 - First real film: Mamu' al-Hob (Forbidden Love).
5. 1949 - Began starring with Fareed Al Atrasch, her lover of 8 years.
6. 1950 - Appeared in LIFE Magazine.
7. 1954 - Appeared in French Movie Ali Baba et Les 40 Voleurs (Ali Baba & the 40 Thieves).
8. 1954 - Appeared in Valley of the Kings.
9. Was married twice - Oil Taycoon, Shepherd King and Egyptian actor, Rushdi Abaza.
10. Set the trend for fashion design in her dance career.

### Badia Masabni
*Mother of Modern Oriental Dance*
1885 - 1970

1. Birth Name: Juliette Masabni.
2. Birthplace: Halab, Syria, now Lebanon.
3. Began her dance career at 17.
4. Married famous play actor and singer, Naguib El Righani.
5. 1926 - Opened Casino Badiya in Cairo.
6. Owned three casinos successively.
7. Adopted a young girl she named Julliette.
8. 1934 - Produced first films: Malikat at Masarih (The Queen of the Theaters) and Layali al Qahira (The Nights of Cairo).
9. One of the biggest patrons of Badiya's nightclubs was King Farouk.
10. Lived out the end of her days in Beirut.
11. Is credited for having discovered many of Egypt's Golden Age era belly dancers.

**Find these trading cards online in printable PDF files in our Bonus Features at www.gildedserpent.com/reader**

**The Gates of Khalif, 1887**
by William Logsdail

# Section 4
# BIZ

One of the goals of many performing Belly Dancers is going pro. But what does that mean? Professional paid performers fall into a variety of different categories. There are the entertainers who work in restaurants, night clubs and hookah joints and are on the front lines of the professional dance world. Somewhat behind the scenes are dance instructors who devote their professional energies to teaching the future generations of belly dance artists. In addition, there are numerous other niches where dancers can cultivate additional income streams, working as event promoters to video producers, touring workshop leaders to local and regional coaches, choreographers and costumers.

Professional practices such as marketing, promotion, advertising, and outreach apply to every niche. From concrete 'how-to's' to more conceptual theories and approaches, Gilded Serpent has supported the sharing of knowledge in support of the professional dance arts. For more articles on the business of dance, visit GildedSerpent.com

# What a Band Needs
## But Doesn't Always Get...

### by Denise of Pangia

At one time or another, we members of the Pangia Band have been at all different ends of production: Dancer, musician, sound man (all facets), show producer, announcer, etc. This includes keeping the dancers line-up on schedule and orderly; often, we've heard it referred to, with good humor, as cat-herding! (Isn't the lovely dancer, *her dance name goes here*, supposed to be up next? Well, then, where is she?)

We band members understand what happens when the communication is either non-existent or perspective-challenged. Your view of an event can change radically with a change in the role you play in the event.

### In a Perfect World
Everyone is on the same page!

- The band knows what the stage looks like, and there is a sound system in place to meet its needs.
- There is a knowledgeable and experienced sound person who is ready to run it for the event.
- The band members arrive at the venue, set up equipment, plug-in, make a sound check and begin to play!

Okay...in reality, that almost never happens without a few heart-pounding moments. If your band plays often and in many different venues, you have to be prepared for anything and everything!

### Make a Reality Check
- The band must know what is expected. A two-month advance notice is a fantastic idea, but in our reality check, this only happens once in a great while.
- You may have to hone your communication skills to get information from the person who is hiring you. Sometimes, the person who contacts you first is not the person who has the vision for the show or the money to pay you! So, you must locate the organizer of the event to find out what is wanted exactly!

### The Band Needs to Know!
Every variation on the theme is possible:
- Is it a 2-hour show featuring dancers?
- Is it to be a 4-hour show as background music for a lavish dinner?
- Entertainment during intermission?
- A festival studded with continuous short dance solos?
- A small living room with toddlers underfoot and great-grandmother singing along with the band?
- Does she need a microphone?
- Will it be outside on a street corner with people milling about?

Just as with dance jobs, a band's gig will almost never turn out the same way twice! The person responsible for bookings must ask questions!

If you can make a site visit ahead of time and also contact the person running the sound equipment, do it! Are there pictures online that you can see to get an understanding of the venue from other events that have been held there? You will want to know if you will be situated in sunshine, shade, wind, or under some lovely trees that just happen to drop sap all over your instruments and your hair! If the people who are hiring are unclear about your minimum sound requirements, and you have your own portable system that you could pack along with you, do it! It will be cheap insurance! (We in Pangia have played at places that have a magnificent sound system, but sadly for us, it was safely locked in a closet and only "Herman", the custodian who went to Bismarck that weekend, had the key!)

### When to Worry
Be wary of someone who tells you, "Don't worry; we have everything you will need!" If this is not the

sound person employed at the venue, you need to check further. "Everything" could be defined as anything from a boombox or an ancient mixing-board to a DJ's professional setup. The DJ setup could work, but if the hall does not have permission from the DJ to use it, then you are out of luck! Bring your own if there is any question about it at all in your mind. Remember that some people think that a microphone and a public address speaker are a "sound system". Only your band knows what is required for an adequate performance.

## Planning the Gig Setup

- If there is a sound person to contact, this is the person to whom you must communicate your setup as well as your sound needs. Send a diagram of your "stage setup" to them and bring a copy of it along with you. This diagram should show your positions on the stage, your preferred types of microphone and stands, chairs, etc. Confirm your setup before the gig begins and also your sound check times; then, be on time!

- Are you allowed to sell your music CDs and DVDs at this venue? Does the promoter demand a percentage of your profit or your gross sales? Will there be a table for you to display your merchandise or should you bring one?

- Yearly Rakkasah Festivals are well-run, and one luxury that bands have there is to be able to set up behind a scrim and get comfortable and ready to play well before their designated play-times.

- At festivals, sound checks happen during the open floors, and bands should remember it is a festival - not a concert. There are monitors, side fills and a separate monitor mix at the Rakkasah Festival so the musicians can hear themselves and each other. However, in a concert situation, you should have from forty-five minutes to an hour for a sound check - with no audience

**Pangia Plays for Isis San Miguel. Member names: Pat, Denise, Casey Bond from NY, Sean McGarry from Pennsylvania. Rakkasah East 2012, New Jersey at Spring Caravan.**

present in the hall. At other festivals, the band just sets up with everyone there and has little or no sound check before the dancer(s) start performing. This situation is disquieting to the band and quite nerve wracking!

- Be sure that you have all the information about your set before you begin playing. It is comical, but unnerving and disruptive to have a stage manager or announcer try to speak with you while you are playing.

## Stages and Special Considerations

There are stages and there are stages. Then, there are stages of staging! Some stages appear professional. Some do not!

- Always ask about the dimensions of your stage, when and where you can load in and out, etc.
- You really don't need to trudge through a hall full of people, carrying all your gear!
- Can you park your vehicle close to unload and reload?
- Is there a place to park where you will not be ticketed?

Some festivals have a true stage while many have only risers, portable and, yes, collapsible platforms! They must be set up so that they do not fall down, and they must be leveled. They must have stable stairs when needed to get up and down. Test it out and make sure you are comfortable with the staging. Safety is truly an issue here.

## Other Surfaces

In addition, there are other lovely and wondrous surfaces on which to perform. Among them: Tile, marble, asphalt, hard wood, gravel, grass (with or without divots, trash, and critters) as well as sand (volcanic and beach). It would be prudent to check to make certain that the sprinklers are not timed to turn on automatically during your performance. Also, sometimes the grass is already soggy since it was watered about an hour before you arrived!

All these surfaces may present extreme challenges. We try to carry carpets because they help with sound if the surfaces are tile or marble. Carpeting also helps the instruments and players

**Tasha of New Jersey kisses Carmine on the head!**

to not slide around! We also carry some furniture pads for an underlayment, tools to level the stage, and things like a pop-up canopy for the elements, extension cords, and a power-strip, towels, antibacterial wipes, hand sanitizer, paper towels, etc. Never underestimate the power of a roll of "gaffer's-tape"! We have insane stories about sinking into the volcanic ash that everyone thought was really cool "because it looks like a desert"! In short, always ask about the proposed performance surface!

## Stormy Weather

Is there a contingency for foul weather? Some places continue on because the stage is protected. Others do not. Make sure to communicate what your plan is if there is a cloudburst or some other act of nature.

## Problems and Solutions

If you are flying to a gig, or your car is small, knowing your solutions to the problems I have mentioned here ahead of time can be critical! These are true situations, and more reasons why we try to get as much information as possible before we show up!

- Is it an intimate private party?
- Is it a surprise party?
- Do you enjoy hanging out in a cold garage, waiting to sneak in before "Mr. Birthday Guy" gets home from work?
- Have you ever heard the embarrassing and threatening line: "Who are you, and what the (bleep) are you doing in my living room?".

## Payment

If you are being paid, write a short "performance contract", stating your fee, set up and play times, etc.

Be clear so that all expectations of both parties can be fulfilled. (Can you play for another hour since Aunt Dodie is not here yet?)

**Setting up for the Asian Festival in a park by the Rogue River. The glamorous part of the job!**

## Dancers

Be clear in your communications with the dancers. If they are not familiar with your music, let them know where they can listen to your music or purchase it. Be sure they understand that if they have a 7-minute solo, that the band must conform to that time constraint. This usually means that they may not be able to dance to a longer version of a specific song or drum solo they want to request. Many dancers do not know the names of songs, so be able to describe rhythms and the feel of a particular song.

## Jams & Other "Get Togethers"

It's fun to jam and get everyone together, dancers, musicians, vendors, the volunteer staff, etc. However, it can also be an insane nightmare of people who just want to make noise and work out their private issues rather than play real music; so they just become louder, and louder, and louder!

If and when we do a jam, we like to play our music for a little while, with drummers who will listen to what we are playing. When it starts to get off-beat (Where is beat one?) and out of control, we just let them have at it - alone!

At one of the "after parties" where we played, the music became totally insane; one end of the room was playing Balady, while the other end was playing something completely different!

An "Open Floor" at the Rakassah Festivals provides our chance to warm up, do a soundcheck, and play some tunes for people to just get up and dance. We love seeing everyone get up and having fun with our music!

## In Conclusion

As much as possible, try to discover what you are getting into. It may not always turn out to be perfect, but you can avoid a lot of disappointment by communicating and realizing the situation in advance. Festivals have to run on time; so it's always a good idea to leave your personal drama at the door and be open to just about anything. Be flexible and professional at all times.

If you are not comfortable with what you are hearing from the person who is trying to hire you, create a performance contract to clarify what is expected of all parties. Contact them a day or two before the gig to review your contract just to ensure that there are no quirky or unreasonable changes. Always expect the unexpected, but nevertheless, have fun while you play. It's always a learning experience and an adventure!

### Denise of Pangia

*Pangia plays exciting and dynamic arrangements of Egyptian, Armenian, Greek, Lebanese, Turkish and Persian dance classics as well as a varying array of original compositions. This band is popular with belly dancers and musicians alike. Pangia's music is sold worldwide, and they have 6 CDs & MP3s available. Be on the lookout for more from this diverse and popular band.*

**Harem Musicians
by Gustavo Simoni**

Leila dances to the Safaa Farid band at a wedding in 2012

# Dancing with Live Bands
## The Little Book of Etiquette

### by Leyla Lanty

Have you ever watched a dancer perform with live music and sensed that something was missing? The dancer was lovely, costume stunning, technique and knowledge of the music and its phrasing, fabulous. The musicians were talented and played beautifully. All seemed perfect, but the sense of a truly enjoyable show was missing. You were left with questions. What just happened? What didn't happen? Did the dancer relate to the live music or could she or he have performed just as well to a recorded piece? Why was there an apparent lack of connection between dancer and musicians? How would a dancer help him or herself to connect with the musicians?

I was inspired to write on this topic while attending and teaching several summers at the Ahlan Wa Sahlan Festival, Raqia Hassan's annual summer event in Cairo, Egypt. Much to my surprise, the musicians often thanked me after my performances at the festival's nightly open stage parties! When I mentioned this to Raqia, she commented that she was not surprised because she saw that I knew "how to dance like a professional." She advised me to watch the dancers performing to live music closely, and I would understand. Following her advice, I found that too often, the dancers paid little or no attention to the band and their singer. The dancers simply entered the stage after their names were announced, danced, then bowed to the audience and left the stage. Almost every time, after just a couple of minutes, the band would "tune out" and play and sing for each other and the audience, no longer watching what the dancer was doing. Back home in the US, I began to notice that many dancers were doing the same thing when they performed in front of live musicians, and I asked myself "Why?" and "What could they have done differently?".

**Yousef Kouyoumjian plays violin with an unknown drummer and dancer. This was probably taken at the Bagdad Night club in the North Beach neighborhood of San Francisco.**

From my observations, I believe the answer to "Why?" is lack of experience. Over the last two decades, the opportunities for dancing to live music have shrunk to a precious few. The majority of emerging dancers today have little or no experience dancing with live musicians. Very likely, many of their teachers also have had little or no experience with live music. If you count yourself among these emerging dancers, you've probably asked yourself: "When a live music opportunity arrives, how can I prepare for it so that it will be a pleasurable experience for both me and my audience?".

My question to you is: "What is missing from your question?". That's right – the band! Few have written about this, but virtually all dancers who have regularly danced with live musicians know how to relate to a live band before, during, and after their performances, in order to create the collaboration that makes the creative energy flow, producing an outstanding performance enjoyed by the dancer, the band, and most of all, the audience.

With the band actively supporting you, each show has the potential to be your best one ever. How do you get the band on your side from the beginning? I've learned first hand that the best way to have a first rate show is to work with the band members as part of their team. If the musicians understand that you have a passion for the dance and the music, they will share their passion with you by playing their best for your performances. Real professionals want to present a "package" to the audience in which the dancer and musicians work together to "make a show."

Over my 30-plus years of dancing, I've had the pleasure of dancing regularly with music played by professional musicians, and I've also had the honor to be asked to play finger cymbals and duff (frame drum) with professional musicians on many occasions. In in my role as dancer, my interactions with bands, and from my experience playing as part of the band, I've learned that it's a two-way street. The musicians want you to be on their side too!

How do you let them know you want their help and support and keep them from "tuning out" and ignoring you while you dance in front of them? It only takes paying attention to a few details each and every time you dance with live musicians. It boils down to one word, as Aretha Franklin so aptly sang it "R.E.S.P.E.C.T." Following are the etiquette guidelines that I recommend for interacting successfully with a band before, during and after a show, even if the only language I have in common with them is the music. It is easier than you might think, and it works for me every time.

## Before the Show

The first tip is about a simple courtesy that will be truly appreciated by the musicians. Introduce yourself to them before the show and tell them you're looking forward to dancing with them.

- Discuss your music requests or preferences. It's best to know titles or to be able to "hum a few bars." On the other hand, don't be surprised if they don't recognize a tune when you "hum a few bars" and you forget to sing a few quarter tones! A few years ago, this scenario happened to me:

Musician: "Oh, you mean ...hum, hum, hum, hum, hum?"

Me: "Yes, isn't that what I just sang?"

Musician: "Well, no, not exactly."

- Be flexible in your requests, always having alternative tunes in mind. If you don't know the names of the tunes, try saying "I'd like a medium-fast ballady for my entrance, then a taqsim or rhumba, a drum solo and a short finale to finish up." Then, be ready to improvise! Remember to write "Learn names of my favorite dance songs" on your "to do" list!

- If you ask the band for a drum solo, do not expect that the drummer will be able to reproduce a solo from a recording produced by the band. Almost every drum solo is completely improvised on the spot by the drummer him or herself, so if you ask for a drum solo on the band's recording, he/she will probably not be able to reproduce it for you. Besides, the drummer for your performance may be a different drummer from the one who plays on their CD! Again, be ready to improvise!

### Showtime

- As you enter the stage or dance floor, acknowledge your audience first; then make eye contact with each of the musicians, giving each a nod of your head or a little salute by looking at him/her and touching the outer edge of your eye or the middle of your forehead with your hand. Acknowledgements like this are short and sweet but appreciated. You will most likely lose the band in the first couple of minutes if you don't acknowledge them. The big stars who employ their own musicians always do this. I've seen Fifi Abdou, Mona Sa-id, Dandash, Dina and many more stars in person in Cairo and all of them acknowledge their musicians at the beginning of their shows and again near or at the end before they exit. All of them recognize that their musicians deserve to be recognized on stage in addition to being paid their salaries.

- Every time, even if your performance is only six or seven minutes long, turn around at least once and dance "for" the musicians. To them it means that you recognize their importance to your show. In the Middle Eastern tradition, music is the foundation of the dancer's performance. Without the musicians, you don't have much on which to build. They will really appreciate your dancing for them personally during your show.

- Be aware of the whole band when you play finger cymbals! By playing zills, you become a part of

**Author dances with the Safaa Farid Band at Ahlan Wa Sahlan in Cairo.**

**Pasha Restaurant of San Francisco in the 1990s**

the band; so, unless you are doing a cymbal solo, try to blend in and support the other musicians. Don't play too loudly and always coordinate your rhythms with those being played by the musicians. If you intend to play finger cymbals with the drum solo, ask the drummer before the show starts. A few (very few) drummers do not want cymbal accompaniment from the dancer, even if the dancer is an expert cymbal player, and they may cut the drum solo short if you play with them without checking with them first.

- At the end of your performance, after acknowledging the audience's applause, step aside, face the audience and extend your arm that is nearest the band towards them to ask for the audience's approval of their work.

## After the Show
- Find the musicians and thank them.
- Tell them how much you liked their music.
- Tell them how much fun you had dancing with them.
- Thank them again! They will remember you in a most positive way next time they play for you.

**Bottom Line:** It's not hard to make a real connection with the band when dancing to live music. Just remember that magic word "R.E.S.P.E.C.T." and mind your manners!

### Leyla Lanty
*Leyla teaches Egyptian dancing, cane, finger cymbals in the San Francisco area. She has performed in belly dance events and many Arab restaurants. She created a DVD "Habibi, You Are My... WHAT?! Leyla Lanty's Essential Arabic for Dancers," teaching Arabic words, phrases, gestures used to interpret Arabic songs. She produced a CD in Egypt, "Golden Days Enchanting Nights."*

# Selling Your Dance: A Series of Elevator Pitches

## by Athena

The concept for this article came from a discussion with a few professional belly dancers at a workshop. We were trading stories of all the crazy things that we, in our business personae, have been asked. During the course of our conversation, I began to notice our attitude towards the entire issue; generally, all of us were annoyed but seemed to accept this as a part of our chosen dance field. While driving home, I thought this over and determined that it doesn't have to be the case.

I decided on four premises on which I would base my responses to these comments. They are as follows:

- I am a hard-working, small business owner.
- I am pleased with my choice.
- This person is probably uninformed or just trying to put me on defense.
- I have an opportunity (even if brief) to educate this person.

Without my four premises, I tend to get upset, lose an opportunity to educate, and speak with a chip on my shoulder. Instead of simply hoping that I will react well in the moment, I have created a series of readily accessible "elevator pitches" to use in these situations. (An "elevator pitch" is a short speech used to sell an idea quickly or secure a gig; it has to be short enough to be said during the average elevator ride.) I have a few examples of my retorts here, but feel free to change them to match your own personality and your dance business. I tend to use humor to diffuse situations, but that doesn't have to be your reaction.

### Aren't belly dancers just glorified strippers?

If you want a stripper, you will be very disappointed in belly dancing! I am a professional belly dancer - a dance that evolved from various folk dances that originated in the Middle East. In performance, belly dance is a positive way to bring people, including women and children, together to enjoy a celebration!

### So, I know you said it would cost around $300 to have you dance at my party, but another dancer said she would charge $45. Why the big difference? Could you give me a discount?

It sounds like you are worried about the wide price difference between the two of us. I don't know why a dancer would price her dance below standard entertainer pricing. She must have some reason, but I want to thank you for calling me back to discuss this. I preform dynamic, exciting shows - especially tailored for your event and with a dignified and professional demeanor. Included in my set price is the amount of personalization that I will build into your specific event. My commitment to a fantastic, individualized show will guarantee that you and your guests will have the time of your lives and it will be worth every penny!

(Note: it's important for you to remember that this person called you back; even though they had been quoted a cheaper offer, they still choose to call you back! Traditionally, I ask for greater detail about their event in order to demonstrate the quality of service they might expect. Choose to ignore the low-ball price mentioned--it may or may not be true--and sell your dance set along with your specialties such as sword dancing or use of other stage props.)

**Do you do anything special for our male guests after the show?**
I preform family-friendly shows only; perhaps you are calling the wrong type of entertainers. Sometimes, I am hired to dance at children's parties; children have fun with belly dance and are very welcome at all of my shows. They sure do know how to have fun! I love to have them join in and dance with me.

**Why do you belly dance? Isn't it for women who are large?**
Belly dance can be useful for fitness and exercise, but more than that, belly dance gives women a safe environment to become more self-confident and to love their body, no matter what shape they are in at the time! I believe everyone is beautiful, but sometimes they just need to be reminded of that and belly dance can help them. You should try it, too!

**Why do you bring an escort? Don't you trust us?**
Bringing an escort is not an issue of trust, but of convenience for your presentation. You don't need to feel burdened with my luggage, or bringing me the right props durng the correct time in my show if I have an escort who takes care of all these details for you. An escort will do all of these trouble-shooting things for your event and guarantee that you have the smoothest dance experience possible.

**Do men belly dance?**
Men do belly dance! There are accomplished male Belly dancers who perform all over the United States and even internationally. In the Middle East, men sometimes perform different folk dance styles of Belly dance in appropriate venues. They are just as entertaining, skilled and fun as female Belly dancers.

**What do you mean by "professional"?**
A professional belly dancer is someone who knows how to bring you the best event possible and who pursues the activity for remuneration. They have studied hard to know the dances of all of the different regions of the Middle East, how to put on a quality presentation and tailor each show to make it perfect for your event. They have colorful and authentic costumes, appropriate music and will give your audience a memorable experience.

**Are you going to try to seduce my husband?**
No, not unless you want a fantasy comedy routine to make your audience laugh! Many times, people just want to poke fun at a birthday milestone, and I would be happy to present this on your behalf--if that is your intention. We can go over my set together and see if we can agree on what is to be presented and determine if you think it would be fun and humorous for everyone to see.

These are just a few ideas. Feel free to create your own elevator pitches. Remember, they are contacting you because they want to hire you. You are in control! If someone says something exceptionally silly like: "Will you rub up against him? It's his birthday!" You can decline even if they think it would be funny; "No!" is the most powerful word in the world.

If someone gives you the heebie-jeebies, just turn down their gig. You can try to teach them how great belly dance is, but some people are just hopelessly fixated on their preconceived notions. They are going to waste your time and frustrate you when you could be focusing on more profitable and rewarding ventures.

Remember the four premises I have listed as examples at the beginning of this article, and you will be successful in dealing with uninformed potential clients.

Lose the chip on your shoulder, good luck, and stay positive!

**Athena**
*Athena has loved belly dance since childhood. Raised in a primarily Lebanese neighborhood. her mother began to take formal belly dance classes and allowed Athena to join her. She began her professional belly dance career in 2008, and has never looked back!*

# Marketing Belly Dance for Fitness
## Is It A Good Idea?

by Meagan Mayada Hesham

Over the past few years, we've seen belly dance classes offered at gyms and fitness centres pop up as part of well-being programs everywhere. Numerous belly dance workout DVDs have entered the mainstream, and famous fitness personalities like Kathy Smith are using belly dance as their gimmick for new videos. I've been belly dancing and teaching professionally for over 18 years and also make part of my living working in the fitness industry as a personal trainer and group exercise class leader. I run a studio that offers both belly dance and workout classes, which I tend to keep separate, except for occasional crossover students.

Indisputably, a belly dance class provides a great workout, but just how does the trend towards *marketing* belly dance as fitness impact the art form? This may be a double edged sword...

On the one hand, it can be a gateway, an avenue to introduce more of the general public to belly dance. People who are looking for novel ways to change up their workout routines, those who might otherwise never consider signing up to learn a traditional, culture-specific dance form - may be tempted by Kili Marti's *Dance Off The Inches: Fat Burning Belly Dance Video* or *Aerobics Oz Style belly dance Fitness for Beginners*. This initial exposure may encourage some people to learn more, register for actual classes, perhaps inspire them to look beyond the fitness benefits and discover belly dance as a wonderful art form in its own right. All are pluses, so far.

The other edge of this particular sword, though, may not be so shiny. I've encountered more and more fitness people watching a DVD or taking a couple of beginner classes, then teaching what they've learned as "belly dance". This results, naturally, in a lack of real understanding of the basics and woefully inadequate technique, which is then passed on to their students. They now believe they know belly dance too! Students think they're belly dancing after taking a few Zumba or Bellyfit classes. It seems harmless at first glance, but consider the efforts made by so many professionals, so many true lovers of the dance, to have belly dance accepted and respected as a true art form, and not just a "shakin' it, hips-don't-lie, flavour-of-the-week".

Workouts like Bellyfit, described as "a holistic fitness system for women with dance-cardio moves inspired by belly dancing, Bollywood, and African dance with Pilates, and yoga based stretch" (phew!), and Zumba: A Latin dance-inspired fitness craze, which also features other world dances like Bollywood and belly dance - are popping up everywhere! All these different styles of dance get mashed together, leading to more confusion and people thinking belly dance is from India, or that Shakira invented belly dance. (I actually heard this the other day!).

Marketing belly dance as fitness requires a whole new paradigm. What is taught needs to be distilled to specific movements, perhaps even combinations that can be closely attached to particular fitness outcomes. Belly Rolls are good for abs, so they're in; Hip Accents - not so much, no point in teaching those. Music used, of course, requires a certain beat to reproduce that workout vibe, which will certainly narrow the wealth of rhythms and nuances that would be used for dance purposes. Often, Arabic music never makes it into belly dance-as-fitness classes, with teachers opting for the loosely-defined "world music" or contemporary Western music with a bit of an exotic feel. These considerations render the experience fairly one-dimensional, pared down for efficiency to accommodate and accomplish specific fitness goals. How disappointing to have people taking a belly dance boot camp class at the gym thinking they are learning "belly dance" when all the history, traditions, the vast range of styles, the richness of context is...missing!

Another issue arises from the reputation belly dance always has enjoyed for being a dance in which women of all shapes, sizes, and ages can come together to dance gracefully, connect with their femininity, and learn to appreciate their bodies. The dance form may attract women who have body-confidence or self-image concerns that would leave them feeling less than comfortable in a mainstream gym or boot camp class. As soon as belly dance is marketed as fitness, however, it's a given that only instructors and dancers with bodies that conform to the North American "fit-look norm" will be featured on posters and in other advertising media. Traditional fitness, with its unrelenting mandate to eliminate all curves, is in direct opposition to belly dance, where these are celebrated. The womanly bodies that belly dance once prized will disappear, and images of six-packs will beckon from belly dance-as-fitness DVD cover photos; this has the power to change the aesthetic of our dance forever.

Also problematic for me is hearing people use the fitness aspect to explain why they belly dance, as if it needs to be excused; of course, who would blame them for pursuing an activity that has such cardio, toning, and well-being benefits? I've overheard this exchange so many times: "Seriously, you take *belly dance?*" - "Well, it's great exercise, you know!". It seems to me to devalue our beautiful and intricate dance form by insisting it require validation as something else in order to be a worthwhile pursuit. I've never witnessed a similar impulse toward justification surrounding Flamenco, Russian Folk dance, Irish Step, or Canadian Aboriginal dance.

Disseminating the beauty and splendor of our dance, tapping into new markets, being pumped about how physically vibrant and healthy belly dance can make people feel, are all valid inclinations. However, marketing belly dance as fitness - it's food for thought. Let's make sure we're smart and sensitive about how this trend may impact our art going forward. Ah, that double-edged sword!

**Meagan Mayada Hesham**
*Meagan is a belly dance instructor, performer, and writer based in Toronto, Canada. She has been belly dancing for over 18 years and hosts Belly Dance Talk Radio.*

## Tip O' the Hat to Tipping
### Practices of Appreciation

**by Samira Shuruk**

Oh, tipping, tipping, scandalous tipping! ...or is it?

For many years, we've been seeing the questions come up again and again online; is tipping okay or is it associated with stripping? Does it (or should it) effect our pay? And the big scandal of course: Tipping into the costume! In the interest of laying myths to rest, it's high time we gather facts based on the experiences of multiple professionals.

First, let me make clear my background as it relates to this subject. My two main dance mentors are Artemis Mourat and Yasmin Henkish. They both have over 30 years experience in the business and teach the profession thoroughly. Before going "out there" myself, I had absorbed their attitudes regarding tipping, one of a collective 60-plus years as performers in multiple states, on multiple continents and with all manner of cultures. That was over 9 years ago, and thus far, my own career has included over three thousand full professional shows and countless tipping situations with tipping clientele originating from every continent.

In my quest for more information to share, so I could present a wide range of experiences and outlooks, I contacted over 20 dancers and musicians with whom I have worked or been in contact, over the years. Everyone has had over a decade of experience--many over 2 or 3 decades experience. I'll introduce you to many as we hear from them in this article.

First the broad question: Is tipping okay? It's understandable that there is controversy. Even in the countries of origin, there are different practices.

According to Tamer Yehia Aziz, an Egyptian folklore dancer and researcher:

> "Normally, tipping belongs to the Oriental dancers, as our habit in Egypt, and it is rare for men dancers... It happened with me as a man dancer...but many times when I was dancing in Iraq...and my type of dance in that time was Iraqi traditional dance plus Egyptian too. In the beginning, I was astonished, but they told me it is normal habit over there."

However, I think Aleya brings the concept home. Aleya is an American dancer originating on the west coast of the US, and now dancing in the Red Sea area and in Cairo. She said:

> "If I get a client who really likes me, they will hand me money, and I just stick it in my hip all the way in my costume, and usually, they will request I dance a song. (...but as tipping is not allowed in 5 star venues, they will just hand it to me as a 'thank you.')".

So, what is the difference between tipping and "handing the dancer money as a gratuity?". They seem the same; right? In Egypt it is considered haram to tip in the 5-star hotels, but Oriental dancers get plenty of tips in cabarets, parties, and weddings. Aleya explained it like this:

> "There is no difference; it still is a tip. It's just that it has to be hidden in the ME--in 5-star places. I think because (maybe) they would think they are "hiring" me for later. He-he; you know, like I'm a prostitute; so maybe it has to be hidden. Everything here is hidden though.

Someone is always paying someone off, but it has to be subtle and unseen."

Tamer also addressed the issues of respect and tips, explaining that folklore dancers usually don't receive tips out of respect; yet, it is expected that Oriental dancers receive tips, and they add significantly to their income. He said the awalim dancers in Cairo learn from their teacher to take tips. So, while tipping is not respectful for folklore dancers and not allowed in 5-star hotels, tipping is commonly practiced in other venues, and a "thank you" of money is allowed, a practice which is seen as the same thing. It's simply a difference of decorum, understanding, and image.

Every single dancer that I asked receives money in tips, with more collecting significant amounts than not. Cassandra Shore, "back in the day" would make 3 times more in tips than she would earn in pay.

> "I bought a car and a house from some of that money!"

Chris Marashlian, my dear friend, wistfully remembers the generous tipping:

> "For many years, NYC's "Eighth Avenue, Greek Town, music scene" (spanning from the 1950s through the late 1970s) at one time, no doubt, had kept many a musician and Bellydancer, very, very happy, on many a night, during that long-lost era in time.

> Most recently, (in the last 20 years or so) many Arabic and Turkish venues have also seen some very good tipping nights on occasion as well. However, nothing ever seemed to compare to "Greek style" tipping, where literally, thousands (and sometimes, even tens of thousands) would end up on the floor some nights."

However, times have changed; they have changed all over. Numerous dancers on the west coast are paying the price. Tipping was so good there that pay was almost inconsequential. Norma Warah, Sabrina, and Princess Farhana all talk about the generous tipping in California that has since dried up. Pay has not compensated for this and the dance market is suffering. When the dance market suffers and dancers get more competitive for the drying-up dollars, owners can take advantage and try to pit dancer against dancer, resulting in even lower pay and (sometimes) disrespectful treatment.

Leyla Amir, who worked in Cairo during the classic era, spoke of her club experiences, when the clientele there was largely Arabic:

> "Tipping was definitely a necessity in Egypt. Although the base pay for the performance was good, I was responsible (out of that) to pay 15 musicians whom I was required to maintain as a 5-star performer. The musicians would get their cut, then have to split it by 15 (for each member). The addition of the private gigs allowed more money for my musicians so they could have a substantial living wage for themselves and their families."

So, while tipping is not seen as respectable for folklore and not acceptable in 5-star hotels, tipping is expected, culturally appropriate and has been practiced for many decades, if not longer.

Except for one respondent, all felt that tipping was primarily for appreciation. That one exceptional respondent didn't have as many tipping experiences as the others and danced more often on stages, than on dance floors.

The second most motivating factor people mentioned was, of course, "showing off." People go to these places "to be seen" and image is important. I have also had Indian clients explain to me that when they tip it is part of "well wishes for the celebration event". So, when I danced at a 50$^{th}$ wedding anniversary, and the husband tipped me a $100 bill, the wife was thrilled--and kissed him on the cheek!

It is vitally important that we overcome our own cultural bias in regards to our dance practices.

Most dancers did say they had a couple of bad experiences, but they were quick to say that incidents were few and far between. A professional dancer is in charge of the tipping process and is protective of her personal space. If she doesn't learn this early on, she doesn't usually last in the professional arena where she will be confronted with these situations. A quality dancer also knows how to use humor and ingenuity to turn things to her favor. Sabrina talks of a woman chasing her around the stage at a venue where costume tipping was not allowed. However, she made it funny and had everyone laughing. To this day, she and the band still laugh about it. Both Artemis Mourat and Princess Farhana became adept at using their toes surreptitiously to pick up big bills from money showers on the floor; quickly shoving them in their costumes to be hidden.

As for splitting the tips: This was done in various ways in different regions. The important thing is that the dancer knows what to expect when she arrives. In all the answers, the tips received in costume belong to the dancer. The split for floor tips (from money showers) differs by region and venue; sometimes dancer and band, sometimes dancer, house and band. Of course, someone else picks up the tips!

Artemis, who has danced in 35 states and 11 countries, talks about the importance of knowing with whom you work:

> "I have experienced a big difference between the way that American musicians and Middle Eastern musicians who have lived in the US for a long time treat their dancers and the way that Middle Eastern musicians who are newly in the US treat their dancers. In my experience, the American and Americanized musicians are more fair and generous in their approach to the issue of tips."

At the venues where the dancer either had to wait until the end of the night to get her share or pick them up the next time, the dancers usually preferred to wait, but by then, their "share" was always considerably less than what they actually earned.

There are various tipping practices and most of the dancers' responses aligned closely with the following:

- Money Showers: Arabs, Greeks, Turks
- Money Necklaces: Gulf Countries, Arabs
- Tipping in Costume: All but the Arab night clubs with a stage area. Stage area seems to create that separation of "show."
- Handed to the dancer (for her to place in her own costume): Same as costume tipping.
- Stuck onto the Dancer's Forehead: Traditional Turkish practice
- Basket or Jar Collection: Haflas, renaissance fairs, festivals, busking
- Gratuity in Envelope: Private & corporate events

Therefore, let's talk about the nitty-gritty of "body tipping". First of all, I believe the term "body tipping" is a misnomer. Most dancers talked about keeping their hand between the customer's hand and themselves. I usually tuck the money in myself. It seems that the more experienced dancers are practicing what I would call "costume tipping", which certainly has a different connotation to it than the term "body tipping."

The professional dancers all talked about protecting the personal "safe zones" which involves using pantomime to guide customers where they may tip, using humor to control the situation, or simply dancing away if need be. Some of us learned from our teachers. In Cairo, the awalim teach their students, but some dancers simply learn from watching other professional shows. Regardless, it is a learned skill. Our customers want to show appreciation, and they want to participate in interaction. Handing us money or tipping us in our costume while saying "beautiful show," "Great job," or "Asal" (honey) is simply part of how people enjoy this dance as an audience. It is important for us to be gracious about their generosity, while balancing this with respect for every-one's private space, not just our own.

One concern often brought up is the "begging" dancer; the wise dancer lets the audience initiate the tipping. With restaurant patrons who don't know that they may tip, dancers often "seed" their belt: Tuck a bill into their costume. It's most polite to have this hidden from view when you first enter. The dancer simply untucks the bill during the first or second song when doing a spin or discarding a prop. There is also no reason to limit the audience's generosity thought process; inspire them by using a $20 bill. It's also perfectly fine to have a friend or venue staff start a money shower. However, the dancer who "doesn't go away until someone reaches into their wallet and pulls out a bill" is a sad sight to see. When an audience member wants to tip, they will initiate. They hold money in their hand and look at the dancer; so you must watch your audience! They start the tipping, and you then guide it, making it comfortable for you.

As always in our dance, reading the audience and understanding its cues is of utmost importance. Chris Marashlian says that some ethnic clients want nothing more than a subtle thank you--or less--even if they've showered the whole dance area and band with money! So, be careful not to assume they want you to hover near them, even if they are quite generous. With experience, a dancer knows which individuals to avoid and which are tipping out of appreciation and celebration.

We are incredibly lucky to have this gift of dance to share. It is a great honor to take part in our clients' life events and celebrations. We gather incredible experiences, whether it is traveling the world with her bird (Shadia of Detroit) or having a client arrange an Asmahan-like entrance at the Smithsonian Women in the Art's Museum atop a palinquin, carried by male models. We have stories ourselves, and we are woven into people's stories of their lives.

With awareness, we maintain our dignity.

With education and experience, we understand the cultures.

With joy, we may revel in stories like Princess Farhana's favorite tipping experience:

"This is the BEST tip I ever got--I swear! It had me (and the whole restaurant) dying of laughing…A toddler saw what was going on with the grown ups giving me tips, and so she toddled up to me and stuck a piece of pita bread in my belt!"

Children tip! This dance is family friendly! Granted, it's usually money, but Princess' story teaches us that despite concerns expressed and myths taught, we can break bread together over this business of making "dough"--above and beyond our pay!

### Samira
*Samira is a full time dance performer and instructor, she has performed over three thousand full shows including for royalty, diplomats, HBO events, international concerts, Turkish and Egyptian embassy events, museums, universities and more. Samira's RaqFit DVD is scheduled to be released 2012, it combines belly dance and Bollywood in fitness format.*

The lady in the photo with Helena Vlahos is a Los Angeles based dancer named IrinaXar. I took that picture backstage at Cairo Caravan 2012, during the vintage costume fashion show. Helena Vlahos created both costumes, "back in the day", Irina probably wasn't even alive when the costume she's wearing was made!

# Section 5
# COSTUME AND APPEARANCE

**W**ithout a doubt, one of the most fun and exciting elements of being a belly dance performer is the glamour and glitz of dressing the part. But where does one begin, in what is truly a vast subject?

*In the following collection of essays, articles and photo spreads, the topic of personal appearance will be explored by costume designers, makeup artists, experienced performers and dance instructors. Each author offers their own unique approaches to cultivating a beautiful hard working dance wardrobe. From details such as makeup and jewelry to the myriad of specialty costume pieces and terms, this section is sure to inform and inspire.*

*Regardless of your individual costuming goals, style, and budget, have fun exploring this section. If this whets your appetite - for more information, visit Gilded Serpent for many more articles on the subject.*

# Raqqin' the Retro
## Vintage Costume Care

**by Princess Farhana**

Vintage belly dance costumes and antique stage accessories are a personal passion of mine ...to look at, to own and to wear. Fascinating in their staggering variety, they can run the gamut from clumsily constructed home-made affairs to Egyptian, Lebanese and Turkish couture costumes, to ethnic pieces that were not made for stage use, but to be worn as real clothing, for every day use or as ceremonial or bridal wear.

Many of the most well-known belly dance costume designers have been in business for years, and like the top fashion designers, have had different design concepts and in many cases, new full collections for every season. Older Oriental dance costumes were made by hand, and constructed to last literally, a lifetime. Of course, there have always been the cheapie 'airport special' costumes - basically souvenirs for tourists - but even those used to be constructed much better than they are now!

In the past five or so years there has been an explosion in belly dance costuming, due to sheer demand as the world-wide popularity of belly dancing grows, not to mention the age-old concept of "making a buck". There is now a wide mid-range of costumes that are not couture; they fit well and look all right, but they're lacking in the detail, workmanship and tailoring of higher-end pieces. These costumes are kind of like the stuff you'd find in a designer knock-off chain store that highlights trends, but does not offer quality.

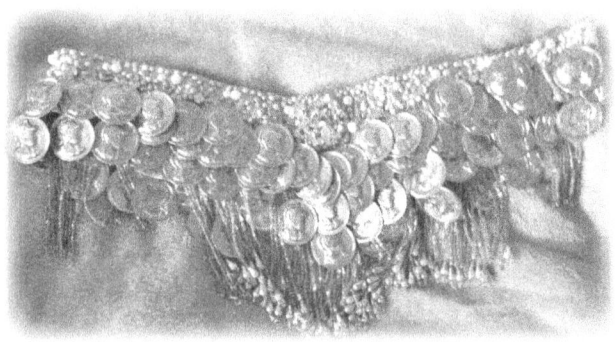

This takes many faces: The stones may now be acrylic instead of genuine crystal and glued on as opposed to sewn on; beading and fringe are done with less workmanship and cheap threads making them prone to fall apart, seams aren't serged, the sizing may be off, and so on.

As with vintage designer clothing, most of the professionally made older costumes were fabricated with much more care than their counterparts today. Compare this trend to what's happening in the world of retail clothing - or even cars, house wares, electronics - you name it... mass production has its drawbacks! Though it makes the items affordable, the quality in design and craftsmanship nowadays just usually isn't there.

Lately there has even been a trend among belly dancers to return to the glamour and over-the-top design of the older style costumes with copious amounts of fringe dripping from every possible area on the garment. It's no secret that many older belly dance costumes can be had for a song and be made beautiful and serviceable again, through a little loving care.

If you are planning on washing a vintage belly dance costume, or a costume that has been fabricated from antique textiles, mirrored fabric, or one that is hung with heavy coins, proceed with care. Many older cabaret costumes were never stored properly - or ever washed, for that matter - and because of the accumulation of sweat or skin oils from the previous owner(s), fabric deterioration due to normal wear and tear or in some cases, exposure to sunlight, the fabric itself may be compromised. And, this is especially true of velvets and brocades.

Older professionally made costumes from Egypt, Syria and Lebanon, even after a number of years, are almost indestructible. This is great because they withstand the test of time, but in some cases, the Egyptian costumes were constructed of so many layers of heavy, thick materials that they may be nearly impossible to alter - even getting a needle through them is tough! And because of the copious amounts of beading, anyone intending to cut into or remove parts of the costume needs to be a cracker jack at re-beading so that the alteration matches the rest of the costume.

Lebanese and Syrian costumes especially used a lot of chunky beads and large pearls on the fringe - and if fringe is missing in spots, it may be impossible to find an exact match. You will either have to hand make your own with similar-looking beads or replace it entirely. Older synthetic pearls may have chipped or flaked or lost their luster due to shaking and rattling against each other. You can either re-bead the strands with new pearl beads or it's actually possible to paint them with nail polish to make them look new again, but this is a very lengthy and intricate process. Vintage Turkish costumes are also tricky to restore; many had wires inserted into the tops of bra or on the belts, to reinforce the intricate cut-out shapes, and these wires may have rusted or poked through the material that anchored them in place. Turkish fringe, though beautiful in appearance, was never constructed as well or as sturdy as its Egyptian counterpart, and may have to be completely replaced.

Turkish costumes from the 1950's-1970's were very fragile, hand-beaded with tiny bugle beads, and featured many cut-outs, including open cut-work on the cups of the brassieres which, as the style of the day dictated, were totally open to show the skin! This spider-web effect is stunning, but because there are no actual bra cups, just an overlay of beads meant to be worn against the skin of the breast itself, they may be impossible to salvage, unless the entire piece is cut apart, glued at the cuts, and carefully sewn in place over a covered bra cup.

Non-professionally constructed vintage cabaret costumes were often made by hand by the dancers themselves, with the bra made from a regular lingerie bra. This is not to say that some of the homemade jobs weren't spectacular, or

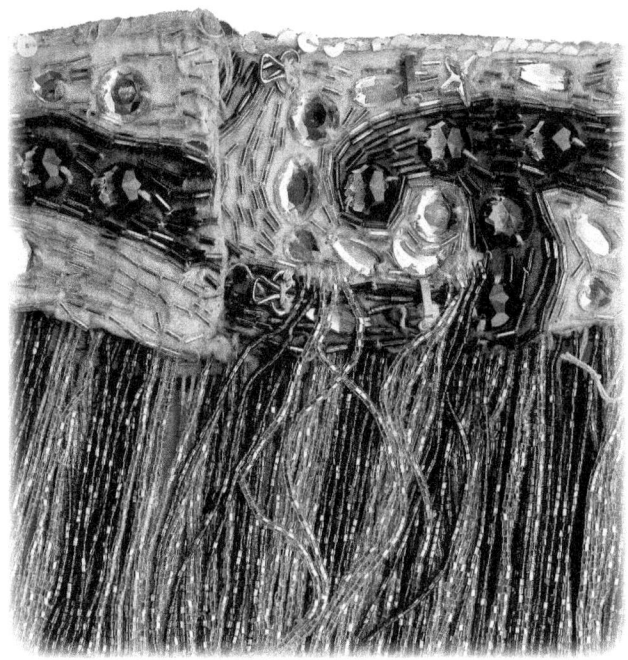

well made. Many of them are simply amazing. But once ten to forty years go by, the older fabric of the base-bra itself, and the synthetic padding, may be breaking down and losing its shape.

Appliqué designs may be fraying or coming off; coins may be missing due to wear and tear on the threads that fastened them; metal snaps, hooks and closures will probably be rusted; and the costume's straps might be stretched out or actually coming off the costume. Since these older costumes were often hand-beaded by the dancer who wore them, sometimes the beads, fringe and loops weren't knotted securely, or the knots themselves have frayed. In many cases, if one piece of fringe falls apart, it will create a chain reaction on the entire row of fringe. Older sequins may have lost their color and sheen and have a clear appearance; some decorative crystal stones may be missing. In order to make these elderly beauties danceable again, you will have to have expert hand-sewing skills, and will probably have to make new straps and closures, at the very least. Dancer Ozma of Japan says she always "bleeds" the cups of the '60's and '70's era costumes she restores, by picking out the deteriorated nylon Tricot padding from the bra cups. I have never done this - I don't have her patience! I usually

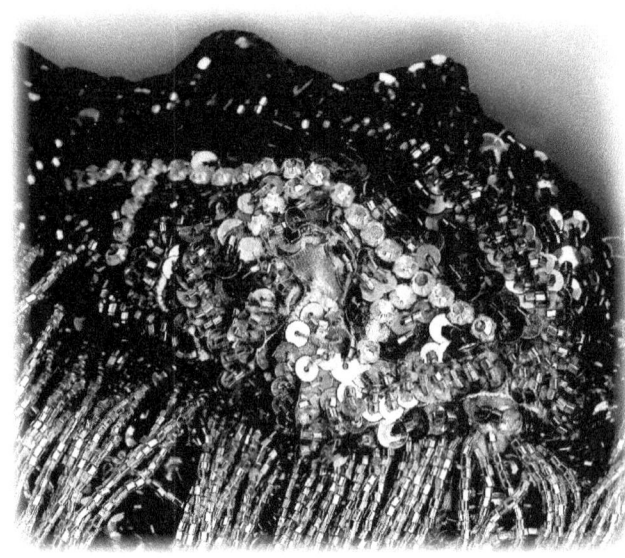

just add new full-cup pads to the brassiere cups (more to hold the shape of the cup than to pad it) and then hand-sew a new lining over the pads.

As for custom made ethnic or tribal costumes, many of the fabrics used in their construction are serious antiques. Dancers hunt far and wide for textile treasures to make their costumes special, and though some of the fabric finds are still gorgeous, they can be extremely fragile. Even older cotton pieces may be delicate in condition and have some dry rot, especially if the material was exposed to the sun, dust or elements - think pieces originally used by nomadic desert-based tribes like Berbers, Kuchi or Bedouins. Also, the more lavishly a piece of older material was decorated with embroidery, variously applied metallic strips, metal alloy buttons, mirrors, or sewn-on appliqués, the weaker it will be, due to age and deterioration of the fibers.

This is especially true of antique Assuit, a traditional Egyptian hand-made cotton mesh fabric embellished with designs created from small strips of real silver, woven and/or hammered by hand into the mesh. Coming from the Egyptian village of the same name, the new Assuit is mostly mesh fabric, with silver designs, while the older type of Assuit was mostly hammered silver (with the designs left in the color of the mesh) which made it extremely heavy. Lengths of vintage Assuit are usually astronomically expensive: The sheer mesh base fabric has become so heavy from the silver decorations, it is prone to rips and tears, plus the fact that as the silver oxidizes due to age, it can weaken the base fabric.

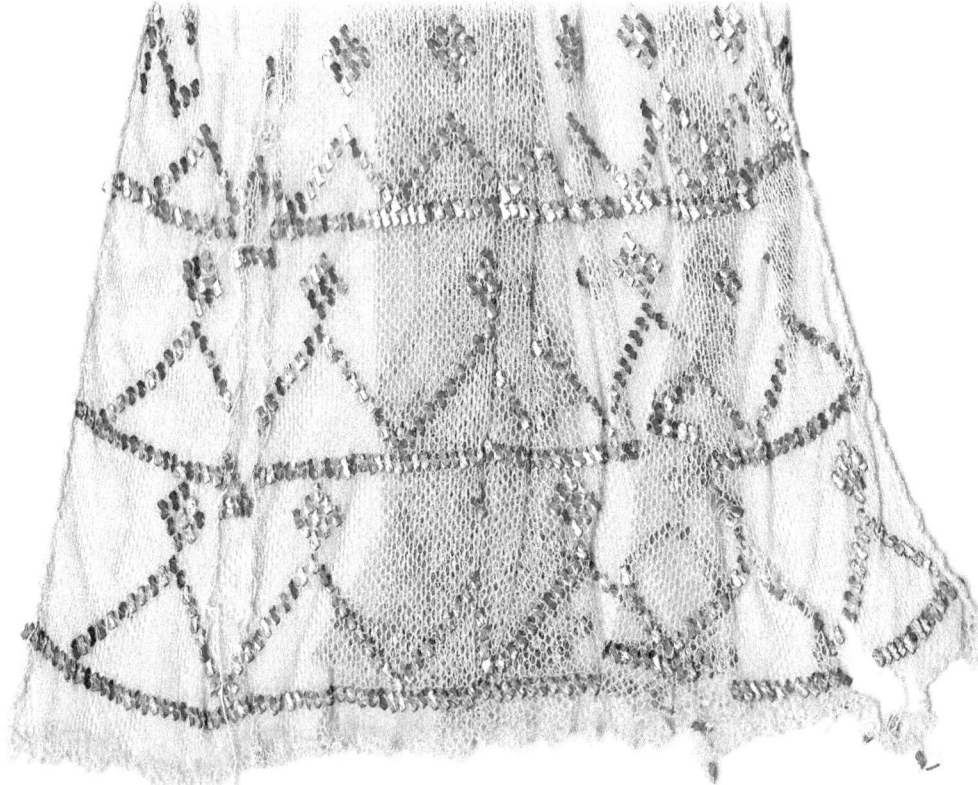

Other vintage ethnic textiles may have been constructed by hand, embroidered with metallic threads, and large beads or pearls; or hung with decorative shells, beads, bottle caps, buttons, small mirrors or bells, all of which will weaken the fabric due to weight. Many ethnic fabrics were woven by hand or embroidered

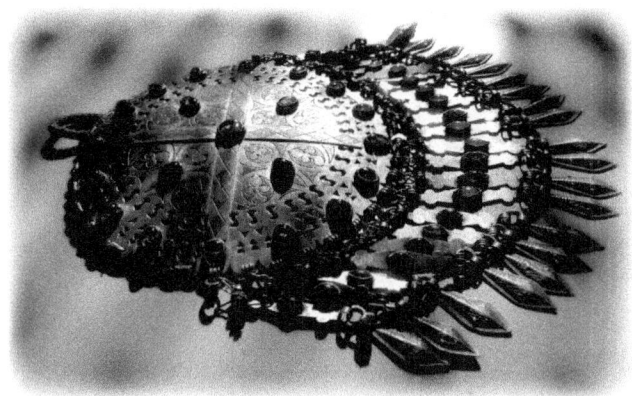

with material threads that were not commercially dyed, and therefore are not colorfast.

Dry cleaning for antique pieces is NOT recommended, however, careful hand washing, in most cases, should be OK. Make sure to use lukewarm water, and a very mild soap, like Woolite or Cool Love. I use baby shampoo. When rinsing, do it thoroughly. Any soap residue left in the garment will put the natural deterioration process on fast-forward. To wash an antique costume or vintage textile, I fill my bathtub with tepid water and a capful of baby shampoo. I gently place the garment or fabric into the water and swish it around with my hands. I never ever squeeze, wring or scrub the piece being washed, I simply drain the bathtub as the dirt comes off the item, refill the tub, and repeat the swishing until the water around the piece is clean and clear. I then rinse it a few times to make sure all the soap has come out.

To dry the costume or antique material, gently roll and pat the item carefully in a towel, then lay it flat to air dry on a few layers of fluffy, clean towels. Do not hang it up or the fabric may stretch out; never put it in a dryer, the heat and tumbling action are the kiss of death!

Have a serious look at your antique or vintage costume pieces, maybe do some research on the Internet or consult a costumer or antique textiles dealer if you possibly can, and try to assess the fabrics used on your costume, its age and durability. You may ultimately opt not to wash them.

If you have a costume decorated with coins that have tarnished and you want them shiny again, you can clean them individually with jewelry polish (not commercial brass or silver cleaner) applied with a Q-Tip. This is a painstaking process, but will shine up the coins and if you apply the polish carefully, it will not stain the rest of your costume. If the coins are sewed on in rows, you can take a piece of heavy paper or cut a length of plastic off a shopping bag, lay it underneath the row of coins, and polish them that way, protecting the material they were mounted on. This works well for both real coins, and manufactured costume coins or coined trim.

Actually, a handy trick I learned from an antique dealer who dealt in estate jewelry is to clean any older metal items using plain old toothpaste, as opposed to any sort of metal polish. This also cleans up rhinestones and crystals. I use this method on all my antique tiaras...and believe me, I own a lot of them! It works just as well for jewelry made of pot metals or "paste" (vintage faux jewelry) as well as Kuchi jewels or ethnic items made from low-quality silver or mixed-metal alloys. The toothpaste is less acidic and much less abrasive than metal or even jewelry polish, and will remove dirt or tarnish without damaging the patina of the item. I usually apply the toothpaste by hand and gently rub it with my fingers, but you could also use a soft child's toothbrush to do this. After you've shined up the item, rinse it off with tepid water, and pat it dry with a soft cloth.

Care for your vintage costumes and accessories properly and lovingly, and you should be able to restore them to their previous beauty, as well as raq them proudly onstage!

**Princess Farhana**

*Internationally acclaimed Princess Farhana has performed, taught and written about Oriental Dance since 1990. She's appeared in China, Egypt, across Europe and The United Kingdom, and throughout North America. An artistic chameleon and a boundary-pushing pioneer, she performs many styles of dance with ease, from traditional to contemporary.*

**EMRA**
VENUS-OF-THE-ORIENT

# Omani Jewelry from the Collection of Nancy Hernandez

GildedSerpent.com is pleased to present a photo essay of Omani Jewelry from the collection of international jewelry and textile scholar, collector and dealer, Nancy Hernandez. Photography by Alisha Westerfeld.

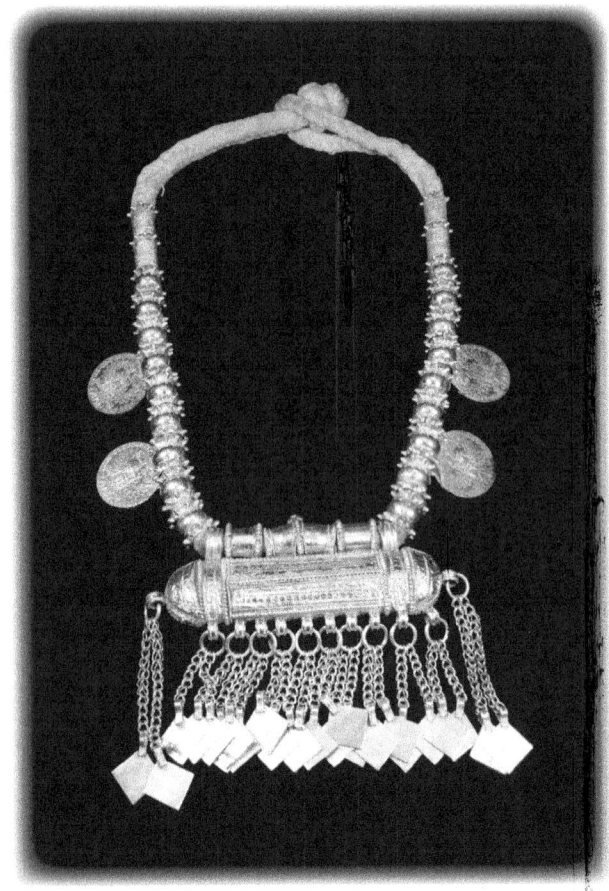

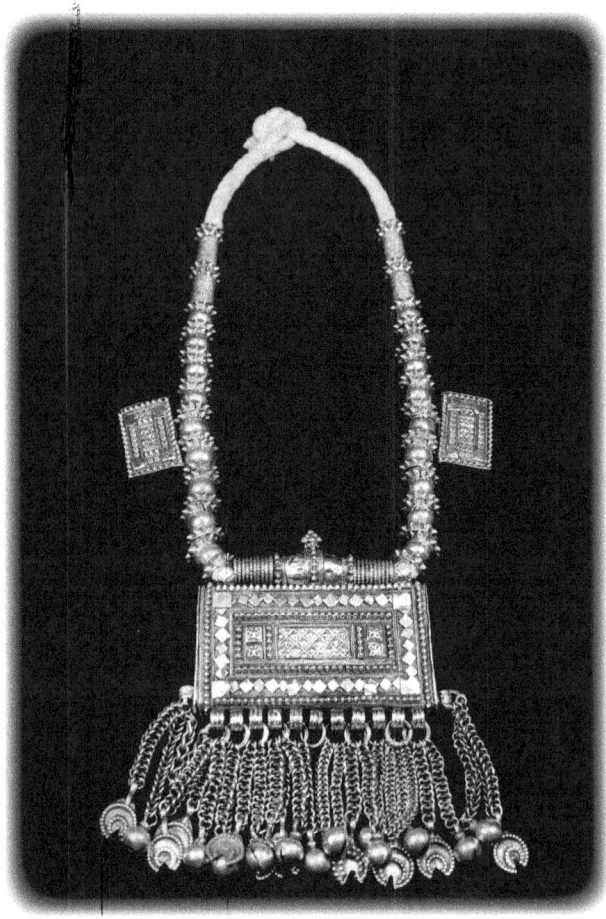

# Practice Makes Perfection
## Make up Artists Share Their Secrets

### by Davina - Dawn Devine

I recently had an opportunity to pick the brains of two belly dance beauty experts for an ongoing research project. My question of the day: How can a dancer quickly improve her image? Adriana Marrelli, professional makeup artist and working dancer has one simple mission, "the goal is to look expensive." Lisa "Firefly" Felton agrees, "Expensive *and* beautiful." Over salads and diet cokes, we compiled this list of thoughts and ideas for achieving these goals.

## Setting the Stage

Both ladies agree – before you pick up a brush or sponge, it is important to set the stage properly. Your skin reflects your vitality and health, and needs to be cared for first, before any makeup is applied.

Lisa, a serious performer, recommends vitamin and mineral supplements to enhance the quality of the skin from the inside out. Keeping your skin hydrated with eight or more glasses of water will prevent that sunken appearance caused by lack of hydration. Of course, every beauty magazine focuses on the importance of daily regimens of cleansing, moisturizing and sunscreen. Which products are the best? The products that work for you and fit your budget. Every skin is different and only through experimentation will you find that perfect combination of products that helps you achieve your goal.

Adriana believes that before you apply any makeup, you should focus on creating beautiful structural details. Eyebrows frame your face and express emotion, and are quite important for appearing beautiful and polished. Dancers should strongly consider investing in a professional eyebrow shaping. A professional eyebrow shaper will evaluate your brows and analyze your face shape, working with you to achieve a brow shape that reflects your style and taste.

Another important, and often overlooked, detail is your teeth. Whitening your teeth has never been easier. From professional dental visits to over the counter do-it-yourself products, there is a tooth-whitening regimen for every budget. A clean gleaming white smile is both beautiful and increases the appearance of your health and vibrancy.

## Creating a Good Foundation

Adriana cannot stress this enough: Foundation is a must regardless of age. For older skin, a primer before the foundation will smooth wrinkles and fine lines and, depending on the brand, can cover spots and balance skin tone. While younger dancers might skip applying foundation, thoughtful application of makeup base will reduce the blotchiness that comes with exertion and the washing out effects of stage or nightclub lighting. A good application of foundation allows a performer to illusionistically sculpt the face. Highlights play up your best features, while contouring will add strength and definition. Unsure of where to begin? A professional makeup artist will teach you the basics of foundation

**Lisa "Firefly" Felton**

and contouring specific to your face to create the illusion of a perfect oval.

Other important tips for achieving flawless foundation:

- Allowing the foundation time to set, a minimum of one hour before sweating or getting hot.
- Powder to achieve the most flawless finish
- It doesn't matter if you use your fingers, a sponge or a brush: Blend, blend, blend.

## The Eyes Have It

The eyes are arguably the most important feature. Lisa, a master of eye makeup, suggests experimenting with color, contour and shape. She recommends checking out YouTube tutorials for ideas and specific application techniques.

Important tips for eyes include:

- If you have oily eyelids, try an eye primer
- Build from a matte base to a shimmer
- Darken your eyebrows to prevent stage lighting from washing them out
- Curl, curl, curl your eyelashes
- Even if you think you have used enough eyeliner, add more.
- Even if you think you are wearing enough mascara, add more, especially to the outer one third of the lashes.
- Do not be afraid of color

A note on glitter: Treat glitter strategically as icing on the cake. As a rule of thumb, glitter looks good alive and in person, on a stage or in a club. For video or photos skip the glitter and only go as shiny as a pearl or opalescent. In photography, glitter can create the unfortunate illusion that your skin is dirty and possibly peeling.

False eyelashes are a potent weapon in the makeup arsenal. The key to wearing extreme eyelashes is to crimp your natural lashes to create a firm base to help support the weight of the false ones. Applying several coats of mascara to your natural and false lashes will weld them together to further enhance the illusion that those are, in fact, your real eyelashes.

## Getting Cheeky

If you have built a beautiful foundation, you will absolutely need to wear blush. Select a color that coordinates with both your skin tone and lipstick choice. The key for blush is learning the most flattering position on your face. There is no one universally correct place for all faces. A professional makeup artist can help you learn how to enhance your unique bone structure.

## Lips

To enhance your smile, chose a richly pigmented lipstick and be sure to apply it right before taking the stage. Your lips can be modified and enhanced by using lip liner to reshape your natural lip line.

**Adriana Marrelli**

Fill in your lips with your lip liner before applying the lipstick and, for the shiniest finish, apply lip-gloss.

### Beyond the Face

Of course, makeup is only one part of your complete image. Your hair is the frame and is an important part of your beauty and look. Before your performance, you should have a modern stylish haircut. Then, when it is time to perform, you will want to enhance it with hair products, combs, extensions and costume accessories. Practice is important not only to master the techniques for a beautiful hair look, but also to practice performing so you know your fall, clip or comb won't fly off in a spin. You don't want the illusion of perfection marred by an unfortunate accident.

### Tools of the Trade

Both Adriana and Lisa agree that one of the best places to invest your makeup budget is in quality tools. Don't limit yourself to only purchasing brushes at a makeup store. Look for brushes at fine art stores and craft centers. Always keep your brushes clean and well maintained. Frequent washing prevents the growth of bacteria.

### Practice Makes Perfect

Makeup is one place where you have the power to create the illusion of perfection, perfect skin and perfectly shaped face. Practice your application techniques, experiment with color and learn to adjust your makeup for different lighting and stage situations and costume styles. Remember, regardless of your dance style or technique, the ultimate goal is to look beautiful and expensive.

Adriana Marrelli: adrianabellydance.com
Lisa Felten ~ Firefly: www.fireflybellydance.net

### Davina

*Dawn Devine aka Davina, is the noted author of DIY information on designing and making Middle Eastern belly dance costumes. Her articles appear in diverse publications from "Habibi" to "Linux Journal". Book titles include: "Costuming from the Hip" and "Embellished Bras". Her current project, "The Cloth of Egypt: All About Assiut", will be available early 2013.*

Lynette Day of the tribal fusion troupe Hipnotica is helped by a friend backstage at the 2012 "Cues and Tattoos". Many tribal style belly dancers draw inspiration from the long history of using khol to embellish the eyes and face. Some dancers like to pull inspiration from the tradition of North African facial tattooing known as a harquus, where tattoos are permanently placed on the skin of young women to identify their tribes. In this photo, Lynette's dotted makeup technique is of a more Indian flavor, reminiscent of facial embellishments on ancient sculptures of the goddess Lakshmi.

# Costume Gallery

Belly dance costuming excites and delights, reveals and conceals; it has the power to amplify movement and exaggerate the body's proportions. All dancers, regardless of technique or style, male or female, young or old, seek out the perfect marriage of costume, music and movement. On the following pages, enjoy this collection of examples of costumes. Want more information on each of these dancers? Visit www.GildedSerpent.com!

Daniella of Seattle, WA wears a red and gold costume designed by Bella of Istanbul, Turkey. Bella is considered by many to be the premier Turkish belly dance costume designers, and her custom creations are exquisitely made and have a price-tag to match.

## Costume Gallery

Asmahan of Florida (via Argentina and Cairo) wears a modern bedlah set in the Egyptian style. The current taste is one of sleek body conscious lines, form-fitting skirts and long wavy free-flowing hair and glamorous makeup.

Ariellah of the Greater Bay Area, performs in the dark fusion style, popularly known as gothic. She mixes vintage lace, modern velvets with accents of metal. Her bra is a classic tribal design by Flying Skirts.

Cassandra of Minneapolis is wearing a beladi dress designed by Sahar Okasha of Cairo. This designer is known for her costumes which not only conform to the body, but also have elements of drape and flow to accentuate movement.

Kamala Almanzaar of Los Angles looks stunning in her couturier-quality Eman Zaki design. This ensemble showcases the popular Egyptian two-piece style bedlah, where the belt has been traded in for simple embellishments on the skirt.

Mish Mish of Anchorage, Alaska (via Los Angeles and San Francisco) In this amazing vintage photograph of the legendary dancer Mish Mish, we can see the costuming taste of the late 70's through early 90's when belts were slender and skirts were full, but quite revealing.

Kristina of the Bay Area favors a more free-flowing and creative style that pulls from an extensive wardrobe that embraces a variety of styles including tribal, ethnic, and folkloric to create costumes that are unique and beautiful flights of fantasy

Kamaal of Los Angeles wears an ensemble that harkens back to the days of the Ottoman rule of North Africa. He's layered a Turkish vest, or yelek, over a traditional Egyptian robe made from assiut. The belt is composed of many layers and is held together by an amazing Turkomen belt buckle.

Diane Webber of Los Angeles, is wearing an amazing vintage assiut shawl that has been slit in the middle and is worn as a torso cover under a coin bra and belt. In the 70's makeup was more natural and hair worn long and free.

Aziza! of San Francisco is seen here wearing a hand-crafted performance costume. In the 60's and 70's, ready-made costumes were nearly impossible to find, so dancers had to rely on their own skills and local costume makers for their wardrobes.

Ma*Shuqa Mirjan of Saratoga, CA, is lucky enough to own a costume from the famed Cost Less Imports of Berkeley. Cost Less specialized in coin and chain bra and belt sets, and were popular for more than three decades with dancers worldwide.

Ilhaam of Spain wears the traditional ATS or American Tribal Style. This distinctive style of dance and costume originated in San Francisco with Fat Chance Belly Dance and their uniform of bra and choli, belt and full tiered skirt, and a complex headdress or turban.

Sherri Wheatley of Los Angeles is a tribal fusion dancer who has a taste for contrasting lace and coins into complex-layered costumes. She has drawn a tremendous number of individual costume elements together to create a highly personal and unique fashion statement.

Ahmad Jarjour, international dancer, strikes a very 60's era pose in this classic publicity still. His costume reflects the loose swashbuckling taste of the era, with narrow harem pants, assiut tunic and low-slung belt.

Malia of the greater San Francisco area shows one of her original designs crafted from a panel of vintage assiut purchased from the famed costume designer Ana of Universal Imports in San Jose. This lovely dress showcases the natural drape and flow of the cloth.

Leyla Amir, International dance performer, wears a nearly transparent beladi dress made of red mesh. Bead and sequin embellishments are applied to strategically enhance her figure and neckline of the dress is expertly cut and fitted to frame her curves.

Iklas, International dance star of the 1960's is wearing a lovely harem-fantasy costume featuring an abbreviated vest, bra, cap and embellished panty. This style of costume crossed over from the world of burlesque and was popular through the mid 60's when dancers switched almost exclusively to wearing belts at the hip.

Anaheed of Los Angeles strikes a classic belly dance pose in a gorgeous costume composed of sheer harem pants, sheer skirt and classic Cost Less chain and medallion bra and belt set. This is one of the original sets, designed and made by the founder of Cost Less, Phillip Au.

Sabah, San Francisco dance performer and instructor, wears a simple and elegant costume with the silhouette popular from the late 70's onward. The full circle skirt conceals the hard working legs, allowing the torso to serenely float above.

Rhea of Athens strikes a pose that captures the essence of the professional belly dancer. She's paid attention to every detail of her professional appearance from the carefully coiffed hair to her model-perfect makeup and costume featuring long Egyptian fringe.

Sheila of the San Francisco Bay Area wears an imported Egyptian costume to perform in. These classic bedlah sets have become widely available in a variety of price points; dancers from students to pros can achieve the classic belly dance look.

Davina ~ Dawn Devine of Silicon Valley showcases the Gypsy, Flamenco or Mediterranean fusion, which takes elements of Romany taste and style and incorporates them into belly dance attire. Here the full skirt, stark black and red color palette, and head-scarf highlight the look.

Nargis, a late burlesque-era belly dancer, posed for this publicity still in a classic professional performance ensemble of the day. Her costume is composed of a belt and bra with rows of looped fringe and an ultra-sheer chiffon skirt. Note her gorgeous hair, makeup and jewelry and her amazing tucked posture that elongates her back, emphasizing her strong dancers physique.

Mahsati of Asheville, NC wears a lovely example of the thobe al-nash'al, an elaborately embroidered, oversized dress worn for formal occasions throughout the countries surrounding the Persian Gulf, and a signature look for the region's traditional dances, known collectively as Khaleegy style.

Michelle Manx of Austin, TX is known for her burlesque-fusion. This image shows how accessories can make a costume and underscore a style. Note how her character-style and fishnet stockings highlight and reinforce her retro pin-up look.

Helwa of Spain (via Brazil) has chosen a sleek costume for performing with a sword. Dancers historically have performed with balance props wearing nearly any style of costume. But these body-skimming pants reduce the chance of having a sword tip catch in a skirt and allow her to strike dramatic poses.

Khairriyya and Raja of the Banat Mazin tribe in Egypt perform in highly stylized costume unique to their tribe. Notice the large moon-shaped necklace, often called a dowry or ghawazee necklace worn as a talisman of fertility, and for specialty dances performed at weddings.

Dina of Cairo wears a fashionable example of a glamorous evening gown designed for dance. Dance gowns allow a performer to control the amount of skin she chooses to reveal or conceal. Here Dina has upped the style ante with a hip-high slit that dramatically frames her legs.

Afet of Detroit, Michigan was captured in this vintage publicity still, wearing the glamorous and iconic bee-hive hair and kitten eye makeup of the early 60's. With her chiffon skirt and looped glass-beaded fringe, she captures the drama and style of the day.

Celena, the Killer Ziller of San Jose, CA wears a costume inspired by those worn by the famed troupe Hahbi 'Ru. The designer, Davina ~ Dawn Devine, married a vintage assiut robe with modern assiut headdress and faux assiut sleeved vest.

Jane Chung How of Mauritius wears a lovely two-piece beldah set designed by Layalie Ahmed. The proportions of this costume are perfect, with a slender embellishment at the top of the skirt and a lovely bra that accentuate her graceful physique.

Scheherazade, in this vintage publicity still, presents the classic features of the ideal belly dancer of the late 1960's. From her bouffant ponytail, nipped in waist and nearly transparent skirt, she is a classic belly dance beauty from a bygone era.

**Women Selling Water and Oranges on the Road to Heliopolis, Near Cairo
by Felix-Auguste Clement**

# Section 6
# REGIONAL STYLES

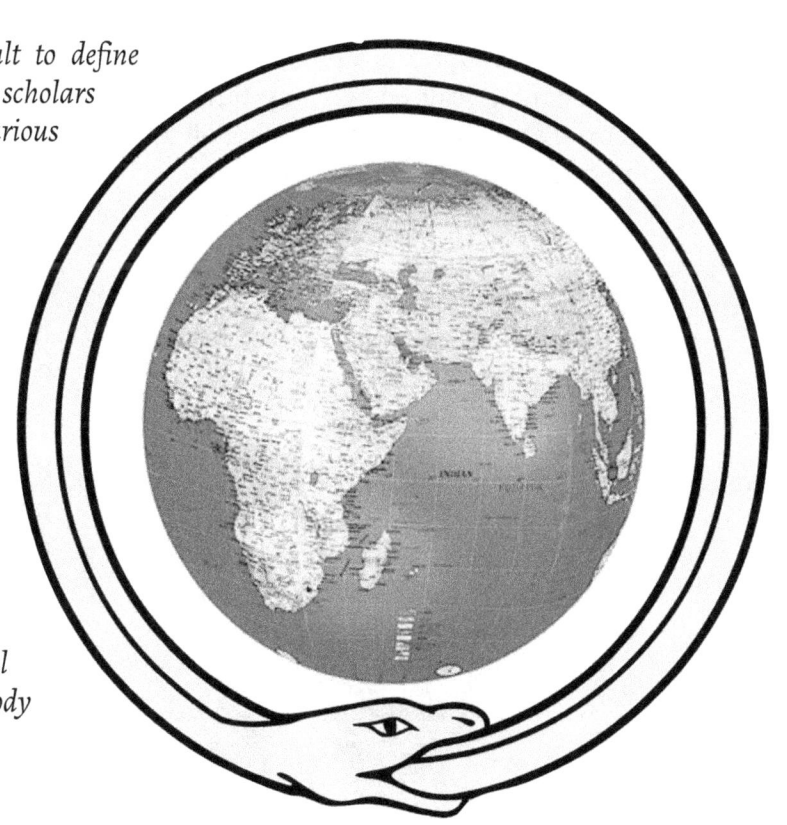

*Middle Eastern belly dance is often difficult to define and complicated to describe. Most dance scholars agree that today's belly dance is a descendent of various regional dance styles.*

*In this section, the editors of Gilded Serpent have compiled a collection of articles about specific regional styles and techniques. These ethnographic dances come from such far-flung areas as North Africa, Central Asia, and the Near East.*

*We are fortunate here at Gilded Serpent to have some of the best contributing authors from around the globe. Professional performing artists and dance instructors pull from this diverse collection of specialty dances to create a richer cultural experience. To learn more, check out the growing body of articles archived on the GildedSerpent.com.*

# Beyond Sequins
## Meaning in the Movement

*by Yasmina Ramzy*

Whatever the current state of belly dance, and whatever its history, there is one profound attribute that people associate with the art form and that is joy. Whether a belly dance student is from Egypt, Argentina, Korea, Canada, the US or Germany, that student will tell you of their experiences when exploring the dance and the parallels that happen in regards to their rise in self-esteem, positive body image, sensual joy and general confidence.

I believe that belly dance is a powerful force for healing on many levels, both for the practitioner and audience. Perhaps it is a possible avenue for healing the damage caused by a long-term worldwide cultural campaign that diminishes all things feminine and sensual.

**Alexandrian style dress with melaya lef by Madame Abla**

I love sequins as much as the next belly dancer, and I am a huge advocate for getting everyone on stage at least once in their lifetime. If it takes sequins, modified technique, simplistic choreography, and pop music in order to make a splash on stage (in lieu of challenging artistic expression based on deep understanding and dedicated training) then, I am all for it. Whether the event is labeled "student recital" or an "amateur presentation," it can be a great vehicle for many to experience the benefits of learning to belly dance.

What a shame though when a student is led astray, thinking that this kind of performance is all belly dance has to offer. It is like eating only the sprinkles and missing out on all the ice cream, cake, and chocolate sauce.

Initially, one is usually attracted to belly dance for a much more profound and emotional reason. Sometimes belly dance students can get so lost in the splash and sequins that they find themselves back where they began, stressing over body image and low self-esteem again. They may get caught up in an endless circle of grasping for yet another technique trick, combination of steps, or a new costume. This can wear thin after a while.

To get to the real guts of the art form in which its emotions, meanings and passions reside, one needs to explore the following types of subjects as examples. Each of these realms of study are so rich, they actually take more time in each category to master than it takes to learn to be a competent belly dancer. Each area of study is limitless but even small efforts can add depth, body and meaning to the belly dance artist's performance, not to mention a limitless experience of joy.

One great place to start is in the study of a myriad of folkloric styles. Each one has a story, a character and a unique message. When a belly dancer has all these characteristics and tools available, then they produce an artist who can exhibit a great range of multi-faceted dimensions. In regard to one's personal journey of self-discovery and enhanced self-esteem, one will find that they already possess each of these characteristics within themselves, and it is liberating to the artist's soul to set them free. Learning folklore is not about gathering a group of steps, appropriate music, and costuming, then fitting all of it together. What the study of folklore has to offer is the study of emotional characteristics and nuance of symbolic meaning.

A second worthwhile subject to explore is Arab music, especially because the movements of belly dancers originated as an expression of the music. Learning about rhythm, maqaam, different styles, how the music is constructed (or lack of construction in the art of improvisation) gives an epiphany of insight into how one's technique may be used to convey what one means. I always tell my students to listen only to the original recordings of Oum Kalthoum 24 hours a day for two years while they are driving, bathing, eating, cleaning, sleeping, etc. For the non-Arab, at first this music can seem morbid and irritating with all of its sad wailing, constantly changing rhythms, and repetitions. Eventually though, one day, the listener "breaks" (like breaking-in a pony) and may become addicted to this music. When this happens, pop music becomes irritating because of its simplicity of rhythm and lack of emotion. At this point, the dancer's understanding changes and consequently, actual physical movements and emotional expressions take on many deep layers.

The next area of discovery is the lineage of the famous dance artists of the past who created the belly dance steps as their personal interpretations of the music and from whom we draw ours today. One will find that, in their own unique way, each artist was a strong and exceptional person and each one contributed some aspect of the art form we practice. I could cite, for example, the showmanship of Nagua Fouad, the articulated technique of Naima Akef and Sohair Zaki, the femininity and grace of Samia Gamal, the strong sensual power of Tahia Carioca and fluidity of Fifi Abdou just for a start. Additionally, one may be inspired by learning that Tahia was arrested three times for fighting for democracy, or that Samia almost became a Hollywood star, as well as the high education of some and lack of it in others. In their own way, they were (or are) all feminists.

Beyond the surface, learning about folkloric styles of dance, Arab music or lineage are entryways to discovering the limitless layers of nuance and expression in Arab art. When one can dance an entire taqsim or song, using one technique, similar to the way in which Oum Kalthoum was able to repeat one word or line with unlimited expression, then one has discovered what lies beyond the sequins and can live forever in that profound emotional joy that first sparked the fires of belly dance within.

### Yasmina Ramzy

*Yasmina is the founder and artistic director of Arabesque Dance Company & Orchestra, Arabesque Academy and the International Bellydance Conference of Canada. Since 1981, she has performed throughout the Middle East, taught in 60 cities on 5 continents, created choreography for many ensembles including the Bellydance Superstars, and produced DVDs and CDs that sell worldwide.*

**Madame Abla Saidi style dress**

# The Rom
## Nomads of the Spirit

### by Sierra Suraci

Dance and other arts have long shared a history of combining creativity and diversity. Within this scope, there is the beauty of blended stories, tableaux, and personal reflections. There are no restraints in the arts; only your imaginative spirit and creativity can take you to the edge of a limitless array of possibilities. There are many pioneers in the field of dance who have captured the world with their own spirit's interpretations of the music. For example, Isadora Duncan revitalized the mythos of Grecian and Roman dance, creating movement and expression unlike anything that had been seen during and just prior to her time. Togas and tunics of flowing, gossamer fabrics swirled upon the Victorians, reminiscent of the Greek and Roman eras, while liberating dances of joy and life. Ruth St. Denis's fantasy tableaux brought the mystery and exotic essence of the Eastern world into a theatrical form of dance. Costuming from the Ballet Rousse brought Middle Eastern fantasies to life, making them seem authentic.

Without freedom of expression and personal display, creativity would be oppressed. Although we are allowed boundless license in what we create, there remains one glaring flaw: cultural assimilation and stereotypical romanticizing of real cultures belonging to real people! I don't propose that everyone should recreate only researched anthropological material, but what I advocate is a dance based on, and guided by, reality.

Some dancers in the field of Middle Eastern dance tend to romanticize a mythical concept to the extreme point at which it becomes a ridiculous caricature of reality.

Because so few of the "Tribal" and "Gypsy" style dances have been researched or taught by a mentor from the Rom culture in their Romani dance style, many dancers perform "Romani dance" that does not reflect Romani dance traditions. Dance artists believe these popular stereotyped styles are a genuine rendering of authentic Romani dancing. Blindly, other dancers follow along, giving little or no deference to the culture and original people from whom this dance springs.

The Romani people, who call themselves "Rom," are commonly known as "Gypsies." The Rom are a multi-faceted people with a diverse culture that contains their main cultural identity as the holding-thread woven into their tapestry of life. When we appropriate an art of another culture in this way, portraying it as our own fantasies would wish it to be, we rob the Rom of their artistic rights and identity. As fellow artists and dancers, we owe greater responsibility to increasing our understanding of this diverse culture, and the Rom's dance variences (upon whom we've historically decided to build a fantasy representation)!

The swirling, five-layered skirts and ribbon bedecked tambourines are no more true to the actuality of Rom life or dance than if we had performed this same dance in a traditional Egyptian cabaret costume.

Western culture is often guilty of borrowing from the most grotesque areas in life around cultures that are beyond our own Anglophile perspective.

One who romanticizes can represent a great menace to the roots of a traditional people and the generations that follow. Always, much damage has been done through stereotyping, whether positive or negative. If you love dancing in the vast stylization that is Romani dance, accept the responsibility of learning what certain foreign words mean, the historical and cultural content and whom it is that they represent.

Become responsible for understanding what it is that you are contributing; either to dilution or the true reflection of a cultural entity.

People similar to the Rom, the Native Americans, as well as other indigenous people, are the peoples of the world who are seen to have been marginalized. Most people have heard of them; however, either they believe the engineered stereotyping of the indigenous artistic and religious culture or prefer to think the culture doesn't exist at all. The Rom are usually treated abysmally in their native countries: They are relegated to forced assimilation and subjugated to hatred because of their ways, purposely not counted as part of the population, and, worse, suffer atrocities because of the sterotypes about them.

Wherever Romani gather, villagers, and other people of the area ascribe to them epithets such as thieves, liars, dirty wanderers, con-artists, and perpetrators of violence. They are prohibited from camping in certain areas in Europe, and many still live poor lives due to the harsh transition from Communism to Democracy. Because of their low rate of school attendance, they are unable to get jobs, or are placed in schools for the learning-disabled due to language barriers. Many are trying to follow the ways of the dominant culture, but it is hard in a world that has long shunned Gypsies as pariahs. Hostility to the Rom's has existed almost from the time they first appeared in 12th century Europe. They live under a clan system, based mostly on their traditional crafts and geography. There is a commonality in the distrust and hatred towards the "gadjo" (non-Romani, outsider, or stranger). The Roms are a nomadic tribe, causing them to be persecuted throughout history, especially throughout Europe. At various times

**Kalderash women on the march in England. 1911**

they have been forbidden to wear distinctively bright clothing, to speak their own language, to travel, to marry one another, or to ply their traditional crafts. In some European countries, many Romani women were sterilized by force under governmental authority. In some countries, the Romani people were reduced to slavery. In Romania, it wasn't until the mid 1800s that they were freed from their enslaved status. Unfamiliar with the history of this last century, many people do not realize that many Roms perished under the policy of ethnic cleansing by the Nazis. Half a million of the Romany were persecuted, tortured and killed in the concentration camps, along with the Jews, Catholics, mentally retarded, and homosexuals. The Gypsies, as "Porriamos", know the Holocaust as "The Great Devouring".

Gypsies no longer live in horse-drawn caravans as they once did. Now they live in homes, motor homes, and apartments. Yet, frequently, they are still portrayed as itinerant, colorful wanderers of the world in their brightly painted caravans. This dated stereotyping is brought into our focus because of the myriad of "Gypsy" styled dances that are currently being performed by the Middle Eastern dance enthusiasts. Most, but not all, of these dances, have little resemblance to actual Romani dancing! Like any regional group of nomadic people, their dance style reflects the region in which they live. Rom music, a mournful, lamenting cantos (song) usually accompanies most dances, reflecting an identity with their pain and suffering in a long tribal history.

Romani performers scoff at the idea of having been trained in dancing. Much like the nomadic or village dancers in Egypt and North Africa, they are not formally trained. They are raised to dance as part of an environment that is based upon music, dancing, and storytelling. As one Rom performer said, "I don't need to train to be a dancer. Training! That's for people who aren't Gypsies." Another young Romani man says," I'm afraid we don't all have campfires, wagons, bandannas, earrings, or violins. We don't steal babies or pick peoples' pockets! Maybe we're not 'Gypsy' enough for you?"

Ask yourself: What is your idea of the Gypsies? Is that faux 'Gypsy' your allusion when you present a dance under the name of a group of people who have their own unique culture?

We dancers must remember to include dignity and respect when we dance in the shadow of a real group of people who have a distinct culture and history, because one may do more harm by not knowing the pertinent history, thereby romanticizing the Rom into unwarranted obscurity.

A Nazi photograph of a Gypsy in the Bełżec concentration camp, marked for reduction by the photographer, 1940

**The caption tells the story**

## References

Goodwin, Peter. "Gypsies the Outsiders". *National Geographic Magazine*, April 2001. Print.

Fraser, Angus. *The Gypsies*. Blackwell, UK: John Wiley and Sons, 1992. Print.

Fonseca, Isabel. *Bury Me Standing, The Gypsies and Their Journey.* USA: Random House, 1995. Print.3 Fonseca, Isabel, "Bury Me Standing, The Gypsies and Their Journey", Published: Random House, 1995.

## Sierra

*Sierra ~ Sadira began her dance career in 1972 in the San Francisco Bay Area and is known for her knowledge in ethno regional dance from Egypt, North Africa, and the Pan-Arabic world. She directed her own dance troupe, Raks As Saidi, for 15 years with emphasis on traditional dances.*

**Sierra-Sadira's troupe portray the Blue Guedra, a North African tribe.**

# Romani (Gypsy) History
## An Introduction

### By Renée Rothman PhD

Romani or *Gypsy* cultures have had a strong influence on belly dance development and their dance continues to be studied by contemporary artists. The term *Gypsy* refers to a population of people who trace their ancestry back to the Punjabi region of India and who migrated through and settled in parts of the Middle East, North Africa, western Asia, Europe, and the Americas over the course of perhaps two thousand years. Their origins in northern India have been confirmed through cultural retentions in language, professional choices, cosmologies, and social practices, as well as by modern genetic testing. Today they collectively call themselves Rom, possibly a reference to their original language, though they are still known by regional and tribal names: Bahlawan in Egypt; Gitano in Spain; Sinti in Germany; and Tsigani and Manousche in France. The term *Gypsy* is now considered pejorative and vulgar by the Rom, although it's used to describe a romanticized character type which persists in America.

Roma are tribal people. The tribe, the family, is more important than any one individual or any outside political state. They are bound by hereditary blood ties. Outsiders cannot marry into the tribe and marriage outside it incurs harsh punishment, possibly banishment, although there is ample evidence that Roma did in fact marry *gadje* or non-Romani. While they may have had a distant matriarchal past, they are fundamentally patriarchal. A tribe is lead by an elected chief, often an elder male, who serves for a lifetime and whose identity may be hidden from *gadje*. The chief presides over marriages, makes migration decisions, and ensures that their demanding codes of conduct are upheld. A council of male elders also upholds laws, resolves conflicts and metes out punishments. An elder female, the *phuri dai*, is the moral leader who advises the chief and council of elders. Individual families or extended families are organized similarly.

Rom are sometimes distinguished from the general population by their professions which tend to be in the lowest economic brackets: Metalsmiths, horse dealers, and entertainers. This may be a vestige of their original low Indian caste placement but it is also due to their previous nomadic lifestyle which was served best by portable professions. Just as one is born into a tribe, one is born into a gender-specific profession. Men tend to be the smiths, dealers, and musicians while women work as fortune-tellers or dancers.

The Rom are legendary for their work as entertainers. The Ursuari of Central Europe raised and trained bears to walk on hind legs, dance, and perform tricks. They are still seen, though infrequently, in the Balkan countryside. Fortune-telling by Tarot and palmistry is both entertainment and serious occult practice still popular today. But it is the music and dance of the Roma that transcends their outcast status.

Even though it was often misrepresented, 19th century Europe saw a brief period when Romani life was celebrated and reflected in painting, literature, and music. Classical European composers of the time, most famously Liszt, borrowed the alluring Asiatic sounds of Romani music. Probably because of portability, stringed instruments seem to be preferred by Roma. Hungarian violinists and Andalusian guitarists continue to inspire passion both within and outside Romani culture.

*Gypsy* historian Jean-Paul Clébert asserts that the origins of Rom dancing dates to their ritual practices in India. According to one legend, the first Roma were the Luri. They were hired by a prince to be professional court dancers but later disbanded and disbursed. As nomads, they contributed to and borrowed from the aesthetic expressions of whatever population they encountered. Nevertheless, they have retained common features which distinguish Rom dancing from their closest neighbors. When Laurel Victoria

Grey witnessed a concert of eight different Romani nationalities, she noted that:

"While regional differences were clear, the common roots of these dances came sharply into focus in a way that volumes of scholarly research could never convey."

The first written record of Romani appearance in Europe dates from 1348. Throughout the next century they migrated in extended family groups to all its regions. This was a time of great social upheaval in Europe when many non-Romani nomadic troupes, including brigands, entertainers and scholars, roamed the countrysides and urbanized areas. The Roma were singled out for special mistreatment. Known by other names such as *Egyptians*, *Bohemians*, *Romanichel*, and *Saracens*, they were suspect for their dark skin and hair, their professions, both legal and illegal, their association with occultism, and even their diets. In 1539, they were expelled from France. In the 17th and 18th centuries they were enslaved in Romania. In the 20th century, they were interred in concentration camps and exterminated at the hands of the Nazis. It has been estimated that between 400,000 and 1.5 million lost their lives in the Holocaust which they call *Baro Porrajmos*, the Great Devouring.

**Famille tsigane en voyage en Moldavie**
**Gypsy family on tour in Moldavia by Auguste Raffet**

The Rom have been stigmatized for hundreds of years causing distrust. Their ambiguous social status, statelessness, and lack of formal documentation, frustrates legal authorities and frightens non-Romani populations. Their commitments are internal and tribal. Their extended family bonds are indelible, and their social customs remain intact, even in the face of continual persecution. In the late 1960s, the Roma began to organize in order to speak publicly about their social conditions and to demand recognition. In 1999, the International Romani Union declared April 8th as International Roma Day, an annual opportunity to discuss Romani issues and celebrate its cultures.

The bleak social situation for European Roma, of which there are an estimated 12 million, continues even in the 21st century. According to the European Roma Rights Centre, they continue to be subjected to segregation, eviction, deportation, and vigilante hate crimes in France, Italy, the Czech Republic, and Slovakia. In September 2008, the European Union Roma Summit created the EU Framework for National Roma Integration Strategies

> "to promote the full inclusion of the RSC people - with regard to both the definition and the implementation of policies for the protection of fundamental rights, in order to fight discrimination, poverty and social exclusion, while supporting gender equality and ensuring access to education, housing, health, employment, social services, justice, sports and culture." (National Strategy For The Inclusion Of Roma, Sinti And Caminanti Communities - European Commission Communication No.173/2011 1.4 pg 10).

The *Gypsy* is a romanticized character type and an icon of social rebelliousness. Although the romanticization of the *Gypsy* began in Europe, it appeals to the American imagination. Non-conformity, individualism, and geographic movement are the foundations of America's zeitgeist. These fictive *Gypsies* are imagined as living a nomadic utopia wherein one experiences the safety of a small-sized community, where music and dance are employed to celebrate life for its own sake, where women and men are equals in social power and sexuality, and where occult magic aids in the resolution of conflicts. This wild, pre-civilized, and free *Gypsy* life is a fantasy of escape from the restrictions of modern society and is depicted in Western film, theater, and literature.

While cognizant and concerned with western Orientalist visions of Rom life, many modern belly dancers do trace their history along the Gypsy Trail, the migratory path taken by Rom tribes in their travels. They study and perform dances from places and historic eras considered to be foundational forms of belly dance: Egyptian Ghawazi with its powerful side-to-side shimmies, Indian Rajasthani and Kathak with an emphasis on rhythm and the use of elaborate hand gestures known as *mudras*, Turkish Rom with its distinctive 9/8 rhythm called *karsilama*, and Andalusian Flamenco which some believe to be the quintessential Romani art form.

Flamenco emerged in the southern Spanish region of Andalusia, historically a politically and culturally volatile area. Ruled variously by Islamic Moors from North Africa and Catholic monarchs from Northern Spain, its minority groups have experienced the worst society can offer: Persecution, deportation, and even extermination. The Rom standards of living were deplorable. Carmen Amaya, who achieved international renown as a great Flamenco dancer, was born into abject poverty in Barcelona's disease-ridden Barrio Somorrosta,

> "Home to bohemians and gypsies, and a place outsiders were reluctant to enter and unlikely to leave unmolested. Against a backdrop of smoke-filled air, factory sirens, and the sounds of the docks, *gitanos* built their crude dwellings on the edge of the sea, on sand blackened by coal dust and littered with industrial debris" (Sevilla 14).

It is said that suffering and celebration are the twin characteristics of Andalusian culture. In the face of this history, and maybe as a remedy to their tribulations, Andalusians also celebrate a great number of public fiestas, religious fairs and harvest festivals with music and dancing.

Flamenco dance, or *baile*, is traditionally a solo improvised dance performed by either women or men. *Cante* are rhythmic but non-melodic songs sung by both men and women who carry in their voices generations of grief and passion. Originally, *cante* was accompanied by *palmas*, intricate, polyrhytmic patterns of hand clapping, and by vocal encouragement. Flamenco guitar was introduced in the mid-19th century.

The arts of Flamenco, *cante*, *baile*, and *toque*, guitar, translate the painful histories of the Roma into music and dance. The Spanish Roma, or Gitano, have a strong sense of ethnic pride which positions them against many mainstream populations. Their arts express the Romani sense of despair, the feeling that the world can be cruel and absurd and arbitrary.

> "In its purest form flamenco is a dramatic collective event, based on centuries of individual but shared experiences. The interpreter's power in expressing his emotions draws his audience into a common experience. He builds upon but goes beyond his personal anguish to articulate what he and his audience have in common..." (Papenbrok 54).

Although each individual suffers differently, a single artist can affirm the realities of the collective experience.

Collective empathy at flamenco performances is felt through the mysterious, spiritual product of flamenco performance called *duende*. Duende has been described as a state of intoxication, of liminal consciousness, or of ecstasy called up by soul-wrenching performances (Claus 94). It is experienced by the artists, dancer, musician, and singer, as well as by the audience. In fact, in the presence of duende, audiences have been known to cry out their own grief, to tear their clothing, to behave aggressively towards others.

In America, belly dancers and musicians cross between belly dance and flamenco with some regularity. Belly dancers view flamenco as a related form deriving from a common source in Rom cultures. Dances with origins along the Gypsy Trail, including Flamenco and North Indian Rajasthani, are often performed together in belly dance concerts as a recognition of their family resemblances.

## *References*

Clébert, Jean-Paul., *The Gypsies.* Baltimore, Md: Penguin Books,1961. Print.

Gray, Laurel Victoria. "Gypsy in Their Souls: The West Preserves Gypsy Dance Traditions." *The Best of Habibi*. 15:1. (Winter, 1996). Web.

Hancock, Ian. *We are the Romani People* Centre de Recherches Tsiganes Hertfordshire, AL: University of Hertfordshire Press, 2003. Print.

Manderino, Amy Luna. "What is Gypsy Bellydance?" *Gildedserpent.com*. n.d. Web.

Papenbrok, Marion "History of Flamenco" in Schreiner, Claus, ed. *Flamenco: Gypsy Dance and Music from Andalusia* Portland, OR: Amadeus Press, 2000. Print.

Schreiner, Claus, ed. *Flamenco: Gypsy Dance and Music from Andalusia* Portland, OR: Amadeus Press, 2000. Print.

Sevilla, Paco. Queen of the Gypsies: The Life and Legend of Carmen Amaya (Flamenco in the Theater Age: 1910-1960), San Diego, CA: Sevilla Press, 1999. Print.

### *Renée Rothman PhD,*

*Renée holds her PhD in cultural anthropology. A scholar, she taught anthropology of dance courses at San Jose State and University of California, Santa Cruz. She maintains a blog dancedocsthinktank.wordpress.com where she comments on dance events. In 2001, she began studying the art and history of bellydance.*

# The Zar
## Dancing with Genies

### by Yasmin Henkesh

It took her under a minute to fall into a trance - literally. One second her arms were flailing, the next she was sprawled on the floor unconscious. The musicians paused while her sisters propped her up, her head dangling forward like a tether-ball on a rope. The Rattler pressed his hands to her temples and twisted her neck this way and that. Then he yanked on her arms. Someone sprinkled rose water on her face. It took a while for her to return; she was a long way away. Fifteen minutes later though, she was back on her feet, dancing. Her jinni liked the music and refused to let her sit out the song. Who knew when she would find another zar? The rituals were few and far between now that Egypt's Islamic conservatives strongly discouraged them.

### What is a "zar", and what does it have to do with belly dancing?

*Zar* is one of three sacred dance rituals performed in the Middle East, along with Sufi whirling and the *zikr*. While the last two are dedicated to Allah (and accepted by Islam), the *zar* is performed to placate possession spirits gone astray. Participants dance themselves into a trance to communicate with a blood-loving sub-species of jinn called the *"Zar"*. Zar is also the name given to the trance inducing movements performed during the ritual. These movements, particularly the wild head tossing, are what belly dancers find so fascinating about this possession cult ceremony.

However, there is a lot more to *zar* than flying hair. *A Dictionary of Egyptian Arabic*, the definitive source for Egyptian Arabic translations, defines *zar* as "a ritual of sacrifices, incantations, drumming and dancing performed for the purpose of appeasing any number of spirits by which a person may be believed to be possessed." Some hold the word was derived from the Arabic root "za'er," (or visitor). Others think it came from the verb "zahr," *"to become visible, perceptible or to manifest."* However, most *zar* scholars believe the word is not Arabic at all, but from Persian or Amharic, the language of Ethiopia.

In reality, no one knows exactly where the *zar* originated. Some Egyptians are convinced a precursor to the cult originated in pharaonic Egypt. Archaeologists have found evidence that Sumerian, Babylonian and Egyptian priests burned incense and beat copper or wooden pots to exorcise unwanted spirits. Certainly, the concept of spirit possession evolved far earlier than the joining of the Upper and Lower Nile Valley Kingdoms. By the time of the Natufians (one of the three world cultures that invented agriculture around 12,000 BCE, from the Levant and Jordanian valley), the belief in spirit possession

**A zar musician playing a goat hoof belt (mangour) and rattles.**

was well ingrained; judging by their grave offerings and shamanic artifacts.

The most likely source for *this version* of possession cult, however, is Africa; Ethiopia, The Sudan or the sub-Saharan states that supplied the world's slave trade. The *Zar* has too many similarities with Haitian Voudoun and Brazilian Candomble / Umbanda cults to be mere coincidence. Surprisingly, the *Zar* is relatively new in Egypt. The great Egyptologist Edward Lane did not mention it in his definitive work about the Egyptians in 1835, but then again, as a man, he would have been forbidden to attend this largely female ceremony. The earliest known European record of an Egyptian *zar* is from the 1870s, although it was described in The Sudan and Ethiopia as early as 1836. In Brazil, the Umbanda cult took root around the turn of the twentieth century, although other Brazilian, Haitian and New World possession cults were well established by then. By the 1960s, the peak of the cult's popularity in Egypt, middle and upper class women considered it chic to attend a *zar*, and participants included stars such as Om Kalthoum.

We do know that today thousands of women from all walks of life turn to the *zar* to cure otherwise incurable illnesses. They believe that *zar* spirits enter their bodies during a time of weakness, then cause pain and suffering to force their hosts to satisfy their needs. During the initial discovery ceremony, the actual *"zar,"* patients literally dance until they drop – from exhaustion or in a trance – as they try to determine the spirit responsible for their problems. At subsequent rituals (called *"hadras,"* after the *zikr* gatherings) the women commune with their possessors and allow them to manifest in their bodies.

In some countries, *zar* gatherings go on for a week - seven days of intense drumming and dancing. In Egypt however, the rituals only last a day or two, if that. Even if the cult is dying in Egypt, it is still practiced (sometimes underground) throughout Africa and the Middle East – from West Africa, Morocco, Tunisia, The Sudan, Djibouti, Ethiopia and Somalia, to Saudia Arabia, Kuwait, Qatar, The United Arab Emirates, Yemen, Oman and Iran.

**What happens at a zar ceremony?**

If modern medicine cannot find the cause of a physical or mental ailment, it is assumed that supernatural forces must be at work. The patient, typically a woman, will consult a spiritual healer (a *sheikha* or *kudiya*), also a woman, to see if she is possessed; *"malbusa - clothed," "milammisa - touched,"* or *"ma'zura - excused,"* as the Egyptians refer to it. The *sheikha* will ask for a personal item, like a headscarf or underwear (an *atar*), to put under her pillow so the spirit can speak to her in a dream. If the *sheikha* determines the patient is indeed with spirit, (or often, several spirits), she will suggest holding a diagnostic ceremony to confirm her intuition - if the possessed woman's finances permit it.

The night before the ceremony, the *sheikha* will set up an altar or *kursi* ("throne") where the *zar* will be held and decorate it with candles and offerings to the *asyad* (spirit "masters"); roses, henna, incense, candy or food and things suggested in her dream (for example alcohol or cigarettes). Each spirit's requirements are unique, so it is important to know which one is causing the trouble. The goal of the ceremony, after all, is to placate disgruntled spirits.

Ritual details vary from country to country, but a few elements are common to all; fumigating participants with incense beforehand, trance induction through dancing, percussion-heavy music and an animal sacrifice in the name of the possessing spirit (that participants eat in a communal meal). The patient is generally a married or divorced woman (spirits rarely choose virgins) who is "marrying" her possessor (because she will agree to a contract with her jinni during the ceremony). She is called an *"arousa"* (bride) and will usually wear white, unless her spirit requests otherwise.

The *sheikha* is also a common element of *zar* ceremonies. She is the leader who will communicate with the spirit world and mediate negotiations. The terms and conditions she arranges will be sealed in blood, so she must know what she is doing. Since she, too, is possessed, she will often draw on her own experience navigating the spirit world or enlist the help of her spirit guide.

### How does the music sound?

During an Egyptian *zar* three different music groups may play, depending on which spirit the *arousa* is thought to harbor. The *harim masri* (or Egyptian women) usually perform first (also called the *Firqa as-Said* because its members come from the *Saidi* region of Upper Egypt). These four or five older women sing *a capella* while they keep time on frame drums. Next come the *tanbour* (or *tambur*) player and his percussionists. This instrument, a large primitive six-string lyre, is the highlight of the evening because it is believed the *asyad* themselves talk through it. It produces music that is heavy and dramatic and particularly exciting to possessed women. One or more percussionists accompany the tanbour player wearing another unusual instrument, a *mangour* (variation: *manjur*). This is a wide cloth belt with hundreds of dried goat or sheep hooves attached to it that is fastened around the hips and shaken using typical belly dance movements. The sound resembles cicadas or the marimba-like rattles the percussionists also play.

The final group is called "Abou al-Gheit" after an Islamic saint from a village north of Cairo where many *zar* musicians originate. This is an all-male group that plays, in addition to drums and tambourine-like percussion instruments, large dish-like *zar sagat* about five inches in diameter (brass finger cymbals) and a *nay* (or reed flute). Their music is light and melodious, almost appropriate for a real wedding. One member, the dance leader (and sagat player), encourages participants to keep moving until they reach an ecstatic state. The sound of bells is thought to please the jinn and their rhythms often push borderline dancers into a trance.

Throughout each performance, and the ceremony as a whole, the music builds into a large crescendo, sweeping participants into another plane of existence. The music may start slow and melodious, but by the end, the drumming reaches a fever pitch, highlighting the ceremony's African roots.

### How is the dance performed?

Participants generally sit in a large circle where they can see the musicians; against the walls of a room, courtyard or flaps of a tent. When someone feels the urge to dance, he or she will rise and face the musicians, their heads and faces covered with a light veil, or *tarha*. Some dance in one spot, keeping the beat with their feet while their upper bodies twist, sway and bob to the rhythm. Others do unique steps in honor of a specific *zar* tribe or individual, such as the *Saidi* or Arab bedouins. Dancers usually keep their eyes closed. Strong

**A zar lyre - the tanbour**

emotions register on their faces as their breathing becomes heavier (a few even pant) while they weave and bob their torsos - until they either collapse in a trance, the song ends or exhaustion overcomes them. Some dance for hours while others only rise for a song.

If a dancer goes into a trance, the *sheikha* and/or her spotter will whisper in her ear and sprinkle rose water, or something more pungent, on her face to bring her back. Opening eyes signal the spirit(s) have left her body, a moment called "*al-radwa*" (or Liberation). Afterwards, the woman will be disorientated, but relaxed and in peace.

Unfortunately, this peace does not last. Entering a trance does not exorcise her spirits; it only pacifies them temporarily. A *zar* stays with its host for life; even when the human upholds their end of the bargain. However, *zayran* (plural of *zar*) are notoriously fickle and rarely play fair or by the rules! That is why hosts end up holding *zars* once a year to appease them - even if they regularly attend *hadarat* (plural of *hadra*).

Not all women who attend *hadarat* are possessed. Some are curious bystanders drawn by the music. Others may want to socialize or release stress through dancing. A few are encouraged to go by their families because of their unusual behavior (like refusing to marry or have children) or their socially unacceptable personalities (they are mean and grouchy or don't obey their husbands). Still others wonder if they are with spirit and if a master would call them to dance.

Sudanese *zars* differ slightly from those held in Egypt. The *zayran* there are more likely to make their hosts do extraordinary things: Speak foreign languages, dance with swords, act out events and perform great feats of strength. Their hosts require numerous props and articles

**Zar musicians during the recording of Zar - Trance Dancing for Women.**

of clothing to appease their masters, similar to Haitian Voudoun and Brazilian Umbanda rituals.

These differences are perhaps due to the relative influence of Islam in each country. Sudan is closer to its animist roots. Egypt has much stronger ties to the Muslim world and its fundamentalist requirements for female behavior. Sudanese women appear invested in their beliefs. Egyptian women pull back somewhat for fear of being labeled as infidels. They take great pains to prove they are not violating Quranic teachings or worshiping the jinn. They call their spirits *asyad*, masters, *qarin (s.) or qurana (pl.)*, spirit doubles that live underground, *ahwat tahtiyeen*, underground brothers and sisters, or *malayka ardiyya*, underground angels – anything but jinn.

Even so, one of the pillars of the Muslim faith is that: "There is no god but God." Fundamentalists believe that entering into a contract with a spirit acknowledges its power, which goes against the orthodox belief that only God has power, and He has no rival. Therefore, women who make contracts with spirits, jinn or not, are transgressing an essential tenant of Islam. They are sacrificing to beings other than God.

### What is a trance?

Going into a dance-induced trance is similar to having an out-of-body experience or a vision. Women describe it as if they were looking at their bodies from a distance - through the eyes of a spirit from a parallel universe. The steady rhythmic beating of the drums allows participants to focus on the music, to let go of the here and now and increase their alpha and theta brainwaves. On the simplest level, as with hypnosis, yoga or just trying to fall asleep, it helps to have outside stimuli to prevent life's everyday problems from hijacking our consciousness. On a more complicated level, once participants experience trance and find personal keys to help them return, each subsequent encounter becomes easier.

It also helps to be familiar with the ritual and mentally open to the experience. *Zar* ceremonies are large group events. In countries where women grow up watching other women go into trance, they are less afraid of loosing self-control because they have seen others come out of trance unscathed. They know those present will not let them be harmed. They have confidence in their spotters and that the *sheikha* will safely extricate them when it is time to leave the treacherous *zar* universe.

Apart from the music, there are other elements of the *zar* ceremony that help participants enter into trance. Panting from the exertion of dancing (these women do not dance on a regular basis) causes hyperventilation and a feeling of light-headiness. The women also take deep breaths of the incense and tobacco smoke permeating the air and may drink alcoholic beverages (forbidden in Islam) which make them feel dizzy - along with the twisting and turning of the dance itself. The change of environment allows them to forget their normal stress-filled lives and relax. Most important, these women want to let go. No one can force a dancer to go into a trance; she has to allow it to happen. She has to want it to happen. If she feels safe and in good hands, she will lose herself in the moment and let go. Then, she will feel better – at least for a little while - until her *zar* discovers a new craving.

*Note: This is an excerpt from Trance Dancing with the Jinn, to be published by Llewellyn International in 2014.*

### Yasmin Henkesh

*Yasmin has forty years of professional belly dance experience in Europe, Egypt and the USA. Her music label, Sands of Time Music, has released the only authentic compilation of Egyptian zar music to date. Her first book, "Trance Dancing with the Jinn", will be released by Llewellyn Worldwide in 2014.*

**Yasmin Henkesh**

# In Search of Zambra Mora
## A Puzzling Dance Mystery

**by Dondi**

My interest in the mystery of the Zambra Mora began around 1995. I was already an established belly dancer at the clubs in Southern California and South Florida and was looking for something a bit different. I returned to my home town of San Diego and heard of a woman named Tatiana who was teaching Zambra Mora and Tajik dance. I wasn't sure what to expect, but loving surprises, and really wanting to do something new, I went to class with Tatiana of Minnesota. This began a journey that led me to workshops in Zambra Mora with Alexandra King and Maria Morca.

Throughout the years, I continued to belly dance around the world. In 2004, when I was touring with The Belly Dance Superstars, I visited Spain for the first time. After a month of performing in the Teatre Victòria in Barcelona, I headed to Andalucía to research Zambra Mora. It was very frustrating. I couldn't find this illusive dance! Records of the forbidden dance didn't exist, or if they did, I could not find them. Since then, I have learned, and I believe, that they were hidden and, finally, lost since the time that Zambra Mora flourished over 400 years ago.

I do not have hard evidence for the existence of Zambra Mora. Even after spending time in Andalusia, and searching for the dance more than once, I can only make intelligent guesses about the dance. Ana Ruiz has researched and written about Zambra Mora and about how elusive the documentation can be. She was at a research center in Jerez de la Frontera, Spain, and asked the librarian about Zambra Mora and its existence as a dance. The librarian let out a long sigh and responded, "This subject is controversial; there is no proof of it ever having existed in this form." This is very similar to the icy reception I received all over Southern Spain, especially when speaking to Flamenco dancers in Seville about Zambra Mora. One Flamenco teacher with whom I studied said, "Zambra Mora does not exist, and it never did!"

This is what I have pieced together from my studies in Spain and from numerous articles, website and books:

Zambra Mora has roots in Southern Spain, mainly Granada, from 711-1492 with the Gitanos or Spanish Gypsies and the Moors who ruled southern Spain for 800 years. This means that Zambra Mora would be older than Flamenco, which was first referred to in literature in the 1700s. If we want to get an idea of what Zambra Mora was, we must search into the era before the Moors ruled Spain in 711, during their reign, and after they ruled Spain in the 1700s.

The Moors were Berbers, Arabs, and North Africans. They landed at Gibraltar, in the south of Spain, in 711, and it took them less than seven years to conquer almost all of Spain. In almost every article and book, it is implied that the time of the Moors was stable and happy, a time of unprecedented cooperation among Jews, Muslims, and Christians. Infrequent conflicts and wars were described as isolated and mild, compared to wars in other parts of the world.

The Moors had an enormous influence on life in Spain. They built beautiful palaces, public baths, schools, and castles, and they introduced sophisticated methods of irrigation and farming. They brought their religion of Islam with them. Many Spanish people became Muslims during their rule; although it is said that the Moors allowed Christians and Jews to follow their own religious beliefs. The Moors were also knowledgeable about math and science, and Spain became a center of learning and culture under the Moors.

The period from 718 to 1491 is known as the Reconquest. Although, art, music and Moorish dance were banned during the Reconquest, the Gypsies continued to express themselves

through these art forms. References to "Gypsy dancers" can be found, and are frequently mentioned, in Spanish literary and musical works from the 1500s onward. When Queen Isabella and King Ferdinand married in 1469, they vowed to make all of Spain a Christian kingdom; together, Isabella and Ferdinand drove the Moors out of Spain.

In 1502, all Muslims were ordered to leave Spain unless they converted to Christianity. Those who did convert were called Moriscos. Most Moriscos were suspected of not being real Christians and, in the 1560s, laws were enacted to rid Spain of traditional Muslim customs like wearing the veil, speaking Arabic, and taking hot baths. Islam was no longer being practiced legally in Spain. Those who stayed, had to practice Islam in secret, but the desire to reclaim power was still strong, and sporadic insurrections were what, in the end, led to the final expulsion of all Muslims remaining in Spain after 1609.

As had happened with the Jews previously, before the Moors were driven out, they began to hide their identities, fearing persecution, imprisonment, and death. They hid their music and dances and changed their names from Arabic, African, and Jewish names to Christian names. People changed their family trees and any paperwork that would reveal their ethnicity and religion. They were forced to convert to Catholicism while mosques and synagogues were destroyed and rebuilt as churches. Jews and Muslims were given a choice: Convert to Catholicism or leave Spain. Nonetheless, those who chose to convert were persecuted anyway.

Moorish influence in Spain goes back thousands of years, but it was the Islamic invasion in 711 that brought with it the main musical influences. The North Africans brought their music and dancing, which was then influenced by Spanish music, dance, and art. To think of this in more modern terms, there was a fusion of Moorish and Spanish creativity and art.

Many people think of Zambra Mora as a type of Flamenco dance. That is not how I would categorize it. Once a person sees a well-trained Zambra Mora dancer, it becomes obvious that it is an entirely different dance. The beat of Zambra Mora is dramatic and slow. It is referred to as a 4/4 rhythm and is free-style, that is, total improvisation--without choreography. The dance has little or no taconeo (footwork), which is often the apex of a Flamenco performance. The footwork of Zambra Mora is earthy, with a stomp and a traveling step while the arms are flowing and the upper body bends, twists, undulates and circulates. Circular hand-and-wrist movement is common and is termed "Floreo". The posture of the Zambra Mora dancer is more relaxed than the extremely upright, and evenly-arched posture of the Flamenco dancer. The Zambra Mora posture tends to be more Gitana (Gypsy) which feels raw and earthy and less formal than Flamenco. There can even be a bending forward in the posture of the Zambra Mora dancer. Zambra Mora embraces the five elements: Wood, metal, fire, earth, and water. The facial expressions in the dance are joyful, confident, defiant, and intense. In Maghrebi (Moroccan Arabic) Zambra means "celebration" or "party" and Mora refers to the Moors, the people from North Africa, of mixed Arab/Berber decent.

The first mention of Flamenco in literature is in 1774 in the book Cartas Marruecas by José Cadalso. The word Flamenco is from the Arabic word fellahmengu, which means "expelled peasant". Those who study traditional Flamenco, like Molina and Mairena, referred to the period 1780-1850 when Flamenco was said to be danced secretly in Gypsy homes. Álvarez Caballero (1998) went further, stating: "If there is no record of Flamenco before the late 1780s, it is because Flamenco simply did not exist." During the Golden Age of Flamenco, between 1869–1910, it developed rapidly in cafes and venues that offered ticketed public performances.

I do not believe that Zambra Mora can be classified as a fusion of Arabic and Flamenco. I have studied both, and find that Zambra Mora is widely different from Flamenco in movement, music, and attitude. When watching a Flamenco dancer, it seems they are isolated and introspective, whereas the Zambra Mora dancer is sharing and communicating with the audience. I don't know who first said it, but I have read, many times that in Flamenco, "feelings are expressed but not shared and the dancer actually ignores the audience, and with the Flamenco dancer, the pain flies freely". This is not the case in Zambra Mora where the dancer expresses joy and envelopes the people who are sharing her space.

Zambra Mora is usually danced barefoot with a coin hip sash or coin belt and bra. The blouse is tied under the bust and the skirt is tight around the hips, then flares out and has a ruffle on the bottom. The costuming is bright, colorful, and flowing. Finger cymbals and/or tambourine are often used. This dance is fiery, passionate, forceful, and seductive.

Since a large part of Moorish rule in Spain was characterized by peaceful times between Jews, Moors, and Christians, I believe that peacefulness would have been reflected in the Zambra Mora. Flamenco is much more emotionally angst-ridden than Zambra Mora. Flamenco dance is the story of the struggle and strife of the Gypsies, and it can be seen in all master Flamenco dancers. If we look at history, it would make sense that Zambra Mora was more joyous, happy, and light-hearted in its feeling because during the Moorish rule, there were peaceful and happy times with different cultures living, working and sharing together. There are many opinions about Zambra Mora, and I believe we have to dig deep into history to get a glimpse of what it might have been. I believe the Zambra Mora has been lost, and we can only guess at what it might have been.

Zambra Mora is an incredibly powerful dance from a time in history that is absolutely fascinating.

Furthermore, it is heart-breaking that an entire dance form probably has been lost because of religious persecution and people having to live in fear. May the ancient memories of Zambra Mora continue to pique the interest of dancers everywhere! It is my hope that, one day, religious persecution will become a thing of the past.

## References

"Zambra Mora." *Wikipedia*. Wikimedia Foundation, n.d. Web. 21 Nov. 2012.

*Cities of Light: The Rise & Fall of Islamic Spain.* Robert Gardner. Unity Production Foundation and Gardner Films, 2007. DVD.

Bragg, Melvyn. "Muslim Spain." BBC broadcast, November 21, 2002. Web.

### Dondi
*Dondi grew up in show business and has performed in over 20 countries. She is a member of SAG, was the exclusive dancer for Omar Sharif's 60th birthday, and was an original member of The Bellydance Superstars. Currently, Dondi travels the world with her family and mom, renowned healer, Donna Eden.*

# Improvisational Tribal Style
## Constructing Self and Community

### by April Rose Burnam

Improvisational Tribal Style belly dance (ITS) is a form of belly dance practiced around the world that started in the US during the first few years of the 21st century, although its basic structure was codified in the 1980s under a slightly different name and its influences reach back to the presence of "Oriental Dance" in America since the 1893 Chicago World's Fair.

A contemporary style of belly dance, ITS is a structured, improvisational dance form performed in a group. All dancers move in and out of predefined spatial arrangements that establish a leader and group of followers. The dancer who finds herself in a designated leader position chooses "stall" moves familiar to the group and is responsible for "cuing" choreographed combinations with a movement cue. At the close of a "cued combination", dancers anticipate the leader's next maneuver through their peripheral vision using a detailed process of categorization which leads stall moves and combinations into one-another, based on pre-arranged transition pathways. The stall moves and combinations must be threaded together in a spontaneous arrangement among a group of alternating leaders and followers. During the improvisation, all individuals are engaged in a commonly defined process of spontaneous decision-making that is informed by the standards and values they have agreed upon (about how long is too long, when to accent the music, where to move in space, etc.).

In the experience of dancing ITS, the dancers put themselves into a situation where the possibility of falling out of unison with each other is confronted repeatedly by the group. They manage to maintain their group-integrity, their relationship to one another, and the choreography, out of which their sense of community is formed and strengthened again and again. Improvisational Tribal Style belly dance does not merely represent the idea of community: The dance form provides a framework through which communities are actually created, realized, and maintained. These communities are constructed by individuals who, through practicing ITS, understand themselves as subjects with agency situated in relation to other subjects.

ITS, as it is currently practiced around the world, originally began in the United States as a categorical offshoot of American Tribal Style belly dance (ATS). Carolena Nericcio of FatChanceBellyDance created ATS in the 1980s in Berkeley, California. A student of Masha Archer, who had studied with Jamila Salimpour in the 1960s, many of Carolena's basic movements began as variations on Jamila's codified set. All ATS dancers around the world know this basic shared set of stall moves and combinations. As dancers of FatChanceBellyDance began their own projects, and other belly dancers became familiar with the ATS cued-improvisational format, troupe leaders around the US began choreographing their own combinations to insert into their own troupe's ATS repertoire, sometimes creating new stall moves and spatial formations. Until around 2008 or so, most cued-improvisational forms of belly dance that used Carolena's structure of stall moves and combinations threaded together in a spontaneous arrangement among a group of alternating leaders and followers were colloquially called American Tribal Style, or the shorter and more popular term, "Tribal" belly dance. The use of the name "Tribal" has become somewhat problematic in the belly dance community, as tribal is also associated with an aesthetic and general style of movement (versus the improvisational structure) that ranges from Jamila Salimpour's Bal Anat "Ethnic" or "California Tribal" aesthetic to almost any aesthetic that differs from traditional "Oriental" or "Cabaret". Carolena Nericcio trademarked the name "American Tribal Style" in 2012 and many group improvisations that do not cohere with her format now call themselves Improvisational Tribal Style (some groups call their structure "Tribal Improv" or "Synchronized

Group Improvisation"). The name ITS, first coined by Amy Sigil of UNMATA, solves the problem of what to call group cued improvisation that does not adhere to all of Carolena's specific codifications, as well as clearly states the improvisational quality of the dance which first-time viewers almost never perceive without having been told.

The experience of dancing within the structures of ATS and ITS is a site where dancers construct their self-identity and group solidarity differently than they may in everyday life. Elaborating on Barbara Sellers-Young's research on community and identity in American Tribal Style belly dance, I aim to demonstrate, through a movement analysis of ITS, how the actual structures and realworld experience of dancing ITS forms communities of interdependent and secure selves.

Barbara Sellers-Young writes:

"In the class, rehearsal, and on the stage, the dancer negotiates the intersections between self, society, and the perceptual awareness of her dancing body. The dancer's body in performance is, therefore, an act of mediation between the physical vocabulary of the dance form and personal conceptions of identity."[1]

When rehearsing and performing, ATS and Improvisational Tribal Style belly dancers negotiate their individual positions together for the common interest of maintaining the synchronicity and solidarity of the group. By confronting, again and again, the challenges that threaten their ability to maintain group composure, such as complex musical structure, each dancer's differing level of confidence and technical skill, the physical shape of the dance space, and the make-up of the audience, they reaffirm their identity and efficacy as a unified community.

**Shelly and Amy of Unmata**

The exhilaration dancers feel from consistently overcoming the threat of falling into dis-unison contributes to their solidarity and commitment to one another in a way that makes space for them to feel confident in their own bodies' ability to contribute.

## Stall Moves and Combinations

Stall moves are short, easily manipulated movement phrases that enable a dancer to stay in line with the music and allow for spontaneous decision-making when cuing combos. Stall moves are the threads that connect combinations, allowing for travel and formation-changes, changes in directional orientation, and time to think about next possible maneuvers. Stall movements can be done for any length of time. The cue for all stall movements is to begin executing it on the initial downbeat of a phrase; effectively, there is no cue, just a committed initiation and follow through. A dancer can vary a stall movement by traveling or turning it in space or by adding a level change.

Most stall moves are appropriated directly from Carolena Nericcio's ATS style, and, consequently, are extensions of Jamila Salimpour's original format from the 1960s. Jamila codified the movements she learned from Middle Eastern and North African dancers performing in San Francisco nightclubs in the 1960s, naming them after the dancers' names or nationality. Most ITS and ATS troupes share the same stall moves, performed as slightly different variations of Jamila's and Carolena's originally codified movements. Some common examples are the "Egyptian," "Arabic," "Ghawazi," and "Maya." Although Amy Sigil does not connect Hot Pot ITS to Middle Eastern or North African history or choose Arabic music to perform to, the names of these stall movements have remained and by their names, inherently reference the Middle East and North African regions.

Combinations are short choreographies that vary in length and may include formation changes. A

**Troupe Hipnotica perform at 2012 Cues and Tattoos Instructor Showcase**
**Corie Brooke, Julia Demarest, Lisa Donohue, Adriene Rice, Julia Sewell**

specific singular movement, called a "cue," which is done at the end of a corresponding stall move, initiates a specific combination. Certain combinations can only be cued from certain stall moves that allow for ease of transition from stall move to combination. These short choreographies allow different ITS troupes to insert their own creativity into the standard organizational structure. Hot Pot ITS combinations tend to employ humorous physical references, such as a line change in which dancers high-five as they pass one another. These combinations, versus the improvisational structure itself and the shared set of stall moves, are where ITS troupes tend to differ from one another and from ATS. ITS troupes often teach their signature combinations to other ITS troupes who collect and add them to their own repertoire.

## Conceptual Variations and Formation Changes

A conceptual variation initiates a combination to be done in a specific manner that varies from the basic combination. Examples of these conceptual variations are spatial orientation changes and/or turns as well as optional formation changes that may or may not result in a new dancer taking the lead role. A series of options may be opened up during the execution of certain stall moves or combinations. In one combination there may be four options, each option "unlocking" the possibility for the next. For example, once a stationary move is done in a spin, the followers will return from the spin and look to see if the leader will now travel with the move. If the leader travels back in space (cuing a line change) the followers will then look to see if the next dancer who finds herself in the leader position will maintain the lead or give it immediately back to the leader who cued these series of variations on that single move. Conceptual variations are also used to change the "front" when dancing for an audience in the round and to add a "cascade" effect created by dancers doing the same movement initiated sequentially at different times, in canon.

All repertoires of ITS have specific line formations or spatial arrangements. The most common are drawn directly from American Tribal Style: stagger, circle, chorus line, and facing duets. Hot Pot ITS includes "V" and "inverted V" formations as well as a circle within a circle, and variations on the classic chorus line. Trybe Habibi Bizarre, an ITS troupe from Southern Louisiana, has a complex spatial formation called a "flower" in which one main leader cues three secondary leaders to whom certain groups of followers, that cannot see the main leader, look to for direction, allowing many people to dance together without compromising the ability of some to see the cuing leader. Formation changes can be tricky to cue because, in many cases, they must be initiated by the leader, then immediately facilitated by the leaders-to-be behind her who must ripple the action through to the group. The spatial arrangement must be cued by the contributing efforts of many dancers not just by the simple direction of a leading one.

## Musical Interpretation

A group improvisation is considered successful not only when combinations, cues, and stall moves are seamlessly hidden by smooth transitions, but also when the combos and conceptual variations are executed to mirror the structure and phrasing of the music. As a phrase of music builds to a crescendo, a leader might cue a series of stall moves, varying them with orientation-changing quarter, third, half, or full turns and arm embellishments until the climax is realized, at which point she would likely cue a combination that varies in dynamic (from smooth and slow to sharp and fast). Hand embellishments called "floreos" are used to set the speed of a current stall move and subsequent combination, and as interpretive filler to finish out phrases in order to stay in sync with the phrasing of the music. This close relationship between the movement and music is one element of ITS that aligns the form with other variations of belly dance. Unlike many styles of belly dance, however, most Hot Pot ITS and ATS movements are motivated by (and accent) the

**Les Shuvanies**
**The duo Audrey and Jennifer are cuing a change of leader to the chorus in the back.**

downbeat of the music, staying rooted in the rhythm versus riffing on the melody.

## Shared Expectations

Experienced dancers who are familiar with one another are able to move collectively in and out of spatial formations based on the decision-making patterns and standards set up by the conditions of the performance. When deciding to change the formation, dancers ask themselves the same questions, and hopefully, share the same answers: How much time has been spent in each formation, on how many sides is the audience, how soon will the song end, and do we want a specific individual to make her way to the lead by then? By rehearsing together over a long period of time, all dancers come to share certain values regarding how long is "too long" to be in one formation and in which performance setting certain arrangements should or should not be used. For example, an inwardly focused circle is less conducive to a proscenium theater stage and more common to informal settings.

## Taking the Lead and Learning to Follow

The cued-improvisational structure of ITS necessitates that dancers move in and out of a leading position. In each spatial arrangement there is a designated leader position and, as dancers rotate through various preordained spatial formations, every dancer passes through this lead-position. If a dancer chooses to become the leader, he or she stops all traveling movement and occupies the lead-position. Here, the leader directs the troupe's movement until he or she chooses to continue the rotation. In some iterations of ITS, when a leader cues the group to do a half-turn or quarter-turn, a follower who occupies a distal end of the line formation may "steal" the lead when all other dancers are behind her, looking at her back, thereby changing the orientation of the group.

> There is a constant awareness among dancers of what their position is and what options they have from that particular position.[2]

An ITS dancer must be aware of her own position in relationship to the group: Whether it holds the possibility for lead-stealing or not and how she will shift herself in space as the formations change while maintaining her position relative to the surrounding dancers. As the spatial arrangement changes, the dancers effectively move as one organism made of constituent parts. All members have a specific and necessary role but each individual must take action with regard for the group and only within the limitations or possibilities of her role. A successful improvisation is achieved by individuals working together from within the boundaries of their individual positions, each person accepting the responsibility of her role.

The calm comportment of the collective dancers is vital to the maintenance of their spontaneous movement together. If a leader appears visibly panicked, the effects on her followers are palpable as their slicing movements begin to halt with hesitation and insecurity, disrupting the set pathways that allow followers to anticipate the actions of the leader and causing the improvisation to fall apart. Elements that help to give the appearance of calm collectedness are the dancers' directed gaze and self-sensory awareness. The leader's gaze and head cue directional changes as she consciously projects her focus toward specific orientations with clear intention. While a core-initiated movement sends energy in multiple directions at once out from the core of the body, a good leader sends all her intention into one direction when cuing half turns, traveling half turns, and quarter turns for example.

With minimal hesitation and confident initiation, the leader must commit fully to her spontaneous decisions. Should she accidentally execute a movement that is not officially part of the repertoire, a good leader will find that her confidence in that unfamiliar movement will cause her followers to execute it before they have had time to process it as out of place. Because every dancer occupies the leader position at some point, every dancer must become comfortable leading the group with confidence. As a dancer inhabits this confident, powerful, director's position she is confronted with the exhilaration of her personal agency and her ability to affect a group and manipulate the experience as it occurs. Inhabiting this leadership role helps foment security and self-confidence in the dancer. The confidence that she instills in her body again and again as a tool for leading is felt outside of performance, as well. About her first experience of taking the lead position in Hot Pot ITS, UNMATA dancer Sarah Stinson said that taking the lead was:

> "terrifying because all of a sudden I was expected to not only understand a language but initiate a conversation on my own with a bunch of people who are very talented standing behind me waiting to hear what I had to say."

Dancers must lead confidently by extending to the fullness of their reach and consciously directing their gaze in the proper direction for the move. If a leader cues a move with bent, questioning arms while gazing down at his or her feet, the followers will be confused and the group will fall out of sync. While in performance everyone has the option to pass the lead, in the classroom every student must take the lead position and cue the new material. A student must cue the new material effectively before they can leave the lead position. Shy, internally focused students learn to take up more space and direct their body and gaze openly and without hesitation. I have observed in students beginning to learn ITS that those who are more introverted, shy, and less comfortable in the front of the room often learn to assume an air of confidence and become more comfortable over time in the leader position. In contrast, students who are very boisterous, confident, and comfortable being the main voice in a conversation often learn through ITS to give others the opportunity to lead and can learn to appreciate the possibility of playing a supportive, following role. If a leader spends too much time in the lead position, or steals the lead at every possible moment, the morale of the group can suffer. Learning how to operate within ITS, where one cannot always lead or always follow, teaches practitioners how to consider themselves as part of a team with a shared objective.

In my experience as an ITS dancer, performing within this structure encourages people to develop a skill that applies to life outside of the dance: Knowing when to lead and when to follow. Students learn to hone finely the ability to lead and follow with mutual respect in everyday conversation and other team-oriented tasks. A student learns to develop an awareness of whether the people around him are looking for a leader, or if he is, in fact, part of a larger supporting structure in which he is expected to follow. Even in conversation, ITS can teach a person when to hold space with their silence versus their presence. Hot Pot Studio "Street Team" dancer Rodin Eckenroth describes the experience of following and leading in ITS:

> "Everyone in the dance is rooting for the leader, the community wants her to succeed and they need her to succeed. When else do you have that experience of knowing everyone behind you is on your team and wants you to do well?"[3]

## Peripheral Awareness and Empathy among Dancers

Dancers must orient their torsos and move their arms along the same planes of movement as one another in order to dance close without colliding arms. Framing arms are always pulled away from one another - either to unfold flat to the front or on a diagonal plane. In Hot Pot ITS, the right arm is always placed in front of the dancer to her right and the left arm behind the dancer to her left to facilitate dancing close to others in a group. The pathway of the arms during line changes and fast spins are strictly set so that dancers transition from one movement to the next through understood pathways of acceptable movement: For example, during a spin sequence the arms draw in close to the body then out in the appropriate plane. The agreement about arm placement allows many people to dance together in a small space at a fast tempo without colliding. As in many other dance forms, ITS belly dancers develop a keen awareness of the space and other bodies around them.

While an ITS dancer's gaze is outward, her focus is inward as she uses her peripheral vision to respond to the movements of the other dancers. In contrast to the gaze of an ITS dancer, which engages the audience but is equally engaged in taking in peripheral visual information from the dancers around her, the gaze of a Cabaret belly dancer tends to play more to the audience. As a sort of nightclub style party dance, Raqs Sharqi performances tend to invite the audience to marvel at the physical feats of the soloist and watch her body. The visible interaction between ITS dancers responding to one another invites the audience to look at the inter-subjective relationships and communication between dancers, complicating the tendency of lay audiences to passively consume belly dance performances with an objectifying gaze.

One result of the inter-subjective experience of dancing Improvisational Tribal Style is the development of empathy and group solidarity among dancers. When students are first learning to lead the group and develop confidence as a leader, or at least the ability to portray an air of calm composure, other students tend to be very patient in that process of discovery because they, too, must learn the same skill. About how she feels when another

**Sarah, Shelly and Kari of Unmata**

beginning ITS student is first learning to lead, new ITS dancer Adria Tinnin says:

"[I feel] sympathy anxiety, like 'I hope they don't mess up' not because it's like 'I hope you don't mess me up' but just because I'm like "Dang, I know how that feels." [4]

Her class-mate Hannah Trimbath adds:

"I go through the movements in my head as-well, thinking: 'What would I be doing?'" [5]

About how she feels when she is leading the group, experienced ITS dancer Leila Maitland says that leading feels:

"familiar, and it's empowering. It's kinda cool to have a bunch of girls doing the same thing you're doing; you know." [6]

Troupe-mate Cory Podielski adds:

"I'd say that being in the stagger is kind of like being in a pack of wolves. It's pretty cool, all your girls are dancing around you." [7]

## Sameness

When learning the movements for Hot Pot ITS, everyone must try to execute the movement exactly the same as one another in order to avoid confusion about what is being cued. If a leader performs a cue in her unique style, because of the speed of the dance and subtle differences between cues, no one will respond in the appropriate way.

A dancer learns quickly that she must perform the movement exactly as it has been prescribed by the format. Amy Sigil has observed that this need to dance the same as one another prevents students from trying to "out-dance" one another. She gives the example that in group choreography, students often try to perform the movement better or slightly different than their peers, whereas in ITS everyone must perform the movement the same.

**Gypsy Caravan Dance Company use body language, directional changes, and the music to cue the movement changes.**

This need for sameness is different than most belly dance forms that encourage all dancers to put their unique style onto a standard movement, stressing the importance of individuality, uniqueness, and developing one's own personal style.

This group-oriented, mutual effort toward standardized sameness draws many dancers to ATS and ITS who are looking for a more structured approach to their dance training and may be a reaction for some against the relative absence of agreed-upon standards and codification in many other styles of belly dance. While this group synchronicity gives some dancers a feeling of rigor or community it also conforms to the values of a "classicized aesthetic" in which sameness is valued precisely for its ability to ensure the dance remains the same across different bodies, spaces, and times.

## Calculated Anticipation and Readiness: Responsive Body, Present Mind

All dancers must hold a catalog of movement pathways and variations in their minds that enable the followers to eliminate and anticipate all possible cues, variations, and sequencing initiated by the leader. Musically, a dancer is always aware of the counting and speed to which the leader is dancing, anticipating changes in the musical phrasing, climactic build-ups, and melodic "breaks." A dancer must recognize the multiplicity of spatial and orientation-changing variations on a single movement to prepare herself to execute the specific variation cued by the leader.

Practitioners generally agree that dancing ITS is an exercise in presence. When engaged in all the decision-making and embodied presence that is required, practitioners are offered an escape from the preoccupations and worries that may consume them throughout their day. Because a dancer must be aware of the movement technique, the bodies and space around her, the musical structure, what the limits and possibilities of her position are, and the leader's cues all at the same time, one's mind must be engaged in the present moment in order to organize the stimulus and information as it unfolds throughout the dance. About this need to be present in ITS that offers an escape from everyday worries, UNMATA and Hot Pot ITS dancer Kari Vanderzwaag says that ITS:

"allows us to not have to verbalize anything. At dance class, you leave it at the door. Who cares what is going on at your job, that you're broke, that you're parents are dying, you're this or you're that? That's gone, and I can go, and I can openly communicate with my friends, and I don't have to talk about that stuff; I don't have to show that sadness on my face. It's black and white. It's not life; it's not grey-scale."[8]

The inter-subjective communities that are created and maintained through the physical practice of ITS, and often belly dance in general, give people a real, tangible experience of relating to other people who share a desire for collective meaning in their lives and productive, intimate relationships with their own physical awareness. Knowing the self by way of bodily experience is a necessary foundation for the claims I make about the role of Improvisational Tribal Style belly dance in the construction of an efficacious self - situated in the context of community. The argument behind this movement analysis assumes, as a given, that bodily experience plays a role in the construction of the self and a subject's perception of the world. It assumes that subjects define their self-hood in a mutually dependent relationship with the objects that surround them as well as in relation to the concept of space. This experiential acquaintance between subject and object sets the groundwork for ways of knowing the world as a self in the context of a whole, a self whose subjectivity and objectivity are fluid, and a self who has an intimate physical relationship to interior and exterior space. The structures embedded in Improvisational Tribal Style belly dance offer a measured and formatted way of interacting with other bodies and minds and the spaces between them, allowing for the realization of specific kind of self; a self that is coexistent and cooperative with others.

## References

[1] Sellers-Young (2005), p. 289.

[2] Sarah Stinson. Interview May 27, 2010. Long Beach, California.

[3] Rodin Eckenroth. Interview October 3, 2012. Los Angeles, California.

[4] Adria Tinnin. Interview April 30, 2010. Los Angeles, California.

[5] Hannah Trimbath. Interview April 30, 2010. Los Angeles, California.

[6] Leila Maitland. Interview April 30, 2010. Los Angeles, California.

[7] Cory Marie Podielski. Interview April 30, 2010. Los Angeles, California.

[8] Kari Vanderzwaag. Interview May 27, 2010. Long Beach, California.

Anthony Shay and Barbara Sellers-Young. *Belly dance: Orientalism, Transnationalism, and Harem Fantasy.* Costa Mesa, Calif: Mazda Publishers, 2005. Print.

### April Rose

*April currently tours globally with Bellydance Superstars. She has researched the transnational history of belly dance since the mid-19th century and the many incarnations of belly dance practice in the post-1960's US, particularly Improvisational Tribal Style belly dance and it's potential for thoughtful self expression, community formation, and challenge of social convention.*

# The Ghawazee

## by Jalilah

The Ghawazee (singular: Ghawzia) are professional Rom or "Gypsy" dancers in Egypt. Although numerous in the past, there are now only a few remaining in Upper Egyptian towns such as Qena and Luxor. Probably the most famous account of the Ghawazee is that of the nineteenth century French writer, Gustave Flaubert, in which he enthusiastically describes their dance as well as his relationship with Kuthuk Hanim, a woman who many writers maintain was a Ghawzia. The writer Edward Lane also writes about the Ghawazee in his book, "The Manners and Customs of the Modern Egyptian", written in 1834. These accounts describe the Ghawazee, also called "Barmakee", as being different from the Egyptians, belonging to a nomadic tribe and speaking their own language. Today it is known that the Ghawazee are indeed of Sind origin and belong to the Nawar tribe and sometimes, to the Halab and Bahlawanat tribes. Some of the famed "Musicians of the Nile" of the Real World Label are Bahlawanat, as well as the two dancers, Najua Tewfiq and Raja Mottawa, who appeared in the film," Latcho Drom". Most scholars are now in agreement that these tribes, including the Nawar, who are known throughout the Middle East, came originally from the Sind Valley and traveled to Iraq, Syria, Lebanon, Palestine and Egypt via Iran.

Legend has it that the Barmakee were a very powerful family of Persian origin living in Iraq during the Abbasid Dynasty. (The most famous Barmakee is Jafar, the vizier of Haroun el Rashid, as depicted in "The 1001 Nights"). Having become too powerful, they were at some point forced to leave Iraq. The Ghawazee and the Nawar claimed to be descended from the Barmakee, but historians believe it to be more likely that they worked for the Barmakee as dancers and musicians. The "secret" language, known as Khotan, that they spoke contained many Farsi and Romani words. Even now in Upper Egypt, some of the older Nawar are able to speak Khotan or at least know a considerable number of Farsi and Romani words.

The Ghawazee were banned from Cairo by the ruler Mohammed Ali in 1834. Most of them left for Upper Egypt to towns like Luxor, Qena and Esna, although a few remained secretly in Cairo. For this reason, most Ghawzee today can still be found in Upper Egypt. They are most certainly the direct descendants of those Ghawzee who left Cairo in 1834.

Some scholars believe Kuthuk Hanim was an Awalim, as well as a courtesan, but not a Ghawzia. They point out that her dancing as it was described by European travelers was very different from the Ghawazee dancing seen today. Other scholars point out the fact that she lived in Esna where the Ghawazee were banished. They would maintain that Ghawazee dancing today is different because the Ghawazee remained isolated for so long and because, being in the Said, Upper Egypt, their dance incorporated many elements of Saidi folklore.

The most famous Ghawazee of recent times are the "Banat Mazin" ("the daughters of Mazin") of Luxor. Jusif Mazin of the Nawar tribe, was the patriarch of a clan with many beautiful daughters. He became very rich from the money his daughters earned for him with their dancing. Unfortunately, he died without telling anyone where he had hidden the money! All of his daughters have since stopped dancing and have married. The youngest daughter, Khariya, got divorced, and resumed dancing in the early 90's. She has since stopped performing in Luxor. She did, however, recently teach and perform at the Cairo Dance Festival.

The original professional dancers of Egypt were either Awalim or Ghawazee. The Awalim were often trained to play a musical instrument or sing in addition to dancing. Being non-Gypsies, and therefore somewhat more respectable, they were allowed to perform inside homes for weddings. The dance of the Awalim evolved into what is today known as Oriental dance or "Raqs Sharqi". In contrast, the Ghawazee were only allowed to perform in the courtyards or out on the streets. After they were banished to Upper Egypt, the dance of the Ghawazee remained simple and incorporated elements of Upper Egyptian or "Saidi" folklore. It has fewer slow, undulating movements and the typical foot stomping movement that is characteristic of Ghawazee dancing is not found in the Sharqi style. Even the costume has remained similar to the style worn at the turn of the century, with the only change being the replacement of the once typical coins with beads and sequins.

Around the mid-eighties, the Ghawazee of Luxor started wearing one-piece dresses, having seen that the folklore troupes of Cairo do so when dancing to the music of Upper Egypt and performing so-called "Ghawzee" dance. By the way, this doesn't look like authentic Ghawazee dancing at all. Fortunately, in the smaller villages, the typical costume is still worn: A skirt, a vest with a shirt underneath, a belt with long strips of cloth and a headpiece.

In the past, if a Ghawzia married in her own tribe, she might continue dancing after marriage with her husband accompanying her musically. If she married an Egyptian outside the tribe, she would normally stop dancing.

The traditional instruments which accompany the Ghawazee when performing indoors are the rababa, a type of fiddle, a tabla drum and sometimes a soffara, a type of flute. Only if performing in a larger place are the mizmar, oboe and tabla balady added, since the mizmars are very loud. At the time of Edward Lane, only the rababa, flute and tabla were used for performances. The mizmar was introduced in Egypt much later by the Ottoman Turks.

It is very sad that the dance of the Ghawazee is dying out. Fewer and fewer Ghawazee are dancing for a variety of reasons. Growing fundamentalism gives public dancing an increasingly negative stigma. Hotels in Upper Egypt now prefer to hire folklore troupes from Cairo, or Raqs Sharqi dancers, instead of employing the Ghawazee and local musicians. In addition, the economic situation in Egypt is not very conducive to the "Gypsy" lifestyle. Most Ghawazee today prefer to leave dancing and lead normal lives. We can only hope that this will change someday.

### Jalilah

*Jalilah ~ Lorraine Zamora Mutke Chamas has toured regularly with the Gypsy group, "Musicians of the Nile", since 1990. Through this experience, she was able to meet and spend time with some of the few remaining Ghawazee in order to learn about them and their dance. The historical information on the Ghawazee, the Nawar, and Mid-Eastern Gypsies was gathered by Alain Weber, music ethnologist and artistic director of "Musicians of the Nile".*

# Two Weddings and a Dancer
## The Beled & The City

### by Leila Farid

Egypt is full of contrast; from the peaceful glide of a falucca (boat) ride at sunset, to the swerving, honking Cairo taxis or from the majestic permanence of the pyramids to the new concrete neighborhoods surrounding them. It seems as if they won't last a generation, let alone thousands of them. Weddings in Egypt are no exception, and occasionally, as a wedding-dancer, you have a night in which the contrast between weddings is so extreme that you have to pause and reflect. Recently, I had just such a night with two such opposite wedding extremes.

My evening began in Cairo at the latest hot-spot for weddings, the Fairmont Hotel in Heliopolis. From the Hummers and Mercedes lined up outside, to the lush indoor garden in the lobby, the hotel is posh! It has become the "in" place for weddings the last few seasons and tonight's was one of the top weddings of the year. The groom is a "rave style" party-planner; so, the wedding became one, giant party. The eight hundred invited guests had swelled to around a thousand people. The DJ, Yasser, was considered one of the best in the Middle East, and he was mixing an amazing set of foreign and Arabic tunes. The garden around the pool had been set with cocktail tables and groupings of low sofas. The entrance had a red-carpet feeling with elegant flower arrangements and crystal chains, leading to a stage made of Plexiglas that spanned the pool, giving the illusion of dancing upon water. Little tables filled with chocolates and petites four cakes were artfully arranged. It had been a sit-down meal instead of a buffet. The bride and groom sat on an understated couch with a casual appearance and an open bar had been serving guests since 5 pm. The guests wore gowns that, obviously, were French imports, most of the girls wore miniskirts and spike-heeled shoes with subtle makeup and hair styles. The men were just as elegant.

I changed in the executive suite that looks onto the garden and started my show. The groom approached me, cocktail in hand, about halfway through my opening music and led me into the crowd. I abandoned the stage and spent the rest of the wedding dancing in and among the guests who were dancing together in small groups of friends. I recognized a few friends as well as many people from other weddings. No less than eight photographers documented everything for the society magazines as well as the video crew unobtrusively filming from cameras on booms. I had danced a lot although little of it could be considered a typical performance. By 11 pm, I was on the road to my next wedding in a villa outside of Alexandria.

We knew the wedding was in a village; so I had changed from my miniskirt into a pair of jeans. The band was snugly packed inside their bus, and we followed in the car. The villa was located on a farm road a little over half-way to Alexandria from Cairo. As we neared the town, the bus slowed down to look for the place. We passed a large hanger (the type where cars are cut up for parts) and judging from the lights, motorcycles and took-tooks that were parked outside, a wedding was going on inside! The main doors were open a bit, and I could see a sea of people. My manager said pensively, "I think this is our wedding...".

Saad il Soyier was scheduled before me on the program, and there he was onstage, inside the hanger. The impresario jumped out of the bus and came over to the car. "Where is the villa?" we asked him. He looked pale and said that he had had no idea the wedding was "so beledi". Just then, the 20-something boys, who were milling around in front of the venue, noticed our car and started surrounding it. The man who was in charge of the wedding had come outside; a big garage door opened, and we quickly drove inside. We got out of our vehicles, and went upstairs to a room that overlooked the warehouse, which had been converted into a gigantic tent with strings of lights draped from the rafters and rows of

approximately 2,500 chairs. A wooden stage, about seven feet high, spanned the width of the building and Saad's entire orchestra (about 150 musicians and dancers) fit comfortably on it.

We stood in the room looking at each other, wondering what to do. The impresario handed us the rest of our money, (we had taken a deposit two months before) saying, "It's your choice to dance or not." I had danced at beledi weddings before with terrible results. One wedding in Nadi Ramaya in Cairo had gotten out of control in the first five minutes of our show as people rushed the stage. Another incident happened in Nadi Asment in the town of Assiut, where a fight broke out just before I went on stage, and our wireless microphones were stolen in the chaos. This wedding was much more beledi (country style) than either of those! Saad finished and we heard an announcer, who at beledi weddings is paid to talk up the bride and groom and keep the energy high between acts, announcing me. From the way he was building up my reputation, I must be the best dancer in the world! My heart thumped. Okay, I was going to dance…

The room in which I was to change was filthy and had a bare bulb hanging from a wire. I recruited three of my duff players, as well as my two assistants, as bodyguards. Since the stage was about 100 meters from my "dressing room" the car was waiting to drive me to it, surrounded by my bodyguards. While upstairs, I learned also that when Saad al Soyier was leaving, some of the guests had surrounded him to take photos, causing him to run for his car, but he tripped and skinned his hands quite badly. I was now a bit afraid, but if I tried to leave, the results might be worse than performing! In a typical beledi wedding, the dancer does not do a 'mergence', instead, she enters dancing straight into her set-list of songs. The crowd sat stone-faced as I danced my 'mergence', albeit with a slightly terrified look on my face. My costumes were also very covered when compared to the typical bedli (dance costumes) that a wedding dancer might wear; sometimes it is just an unadorned bra and tiny miniskirt. After the mergence, we launched straight into Shabby songs (popular well-known music) and the crowd started to loosen up. The bride and groom sat at one end of the stage, surrounded by white satin. I went over to have photos taken with them and realized there was no photographer - just the videographers who were stationed within three feet of me for the entire show. The bride and groom sat stiffly on their elaborate sofa, barely smiling and with no intention of dancing with me. I descended from the stage onto a dance floor in the middle of the chairs surrounded by security - just regular guys whom the father of the bride had hired to keep the peace. They held hands and surrounded me. This was a bit too much for the guests, and they began to push closer to take pictures with their phones. Smoke hung over the entire room and the smell of "Bango" (marijuana) was intense. I was ushered quickly to the women's section (about 10% of all the guests) to dance with the mother and grandmother of the bride. All the women were dressed in black abeyas with their hair covered and quite heavy makeup; gold bracelets covering each arm from wrist to elbow. They were lovely and happy to be up, dancing. After my set, I was driven back to the dressing room. I asked about the buffet and learned that typically, the guests receive paper boxes filled with rice or macaroni, chicken, and a little piece of cake.

From what I could see, this wedding was much more controlled than any other to which I had been. The guests and I had warmed up as the show progressed and many had left their chairs, dancing in front of their seats by the end of the show. After the show, I was quickly shuffled out of the dressing room and into the car. "Please come back again...You have brought us light," yelled the ancient doorman who had been sitting outside the door of the dressing room, watching the show. I was glad to have danced.

My dresser, when she saw the second wedding, joked, "We have come from the sky and been thrown to the ground!". Although an overstatement, the contrast between the two weddings was telling. It reflects the glaring economic disparity that exists in Egypt: A disappearing middle class, leaving masses of the extremely poor and a handful of the opulently rich. Even with such extreme social and economic contrast between the classes, there are common threads that bind all people together; weddings are a reason to celebrate, whatever your economic status. They are a reason to cut loose, socialize, and watch a live show, which most people rarely see - with the exception of weddings. Weddings are a reason to have fun; sometimes, with a few thousand friends and neighbors! What could be more fun than a belly dancer? I can't think of anything.

### Leila Farid
*Leila is an American born dancer and rising star in the Egyptian dance scene. She is a sought after performer for weddings, parties and nightclubs of Cairo's five star hotels, having collaborated with many superstar singers such as Sameera Saeed, Hishem Abaz, Moustafa Amr, Khalid Seleem, Ali Haggar, Hakim, Ahkmed Fathi.*

## Zeffat Al 'Aroosa
### Ritual Procession for the Egyptian Wedding

by Sahra Carolee Kent

Even from my fifth floor room, I could hear the zaghreet (vocal trilling) from the street below. I listened for the informative iqa zeffah (the rhythm of the zeffah) through the noisy fanfare of drums. There it was: "Dum, tec-a tec tec, Dum tec tec" the rhythm that communicated that this was a marriage procession. I had time to get ready and dress up; zeffahs proceed slowly. Traditionally the zeffat al 'aroosa accompanied the bride from her family's home, continued through local neighborhoods, eventually delivering her to her new husband's family home. Nowadays the zeffah, which today often includes the groom as well, might only proceed a couple of blocks, or through the lobby of a hotel or club to the ballroom where the marriage is to be celebrated.

I arrived in the hotel lobby to see a multitude of happy Egyptians dressed up for the evening. First in the procession line-up there were announcement horns and a large video camera, complete with bright lights to guarantee a good wedding video. Next, forming two long lines were 16 drummers (one *tabla*, 5 *muzhar*, 10 *riq*, all male musicians), then, continuing these lines, were 10 unmarried females of engageable age each carrying a s*hamma' al zeffah* (tall, decorated, lit candle for the zeffah). Finally, the bride, groom, their mothers and female relatives completed the far end.

I was happy to see that this *Firqet Zeffah* (Zeffah Troupe) included *awalem*, one of whom was wearing a *shamadan* (candelabra). I could also see folkloric dancers waiting near the side as well.[1]

The *Zeffat Al 'Aroosa* is a ritual procession traditionally occurring after the marriage agreement (between the 2 families) and engagement. The procession physically accompanied the first-time bride from her family residence (where her identity was as a daughter) to her new husband's home (where her identity is as a wife and future mother). Once at the husband's home the *Katab* (signing of the book to document the marriage as official) occurs, after which time the marriage festivities *farrah* (happiness) occur. There are many minor zeffah within the marriage events (moving the bride's goods to her new home in an open cart; the groom's friends accompanying him to the barber shop; etc) but the Zeffat Al 'Aroosa is by far is the most celebrated and important.

To be noted, there are other types of zeffah for different occasions, with different *iqa zeffah*, for different occasions and changes in a person's status.

The word "Zeffah" means "procession with noise". It is the noise that calls people to witness the change in status. A secret wedding, a quiet wedding, isn't really seen as an actual wedding, it needs to be announced and publicly witnessed.

### Zeffah of the Past

Edward Lane spent several years in Egypt (1825-28, and 1833-1835) and has left us one of the most quoted sources on the private lives of Cairenes of his time. He describes several types of *Zeffat Al 'Aroosa*, and indicates which social class followed each particular tradition.

For a middle-class bride in Cairo, the zeffah was led by musicians playing drums and "hautboys" (an oboe, referring to the mizmar) and singing popular songs. After the musicians walked a group of married women, relatives and friends of the bride, wearing the customary black veils of modest streetwear. Following them, walked a group of unmarried young women, also relatives and friends of the bride, distinguished by white veils. Finally the bride herself appeared; she and two female relatives, all veiled, walked under a canopy carried by four men. At the end of the procession were more drummers and musicians. It was also possible to add more participants;

sword fighters, stick fighters (*assaya tahtib*), magicians, strong men, etc.[2]

Brides of "great families" rode on donkeys and added more participants. Brides from the villages rode on camels. Poorer families provided the music by their own singing.[3]

## Zeffat Al 'Aroosa of the 1930-1950s

Moving forward one hundred years, we can see how bridal processions have changed. Literally, we can see, because Egyptian films of the 1930s through 1950s (and even today) often include wedding scenes. The principal participants described by Lane are still there: Musicians, married female relatives, unmarried females, and the bride, but there are some new features as well. Now, the groom is sometimes shown walking with the bride, the unmarried females walk in two rows, parallel lines and carry tall candles, the married women walk in a group to the sides and behind the bride. There is often an *almeh* (belly dancer) directly in front of the bride, and drummers are female.[4]

So, at this point, in the "Golden Age of Egyptian Cinema" we see the inclusion of the *Awalem* (*Almeh*, singular), the indigenous female entertainers of Cairo, both as dancers and drummers. And in addition to dancing at the *farrah* celebration, as they did in Lane's day, the *Awalem* are also included in the zeffah. In these films we can also see the addition of the *shamadan* (candelabra balanced on the head), not mentioned by Lane.

## Modern Zeffat Al 'Aroosa

In 1989, when I arrived in Cairo, Egypt to do research for my Master's thesis (Dance Ethnology, UCLA, subject *Zeffat Al 'Aroosa* in Cairo) it was an interesting moment in the history of this zeffah. I had access to women of many ages, mostly of the middle class, the educated elite, and the educated middle class. Of the women who had married for the first time in the 1950s and before, the information supported the film representation (if one had enough money to hire the *awalem*).

Of the women who married for the first time in the 1960s, the view of the zeffah was more complicated; some felt it was old fashioned, the more traveled educated elite felt it was unsophisticated. Some felt that to believe in the zeffah having an affect on fertility was superstitious.

One bi-cultural and traveled Cairo woman kept referring, with disgust, to the hypocrisy of her zeffah, that it was a ritual for an unknowing, home-protected virgin to be handed over to a different male to rule her. They also criticized the superficial display of wealth whom zaffaf-ed the bride, since now, not only awalem could lead the zeffah, but so could expensive movie-star belly dancers such as Sohair Zaki or Fifi Abdou; the fame of the dancer was a status symbol.

Lower and middle class women complained that there were too many strangers in the streets that should not know where a woman lives (the zeffah leads directly to her new home), and it brought too many people to their home that, by hospitality etiquette, should be fed and served something to drink. I interviewed many that did not have a zeffah even though they, or their family, wanted one for these very practical reasons. Problems such as delayed pregnancy or early marriage problems were blamed on not having a real zeffah.

Also mentioned was that having a woman dancer on the street, out-of-doors, was unseemly. The female awalem drummers wore long dresses but were deemed by some as a little risque, and they were expensive as well.

Then, suddenly, in the late 1980s a new solution appeared (from the delta north of Cairo) which remains the main Zeffah entertainment today: The *Firqet Zeffah*.

## Firqet Zeffah

The name Firqet Zeffah literally means "group of the zeffah". The concept spread rapidly! When I arrived to do my research on the Zeffat Al 'Aroosa in 1989, the new zeffah troupes were generically called *"Dumyati Zeffah"* (after the Delta city of Dumyat, one of the cities that made this concept famous.) This type of zeffah entertainment organization, designed and run by young men from universities, solved all the problems.

For those who did not want women on the street, these were all men; for those who did not want strangers to know where the bride and family women lived, the zeffah started in a public place and finished in a public place with decorated cars providing transportation for the wedding families; for those who felt the zeffah was old fashioned, this was new and fun. For women who were shy of letting people call them superstitious, it could be called entertainment.

For those who did not want to be near professional entertainers, these young male drummers were billed as university students, wearing bright suits or almost sports type clothing, and not billed as musicians since "everyone knows how to play a drum".

These Firqet Zeffah groups can perform indoors or out, as a large group or small (the others waiting in a bus), prices arranged for 15 minutes to 2 hours. It is still possible to hire awalem dancers (I saw many) or awalem drummers (I only saw this once).

Most Thursday nights you can hear many Firqet Zeffah on neighborhood streets. You can usually find a Firqet Zeffah in the major 5-star hotels, processing the bridal party through the reception lobby, up the stairs, into the reception with the assembled guests, escorting the bride and groom to the two thrones where they will sit for most of the rest of the farrah celebration.

There also are numerous military clubs where families with some connection to the military can hold the wedding reception in one of the ballrooms. Scheduling the lobby became as important as the ballroom, since the zeffah would start at the front door and have a certain amount of time to do the entertainment there before entering the ballroom.

The line-up was the same as before: The bride, and possibly groom as well, standing, surrounded by female married family, at one end. Preceding them are two parallel rows of unmarried young women each carrying a tall candle, then continuing the two rows are the Firqet Zeffah drummers, ending with the video camera and any other musicians.

The drummers play the ritual iqa zeffah and all proceed slowly. If there are awalem participating, they are between these two rows, in front of the bride; if there are no awalem, this space stays unoccupied during the ritual rhythm. I call this the "ritual dance space".

The big change is that periodically the procession stops, the lead tabla drum changes the rhythm, and what I call a "mini-entertainment" ensues. This can be one of the many regional dances made famous by the Reda or Kowmeyya National dance companies, or it may be a *tanura* (Egyptian Whirling Dervish), or any number of creative scenarios, or formations made by the drummers. They can also play dance music and encourage the mothers of the bride and groom to dance, the mothers dance to show their support of the union. It is a good sign if the mothers dance, and especially auspicious if they dance together.

Do the awalem still perform zeffah? It would seem as though the awalem have lost their jobs, but I saw several indications that they have entered this market. I have seen awalem perform in the indoors zeffah, between the two rows, some wearing the shamadan, some not. Within the first couple years, I noted that the Awalem were owning some Firqa (groups) having their sons being the figurehead director rather than a woman as in former times.

A meaningful, flexible, new tradition in an old land.

## Zeffah in Diaspora

Another contemporary version of the wedding zeffah is found in diaspora. The hotel zeffah is very popular among Arab-Americans. Similarities to the modern Egyptian Zeffat Al 'Aroosa are noteworthy. Because Egypt is the film capital of the Middle East, those films became standard fare in theaters all over the Middle East; viewers became familiar with Egyptian colloquial Arabic and cultural conventions. The zeffah wedding procession with a belly dancer, years later, on another continent, became the a new sophisticated style for Arab-Americans to emulate. Said one Lebanese man; "At home we have men on horses ride through the streets, sabers raised. You can't do that in Los Angeles; so we have a pretty girl, with candles on her head, leading the bride."[5]

A firm, flexible, old tradition in a new land!

## References

Lane, Edward. *Manners and Customs of the Modern Egyptians*. London: Ward Lock and Co., 1890. Print.

Sahra Carolee Kent and Marjorie Franken: "A Procession through Time: The Zeffat al-ꞌArusa in Three Views". *Images of Enchantment: Visual and Performing Arts of the Middle East.* Editor Sherifa Zuhur. Cairo, Egypt: The American University in Cairo Press, 200), p 72. Print.

Kent, Carolee. "Arab-American 'Zeffat al-Arusah' in the Los Angeles Area." *UCLA Journal of Dance Ethnology*, 13 (1989). Print.

Aroosa = bride
Ariis = groom

### Sahra Carolee Kent ~ Sahra Saeeda
*Sahra currently performs and teaches Orientale and Egyptian Folkloric worldwide. As a Dance Ethnologist (Dance Ethnology MA from UCLA), Sahra developed and directs "JtE" series. After living, researching and performing (with over 1600 shows in Cairo, Egypt) in Cairo for 6 years (1989-1995) she continues researching in Egypt annually.*

**Yasmina Ramzy teaches a class in Toronto**

# Section 7
# THEORY & TECHNIQUE

*Theory and technique are some of the most ephemeral and yet important fundamental concepts that dancers need to understand in this ever changing art form. It is nearly impossible to describe in words the subtle nuances of body articulation or to describe that essential "it" factor which separates students from teachers and performers from stars. It's difficult to describe a basic hip lift at the best of times, and even more difficult to quantify and explain passion, intensity and drama.*

*The editors and writers here at Gilded Serpent have produced a great body of articles that, when taken together, form the foundations for creating a unified vocabulary of dance so performers and teachers from around the world can effectively communicate. In this section, The Belly Dance Reader continues this process and the debate over terms, moves, and styles. To read more, and join the dialog, visit us on line at GildedSerpent.com*

**Bert Balladine & Najia Marlyz**

# Belly Dance Motivations
## Context & Content of Performance

### by Jezibell Anat

At one time, the term "Middle East" conjured up visions of the Arabian nights, of opulent palaces and masterful sheiks and sultry harem girls. These Orientalist fantasies ranged through time and geography, freely blending images of Pharaonic Egypt, the Baghdad Caliphate, the Ottoman Empire and other exotic cultures into a mysterious melange of intrigue and passion. In many ways this view was inaccurate, racist and sexist, yet this romantic (and often lurid) depiction of the Middle East aroused a surge of art, literature, and dance.

Nowadays, many people associate the Middle East with war, terrorism, jihads and burkas. As I was working on this article in 2012, the United States embassies in Libya and Egypt were attacked, and I wonder what will be happening over there by the time this book is published. Dance is art, not politics, but international tensions affect the Westerner's point of view when we practice and perform a genre that began in one of the most volatile areas in the world.

One of the foundations of American democracy is the long-cherished right to free expression. We want to choose our music, costuming, combinations of moves, yet we want our dance to be well-received, and we would rather not inflame sensibilities. So how do we respect the roots of belly dance without being limited by the current strictures of traditional religion? Belly dance in the West has taken on many forms: Glittery cabaret, ornate tribal, earthy folkloric, atmospheric Goth, and all sorts of fusion and fantasy blends. Most of the tribal and fusion styles have flowered in forms that bear little resemblance to their ethnic roots, and a lot of us prefer it that way. In promoting dance to the public, the term "belly dance" usually gets a much more positive reception than Middle Eastern dance.

Performers who live in areas with large Middle Eastern populations have opportunities to dance for Turkish, Lebanese, Persian and other ethnic audiences where authentic dance is appreciated. Many dancers study and research specific regional styles, and they strive to present these dances preserved accurately. However, where there is a limited or nonexistent Middle Eastern audience, dancers who want to perform must expand their

**Jehan of New York**

appeal and find appropriate ways to present this dance to a mainstream audience.

Some of us perceive ourselves as creative artists, unbound by traditional mores, and we absorb belly dance moves as a basis for individual improvisation and experimentation. We have incorporated new and increasingly flamboyant props including fan-veils, poi, hoops and fire. Many dancers do not agree as to what constitutes belly dance in the twenty-first century because this art travels further and further from its countries of origin. Some claim that all these fusion forms simply lead to confusion; others welcome this variety as it offers new ways for the dance to evolve and develop.

Our modern Western search for personal growth and transformation has led to the popularity of organic, sensory movement systems, such as NIA or Gabrielle Roth's Five Rhythms, and this approach has filtered back to belly dance. Many dancers practice Yoga and Pilates for centering, body conditioning and kinetic flow. These methods have engendered a more conscious awareness of the patterns of belly dance moves and a deeper connection to the dancer's emotional life. For some of us, this dance has become a spiritual practice drawing from many sources, including Sufi mysticism and feminist spirituality.

How do we convey all this to an audience? The general public does not know much about our art, and often we are offended when our dance is confused with striptease or exotic dance. Many of us insist that our dance is not "sexual" and strive to present an image of grace, elegance, and femininity. Some chose to frame the dance as genuine folklore and present it in an anthropological or historical context. To bolster this impression, some dancers insist on wearing several skirts and pants even when performing at a summer festival where the audience is dressed in shorts and tank tops.

Others take the approach of "I'm sexy and I know it; so what's wrong with that?" Our dance, with its freedom of movement, dynamic torso motions, and intense music, might be perceived as a rebellion against patriarchal control of women's bodies and lives. Some belly dancers have joined in the revival of burlesque, with its focus on teasing and playful expression. Thus, we flaunt our sensuality as a reclamation of female power and joy.

Purists may insist that such an approach degrades and debases the essence of Middle Eastern dance, but this dance has been renamed and re-framed to suit foreign audiences for centuries. Authenticity does not always equal theatricality. The belly dance that we perform today is a derivative of communal folkloric dances. These dances provide a great deal of fun for the participants, but they are often not interesting for an audience to watch.

Accurate gestures and styles can appear strange or humorous to someone of a different background, and Westerners frequently find the sound of Middle Eastern music to be dissonant and whiny. In many cases, imaginative interpretations have become much more appealing than realistic presentations.

Orientalist portrayals of harem girls dancing for the sultan's favor and myths such as Salome and the Seven Veils gave the dance the lure of the forbidden. During the various colonial occupations of the Middle East, the dance appeared in tourist shows and was a salaciously marketed highlight of World's Fair Expositions in Europe and America.

In 1926, Badia Masabni opened a nightclub in Cairo that presented Arab music and dance to a European audience. She brought in Western choreographers to adapt the Egyptian dances to the stage and presented dancers in the beaded, sequined Hollywood-inspired bra and belt for a more glamorous and seductive appearance. Thus the dance gained recognition as a performance art and launched the careers of the first Egyptian stars such as Samia Gamal and Tahia Carioca.

Western dance forms, including ballet and samba, influenced the styles and rhythms of Middle Eastern dance. Fred Astaire, Gene Kelly, and the dramatic creativity of the American musical theatre inspired Mahmoud Reda. He applied the concepts of large choreographed numbers with characters and stories to folkloric dance when he started the Reda Troupe in 1959. Even before belly dance gained popularity in America, it was affected by the dancers' desire to expand their repertoire and to appeal to a wider audience.

Laws, attitudes, fashions, and technology have advanced tremendously since Sol Bloom presented belly dance at the Chicago World's Fair in 1893. Our dance is not as scandalous as it used to be, and the rise of hip-hop has changed the dance landscape. Our cabaret costumes were once considered risque, but seem much less titillating now that body-baring fashions have become mainstream. Compared to the choreography and outfits on today's music videos, our dance is tame.

The entire entertainment landscape has changed since the nightclub era when bands, singers and dancers performed several sets every evening. Now, live performances, theatre and music as well as dance, are suffering because people can enjoy a plethora of cable television channels and streaming videos in the comfort of their own homes. Economics are also a factor. The post-recession has decreased the funding of many arts organizations, and people have less disposable income.

At the same time, twenty-first century audiences are becoming more sophisticated about dance. With the popularity of television shows such as "Dancing with the Stars" or "So You Think You Can Dance", viewers may even know the meaning of dance terminology such as paso doble or lyrical. Sometimes, television talent shows feature belly dancing. With a lot of focus on competitions now, audiences are looking for "wow factor."

Where does this leave the modern belly dancer? Do we choose to honor ancient traditions or do we dance to express our innermost feelings? Are we entertaining, educating, or offending? Do we create our own fantasies of feminine power? However we choose to dance for ourselves in private is our own business, but those of us who wish to dance in front of others have to consider the audience, their needs, expectations, and perspectives.

What kind of dance do we want to present, and why? How are our own performances affecting perceptions of the dance in our communities? We need to be aware of our audience and try to view the dance from their perspective. In many cases, our dance might be the first belly dance they see, and they will judge all belly dancers and shows by our presentations.

We are in an era of niche marketing and increasing customization. Attention spans are shorter. Belly dance is a niche in most parts of the country, and many dancers are searching for ways to broaden its appeal. Using Western music can make our dance more accessible, and different fusion styles can attract unique audiences. Goth belly dance incorporates the fashion and attitude of this nocturnal subculture. Hip-hop belly dancers flaunt an urban edge, and medieval fantasy belly dancers perform at Renaissance Faires.

**Samia Gamal**

Local mores and attitudes definitely influence the practice and performance of belly dance, and some parts of the country are much more conservative than others. Some performers are blessed with a dance-friendly audience, or live in open-minded areas where people appreciate all types of artistic expression. In other regions, all forms of live music, theatre and dance shows struggle to fill the houses, and belly dance is still considered shady.

Hopefully every dancer will have the opportunity to perform at a hafla (dance community party) with an appreciative gathering of fellow belly dancers, family members, and friends who will shower her with applause and love. Dancers of all abilities and styles feel welcome and appreciated, and this is a beautiful communal aspect of our dance. Often the emcee will urge the crowd to make noise and will even tell them the segment of the dance where they should clap, cheer, zaghareet, or hiss to encourage the performer.

However, there are major differences between dancing for personal pleasure and dancing for an audience. Remember that a hafla is not a professional performance, and an emcee should be careful about giving this type of introduction to a general audience who may never have seen belly dancing before. This cheer-the-dancer-spiel makes us look amateurish, like we're either divas who must be showered with attention or needy dilettantes begging for support.

As performers, we earn our applause through stellar performances, not by haranguing our viewers for a response. Besides, if every move must be validated, how does the audience distinguish a truly spectacular feat? We do not want the quality of our dance to depend on how much noise the audience makes. People may be quiet because they want to focus on the details of the performance. Performers are wise to prepare for all kinds of audience responses, including an audience that is silent, hostile, or even disruptive.

**Ariellah**

A common fallacy states that if the dancer is having fun, so will the audience. When she performs, a dancer may have a feeling of personal transcendence, but an audience must be able to share it. Perhaps the dancer may be jamming away to the music and thoroughly enjoying herself and the audience appears bored, disinterested or disgusted. Even worse, she may not realize she's lost them; part of our job is to make this look easy!

One technical point to consider is the size and location of the venue. Will the dance be in a 21-and-over nightclub, or an outdoor community festival? On a large stage, the detailed, intricate movements that we spend hours practicing will be lost. Sound amplification often drowns out the nuances of our zils, yet in an intimate venue, zils can overpower sensitive ears.

In some areas, dance in general is perceived as an activity for children, so people will show up to see the kids once a year in Nutcracker or some other crowd-pleaser, but adult performers don't have that same appeal; we have to show them something more substantial. If the audience sees an enthusiastic but awkward student, they will think of this as a dance of cute girls having fun rather than as a professional performance art.

Because of shortened attention spans, people need to see something happening, more than sustained poses and smoldering looks. An audience will not be interested in sequences of repetitious moves to consistent beats. They want excitement and intensity. The public will be drawn in by beautiful lines, interesting moves, unpredictable combinations. Some dancers reach out to their audiences, others pull them in, but they make sure to present something worth seeing.

One danger is that we can be self-indulgent. Every dancer has the right to express herself as she chooses, but that does not mean that others will care to watch. An audience of aficionados may love a presentation of belly dance as a personal or sacred journey, but much of middle America will find it weird. When we present a fun, dynamic, diverse show, we have a better chance of attracting a mainstream crowd.

Another danger is that some of us are so insistent on building respect for the dance that we simply try too hard to educate our audience. We want them to understand the real cultural origins, and we want them to be able to distinguish between the different styles of belly dance. How many shows are structured around belly dance history, or a world tour of dance? This can be very effective for an audience of dance enthusiasts, but can be pedantic for the general public who just wants to be entertained.

Our advantage is that we can harness the power of the imagination, for dance has the ability to bring the audience into a different world, which may be a lake of swans, the streets of the Bronx, or a desert oasis. We have another great advantage in our wardrobe. These colors, textures, and jewelry make a terrific visual impact. The diversity of dance styles has sparked creativity in costume design, as the flow and fabric of our clothing are designed to enhance particular movements and establish specific moods.

Should dance be presented as fact or fiction? Certainly, those dancers and teachers who research and perform accurate folkloric dances deserve to take appropriate credit. However, a dance may be ethnically correct but mean nothing to people outside of that particular culture. Accurate descriptions of the performance are crucial, so that people will know whether they're seeing a traditional Egyptian Saidi or a fantasy dancer portraying Mata Hari. The people watching do not have to understand all the different styles and nuances of belly dance to be able to enjoy the performance.

For many viewers, a fantasy dance of a free-spirited Gypsy is far more appealing than an accurate dance of the harsh reality of the lifestyle of the Rom people. We will usually be more effective if we draw them in and engage them instead of lecturing to them. They want to see art, not anthropology. From a creative perspective, as long as the fantasy dancer does not claim to be presenting the genuine article, her dance is perfectly valid. When the audience members like what they see, they will become interested, and then they may want to know more.

One valid concern is whether or not our dance is offensive. Dance has been banned by religions throughout history, and the fact that we dance at all is offensive to some; not everyone will like us. Even if our bodies are covered, our connection with our physicality, with our emotions, along with our openness and joy of movement challenge those who impose rigid codes of behavior upon women. We may be able to engage in dialogue with our detractors and open some minds, but we will not be able to undo centuries of repression overnight.

Many Muslims in the West may enjoy our dance if we use secular Middle Eastern folk or pop songs, but they will be upset if we use their sacred music, especially the call to prayer. This is frustrating for some Western women who feel that they have the right to dance to whatever they please, including these lovely but sacred Islamic melodies.

Certainly, in private, we can dance to whatever music we want, but in public performance, we have to be aware of appropriate choices, especially for ethnic audiences, and we need to know our songs if we're choosing Middle Eastern music. This is another reason why some dancers prefer to use Western or fusion music.

For others of us, our dance has also become a tool of social transformation. Most of us have performed at charity fundraisers and benefits for causes that help others. Some of us have participated in large scale processions where we dance for peace and healing, or as part of belly dance flash mobs to raise awareness of specific social issues.

The tragic dichotomy of belly dance is that it has become an incredible source of inspiration, affirmation and power to women in the West; yet it is considered disreputable for women in its countries of origin. The misogyny of much of Middle Eastern society is one of those dirty little secrets we prefer to avoid because we want to be open-minded and politically correct, and many of us know plenty of exceptions. Ironically, there are Arab women who do not understand why American women, with all their access to education, jobs, and other opportunities, would choose to dance. Essentially, we Westerners have taken the ethnic origins and meanings of this dance as a platform for our own creativity, while rejecting the limitations of its culture. This could be described as cultural appropriation, especially when it is presented as a taboo dance of sexual decadence.

Western women have developed a dance of beauty, creativity, and joy that celebrates our bodies and lifts our spirits. We have imbued belly dance with our own love and passion, and it has brought us healing, inspiration and community. The best way to present the dance to others may simply be by bearing the truth of our unique artistic expression

### *Jezibell*

*Jezibell studied and taught at Serena Studios in Manhattan, New York, performed with the Egyptian/American Folkloric Group, Serena Dance Theatre, Gamila el-Masri's Nileside Dancers, PURE, and was a staff writer for Bennu. Now in Augusta, GA, she dances locally as a soloist and directs Eastern Star Dance Theatre.*

**PURE (Public Urban Ritual Experiment)**

# Contextualizing
## Giving Your Dance Context!

### by DaVid of Scandinavia

When we dancers think of bringing context to our dance, we imagine ourselves as if we were watching our own work, projecting thoughts, knowledge, and preferences outward to our audiences. Audience feedback fuels how we place our performances in context. Although it is valuable information to know what sentiments and sensibilities the audience might experience from our efforts, this information will not be available to us until our creative process is complete. Obviously, we cannot go back into the past and change the quality or integrity of the completed presentation!

Another way to give context to one's dance is to make evaluations and choices about the content of our presentations long before the potential viewer becomes part of the picture. There are two quite different approaches: One involves motivating your composition by using outside sources, while the other uses perspectives from the "inner you". Both will be guided by the dance style that you dance, and your artistic visions, representing the strengths and aesthetics of your particular "dance pedigree".

As dance artists, it is our ultimate goal to cause our audiences to experience a vision, an emotion, or a connection to music by our dance movements. We expect members of the audience to "lose themselves" in our performances. Every dancer wants audiences to appreciate their dance work, and it feels frustrating when our efforts do not receive the praise or reception that we have come to anticipate.

These questions will arise:

- What can we dancers do to help the audience share our visions, respond to our emotions, and feel the connection between the music and movements of our performance?
- Through application of context, can we bring clarity to our work?
- How can we performance artists better articulate our statements?
- How can we artists refine our skills so that we may deliver a coherent dance message?
- How can we display technical proficiency while retaining a human aspect to our presentations?

As dancers, we are communicators. It is important to understand exactly how an audience meets our work. They approach the performance from a completely different aspect than we do. Although a dancer may focus on good posture, technique, combinations, flow, rhythms, musicality and expression, it is only at the point of expression that audiences meet our work; they focus upon the way in which they experience the personality (or lack thereof) that they see before them. If the expressive ability of a dancer draws them in, they may dig deeper to see the other elements as well. If not, further investigation may be overlooked. Sensibilities of audiences - both good and bad - inevitably, have an effect on how they will receive our work.

In the first belly dance class we attend, we will probably encounter dance concepts such as: Posture, alignment, and centering. These concepts are of paramount importance as they can prevent injury and promote injury-free, strong dancers. An injured dancer is one that is unable to dance or is prevented in fully pursuing a message through dance. That is why a continuous effort towards proper posture, a strong sense of alignment, and a passionate relationship with one's dance center is so precious in the dance world. Not only do concepts and proper technique of dance prevent injuries, but they establish a strong relationship with the body in a neutral position. This concept of neutrality works much like a blank canvas does for a painter. A dirty canvas will interfere with the clarity and articulation of the final artwork. Development of a strong, neutral position promotes expressive dancing as well as physical and mental clarity.

Different styles of Belly dance may approach the body alignment with slight differences, but the purpose of how the limbs are aligned will still be "to achieve the best possible way to stay balanced and stacked upright", as well as the best alignment to accommodate the movements the dancer expects to use.

Once the physical sensation of being in balance feels natural, the dancer may still think about many things that distract the mind while dancing, preventing the achievement of complete focus – or providing the dance with a blank canvas. One may try to concentrate harder on creating a "blank canvas" by returning consciously to the tasks of alignment, movements, music, direction etc. Inwardly, one can ask: "Am I still thinking about all the different elements of my dance?". However, a better way to achieve a blank starting-point is to practice detached mindfulness. By use of the term "detached mindfulness" I mean: While thoughts or tasks enter your mind, acknowledge their existence, but do not let your mind focus on them. Although this skill is a virtue most often practiced in meditative and yoga practices, it may bring unexpected benefits to a dancer's technique as well.

Other valuable tools are breath and music. Training yourself to focus on bringing enough oxygen into your body, and listening to the music – the continuous flow of it, the pulsation of it – one can learn to keep one's breath synchronized with the slowest common denominator in the music. This implies that one will not end up hyperventilating or holding the breath and develop the skill of remaining in sync with the music.

Through diligent practice, a dancer can create a blank canvas that on command can accommodate desired visions and statements to showcase in the dance. It is a pretty nifty tool!

The next step is to bring articulation and clarity to one's dancing. How well the dancer's body translates movement to a viewer depends on several things, but the most central elements are balance, produced by proper alignment, and one's relationship with gravity, resisting it or giving in to it. Giving in to gravity is a central concept in belly dance. Sometimes this concept may be referred to as "staying grounded" or as "grounding". Other times, it may be referred to as the quality of "staying or becoming heavy". Used together, alignment and grounding permit the dancer to achieve articulate, deep movements with an enhanced range of motion.

Combined with strong practice of technique, a dancer can improve the delivery of a dance statement immensely. For the dancer, the combination of good alignment, a fine sense of grounding and a dependable practice of technique, allow a dancer to feel better energy flow of the music and movements through the body, allowing more assertive and effective delivery of the dance message. An assertive and effective delivery emphasises the music, and the audience can experience the connection between the dancer and music or musicians. We refer to this quality as "having musicality". Good musicality means that the dancer has made educated evaluations in regards to dance style, musical traditions and heritage, cultural information, costuming, venue, the viewers' psychology, his training, and his personal style. Further, it shows that the dancer has made clearly defined choices that enhance both their dance movements and the music, while maintaining the integrity of these two different areas.

In dance, as well as in other dramatic arts, we speak about "expression". We often refer to expression with abstract visualizations, and visual emulation. Many times these visualizations are quite difficult to grasp, and therefore, they may be misunderstood. Often, expression becomes restricted to an element of facial mimicry or even a cliche that triggers a particular facial expression; smiling, happy, sassy, etc. Dictionary.com defines the term "expression" as "the manner or form in which a thing is expressed in words; wording; phrasing; delicacy of expression". Further, the definition says, "the power of expressing in words: Joy beyond expression" and "indication of feeling, spirit, character, etc., as on the face, in the voice, or in artistic execution: The lyric expression embodied in his poetry". In dance, this definition would translate into the power, quality, manner(s) or form(s) in which movements are expressed, indicating feeling, spirit, character, etc. throughout the body.

In the philosophy of Kathak dance, this element of dance is referred to as abhinaya (expression) bringing importance to style, manner, feeling, refinement, softness, delicacy, grace, elegance, contrast, and masculine versus the feminine - among other qualities. In the Egyptian dance philosophy, huge emphasis is put upon feeling – ihsaas/ehsaas/eihsees. The dancer's ability to become immersed in the music, letting the music flow through the body's fibers is regarded as a desired skill, and it is considered the manifestation of the dancer's instinct - based upon training and perception of the music.

As artists, we dancers are more than people who move about while music is playing. We are actors, musicians, and dancers; all these factors play a role in how we approach the subject of expression. Our body language, gestures, and facial expression can convey concrete or abstract qualities, as can our body through movement; i.e. how we play our instrument. We write concrete or abstract stories with our bodies; so, this makes us writers as well. All these skills: Acting, playing music, dancing, and writing, give us quite a few ways to think of expression across all modes of the dramatic arts.

A piece of music may inspire us to have a vision that we want to place in context through movement. The musical tradition and heritage behind a piece can evoke certain movements. The philosophical, cultural and societal context of the music that we use can give us parameters to motivate our creative processes. A song may have lyrics that move us emotionally and move us to dance. The freedom provided by the form of a dance style or genre could give us a foundation to express meaning in a certain way. We may use intent to motivate our movements and statements as well as place emphasis upon the most important part of a movement, choreographed dance, or statement. We can use a character or story to place our dance in a context. We could have short or long-term developmental goals as artists or dancers that give us a specific purpose each time we move, perform, or practice.

The venue in which a dancer performs plays a significant role in how one may portray these qualities. Skillfully, the dancer needs to tune and adjust:

- Intensity of movements.
- Physical and communicative distance kept from the audience.
- Intensity of commitment through their performance focus and direction.

The dance presentation needs to fit the type of venue in which you are performing. If you perform an artistically charged piece at a wedding or a party or in a restaurant, it may not translate as well onto a stage, merely because the audience expectation is different in these venues. Yet, if one were to perform on a stage exactly like in a restaurant, the audience may feel that the artistic vision and dance content is lacking in the performance. This does not necessarily reflect upon the dancer's abilities, but on the choices they make within their skills of portrayal and delivery. Being as versatile as possible in tuning and adjusting your intensity and delivery is a skill that should be rather highly desired, since it immediately impacts the audience's experience and ability to appreciate the performer.

While maintaining our regard for skill, artistic distance, and uniqueness, it is desirable for a dancer to show humanity and compassion. Most of all, dancers must relate to a common and communal groundwork of truth that invites the audience to appreciate the dancer's efforts emotionally and psychologically. Essentially, all these qualities and thoughts tie into the question of how to weigh, charge, and motivate our work before it can translate in the best possible way to the public. By brainstorming how these subjects play into our dance, we can better articulate, connect, and deliver our messages to our fans, while allowing a balance of humanity, technical proficiency, artistic vision, and humility to enter all our performances.

### DaVid

*DaVid of Scandinavia is an internationally touring Middle Eastern and Indian dance artist, choreographer and dance coach based in San Diego, California and Oslo, Norway. He is the artistic director of the Ethnic Dance Academy and has been hosted in many countries as a guest artist, dance coach and choreographer.*

# Performance Enhancement

## by Mahsati

You know the moves, now we need to look at how to present them on stage in ways to showcase your performance: Concepts like emoting, characters/archetypes, movement variation in speed, direction, and use of concepts like effort shape.

Every dancer and audience member knows it; when some dancers perform, the performance leaves you breathless! There is just something about them that draws your attention and doesn't let it go. Where does that come from? It is one of the things that can be there from day one of the first class or something that the student has consciously developed over many years. What is it that turns a skilled dancer into an unforgettable one? A combination of technique, stagecraft, performance skills, personality, and the intent of the dancer come together to become more than the sum of its component parts! Let's look at some of the elements other than excellent technique that need to come together to advance a performance from simply nice to absolutely amazing. To start, let's work on how to present your performance to showcase the best of your potential. Concepts like energy flow, emoting, characters and archetypes, movement variations, effort shape and emotional direction and intensity give you more options and opportunity to customize your performances.

## Using Your Stage

What is the base layer for your performance? The venue! Different kinds of venues and stages will lend themselves more readily to different types of performances. From your costuming to your music, tailor your performance to the type of venue in which you will dance to achieve its best reception. Is it a dark and smoky hookah lounge, where you will be dancing closest to your audience? If so, choose music that gives you a lot of options for stationary work with some travel possibilities. Will you be performing on a theater stage with great lighting? Go for the costume that looks perfect even when it is seen from far away and flexible enough to accommodate music that will let you make intriguing poses and allow for your ability to travel across the stage. A dancer who keeps the venue in mind during planning can build a strong base for her performance. She or he can go into a situation knowing the most likely variables, having prepared contingency plans for most common issues that are likely to exist at that type of venue.

The venue can give you a general idea about the performance, but once the performance starts, your stage is going to be the key. If possible, find out prior to your show if you will perform on a stage, what kind of stage you will have, and if so, its dimensions. In some cases, you won't have a stage at all and will need to perform in the aisles at a restaurant or on uneven ground during an outside performance. Think it through when making your plans. If it is an outside performance without a stage, check to see what the flooring will be made of – there is a huge difference between grass and asphalt, especially in the summer! One recommendation is to have different types of footwear available to protect you in any performing environment. Sandals, dance slippers, half-shoes, high heels, and bare feet will all work for different performances, so check your venue and be prepared for anything.

Okay, so now you've covered the location and type of stage. If possible, arrive early and have a rehearsal or a stage check to confirm everything before you dance. Make sure to check the stage area, ask about your music, confirm any special requests, and any last minute details or needs for either the dancers or the audience. Being well-informed and ready will keep you from feeling unsure or uncomfortable during your performance. Confidence is part of what gives a dancer that mesmerizing quality. Anything you can do to increase your comfort and confidence will be useful to improving your performances.

Once the dancer has prepared as much as possible, it is time to perform. This is where your staging comes into the equation. This requires rehearsal just like your technical skills. Plan the performance from the audience's point of view. What they will see is as important, if not more so, than what you are trying to convey. An audience will only be able to understand a message that they can see. A practical example of this is not to perform floor work where a significant portion of the audience will be unable to see you once you have descended to the floor. No matter how amazing that part of the dance may be, it will be lost on those people who were unable to see it and they may lose interest during the time while you aren't visible.

Dancers need to learn professional terms such as stage directions to help them communicate with lighting designers and other performers about what will happen on stage. It can be difficult to describe dance movements and staging accurately when everyone is using her or himself as the point of reference. Using standard stage directions will give all of you a consistent point of reference.

- **Up Stage** – If you divide the stage in thirds, the third farthest from the audience is termed "Up Stage". You can also use Stage Left and Stage Right to clarify specific areas within the Up Stage portion of the stage.
- **Center Stage** – Continuing with the stage divided into thirds, the next third moving towards the audience is designated "Center Stage". Again, you can also use Stage Left and Stage Right to clarify specific areas within the Center Stage portion of the stage.
- **Down Stage** – Finally, the third of the stage that is closest to the audience is called "Down Stage". Down Stage Left would mean closest to the audience on the Stage Left side.
- **Stage Left** – Looking towards the audience, Stage Left is the performer's left.
- **Stage Right** – Looking towards the audience, Stage Right is the performer's right.

**Mahsati Janan**

These directions can be used when talking with your stagehands, lighting techs, or other performers to keep everyone on the same page.

This all seems pretty straightforward so far; so now we are considering the actual performance. Think about those dancers who hold your attention the most. Do they stand in one place for their entire performance? Unless intentionally choosing a dance done in place, they probably travel around their stage, but it doesn't seem random or out-of-place when they move. This is due to their choices in floor patterns and use of space. A good dancer may make sure to move around to all areas of the stage, but it might feel forced at times. An extraordinary dancer makes stage positioning look effortless.

Floor patterns are a reasonable and logical way to plan your use of space, whether the piece has been choreographed or the dancer is performing an improvisational piece. Drill some basic floor patterns to keep them fresh; this is where you will be able to play with geometric and other shapes.

## Pattern Examples
- Arcs – An arc is any part of a circle, so a curve, starting at one point and ending at another.

You can think of this as positions on a clock; so, from the dancer's point of view, you may choose to travel from left to right on an arc starting at 9 o'clock and moving to 3 o'clock or moving right to left around the back half of the circle from the same 9 to 3.

- Circles or Rounded shapes – Draw an imaginary circle on the floor and keep your travel steps on this imaginary line.
- Figure 8 or Infinity
- Lines
- Squares or Rectangles
- Triangles
- Letters, flowers, or other unusual patterns – You can use any pattern that you will be able to remember and train yourself to use.

## Variations

- **Directionality** – Your shapes have both an inside and outside; so you can play with the direction you are facing at different points in the shape. Also, don't hesitate dancing while you are traveling backwards. The variation between seeing you facing the audience, transitioning to angles or away gives you more options for visual impact.
- **Mixed patterns** – Try planning a circular pattern that turns into a square pattern. By designing different custom patterns, you can add interest to your performance.

## Expressing Your Emotions and Presence

Most Middle Eastern based dance styles are non-narrative, meaning that they do not tell a specific story. Other dance styles, such as Ballet, commonly tell stories in a theatrical way like plays. In our styles, we are generally expressing emotions and musicality, but not focusing on a step-by-step story. This doesn't mean that you can't have a fabulous narrative show based on Middle Eastern dance styles. However, it is less common than the non-narrative versions.

Just because we aren't trying to convey specific stories doesn't mean that we don't have a lot to communicate to the audience. There are shortcuts to help a dancer convey specific attitudes or ideals. One way of thinking of these is the use of characters or archetypes. For our purposes, archetypes are like templates for your stage presence that delineate specific presentations of yourself to the audience.

Stage presence can make the difference between a good performance and a great one. There are many different ways to enhance your stage presence, but finding what works for you is important to communicate your energy and intent to your audience. Remember, these are only to help your dance reach that next level; don't lose yourself and your own art while working on adding more tools to your toolbox!

Archetypes: Some dancers find that using a set of dance archetypes is a good way to help them determine a persona for specific performances. The archetypes listed below encompass full personalities and worldviews, but while typically written towards women, the same characteristics can be chosen and used by men as well.

## Common Archetypes

- **Bint al Balad, the Country Girl** – Simple, innocent, sweet, girlish, girl next door, cute, cheeky
- **Dala'a, the Coquette/Flirt** – Playful, flirtatious, teasing, sometimes sexy
- **Ma'alima, the Boss-Woman, Lady in Charge** – Sassy, confident, in control
- **El Sitt, the Wise Woman** – Dignified, spiritual, serene, matriarchal
- **El Malika** – the Queen
- **El Sitt/Ma'alima** – serence, secure, confident, powerful, gracious

## Personalized Characters

Create a dance persona based on anything that calls to you. Feel like a princess? What about a rogue? A priestess or priest? A warrior? Think about what you want to project. Make a list of the characteristics you want and study similarities among people who project those characteristics.

Another thing that will help you to make your dance come alive is to learn the cultural clues, like body postures and expressions, to give your performance a strong feeling of being part of the culture you are representing. Don't try to use movements from other cultures if you haven't first learned their meaning, if any. Some movements that look great and seem perfect may have unexpected meanings that would conflict with the performance you are presenting.

## Emotions

Dancers who are able to express a large range of emotions will be more engaging than those that are expressionless or stick to only one or two emotions. The problem here is one of blanking. Dancers want to express more emotions, but in the moment of performing, sometimes end up defaulting to a constant smile or a thoughtful expression. Both of these are good, but without any variation, the audience will soon waver in their engagement.

Even with a happy song, you can vary the type of happiness you want to convey. Are you wistfully happy, waiting for your loved one? What about ecstatically happy to see them again? Then again, now that they are home safe, what about a mischievous happy? As you can see, there are a lot of options! The good news is that you already know how to express all of these things. You may need to dial it up to a higher intensity for stage, but you can draw on your own life experiences to make your emotions feel true to both you and your audience.

**Plutchik's Wheel of Emotions** (Plutchik, 2002) is another tool to help with your emotional presentation. This graphic shows the relation and intensity of different emotional states. A dancer can use this to design the emotional progression within their performance by considering the distance and difference between the emotional states they want to convey.

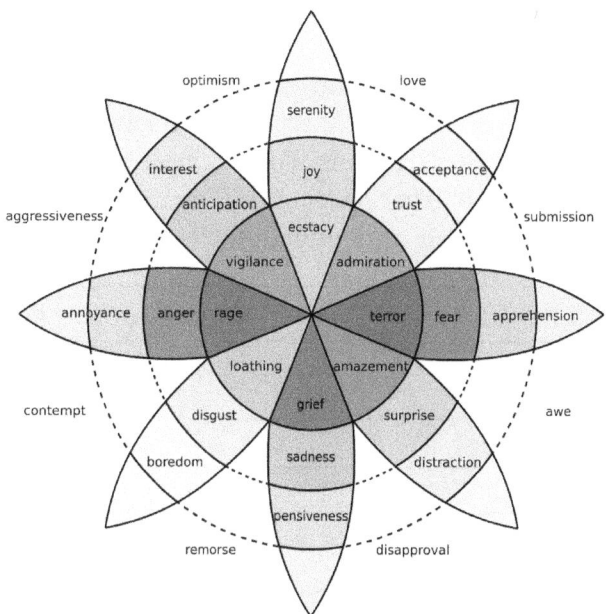

**Movement Quality** – Expressing emotion through your face and posture is one tool. Another is varying your actual movement technique to engage your audience by bringing them through different variations of movements with qualities that match the mood that you are trying to set. Each dancer has his own way of understanding movement quality and options. The guide I use is below. You may find that you need to add, remove, or change this list to be more useful for your needs. Each of these is a variation that can be used to either plan or evaluate specific movements.

- **Energy** – Where is the movement generated? Is it powered through the entire movement or only on parts?
- **Execution** – How well is the movement completed? Which muscles are used? Is it consistent? Is it evenly replicable?
- **Timing** – Is the movement on the beat? Where does it fall on the beat?
- **Quality** – What is the intention and where is the attention? What qualities does the movement have: Soft, hard, fast, slow, floating, flowing, striking?

- **Style** – Is the base movement being modified by a specific style accent? Egyptian, Lebanese, Greek, Turkish, ATS, Fusion, etc.?

By modifying your technique intentionally, you are able to convey a lot more than if you always completed specific movements with the same intent. Each movement type lends itself to different types of variations. For example, a circular movement will have a lot of fluidity in the options for your speed and directionality. If you want to switch from a sultry, slow movement into a fast crisp movement to signify a change in your emotion, a smooth circle into a sharp accent is an appropriate choice. Thankfully, there is already a great rubric for different types of movement quality; the concept of "Effort Shape" brings a consistent shorthand to movement descriptions. (Dell, 2007)

**Effort Shape** – Each Effort Shape combination is actually a combination of a specific spatial focus, weight, and timing that has been given a name for quick reference. (Dell, 2007). These concepts were first developed by Rudolf Laban who also created a system for movement notation. (Chi, Costa, Zhao & Badler, 2000) The key elements to understand this shorthand are Space, Weight, Time, and Flow.

- **Space** – This can be either Direct or Indirect and refers to the attention or focus of the movements. Indirect movements would be meandering, wandering, multi, or unfocused. Direct movements would be focused with a specific clear intent. (Chi, Costa, Zhao & Badler, 2000)

- **Weight** – Weight can be either Light or Strong and refers to the sense of impact of the movement. Light movements are characterized by a lack of or lessening pressure. Strong movements are powerful and have a sense of continued or increasing pressure. (Chi, Costa, Zhao & Badler, 2000)

| Effort Shape | Space | | Weight | | Time | |
|---|---|---|---|---|---|---|
| | Indirect | Direct | Light | Strong | Sudden | Sustained |
| Flick | X | | X | | X | |
| Float | X | | X | | | X |
| Glide | | X | X | | | X |
| Dab | | X | X | | X | |
| Press | | X | | X | | X |
| Punch | | X | | X | X | |
| Slash | X | | | X | X | |
| Wring | X | | | X | | X |

- **Time** – This refers to the timing of the movement and its sense of urgency. Sustained movements are unhurried and continuous through the full motion. Sudden movements are quick and feel urgent. (Chi, Costa, Zhao & Badler, 2000)

- **Flow** – Flow is not always used when describing effort shape, but it can be useful for dancers who want to express even more of their intent through their motions. Flow refers to the amount of tension or control to a movement and can be either Free or Bound. Free movements feel wild and uncontrolled, but Bound movements feel controlled and restrained. (Chi, Costa, Zhao & Badler, 2000)

Using the combinations of the first three of these movements attributes, Laban developed a set of basic Effort Shapes that can be used in any movement art, including Middle Eastern derived dance forms. A quick table will show these options below. (Dell, 2007)

Think of your movements. Which movements might be a glide? An arm raising overhead or your hips sliding to the side can be a glide, but, then change it up. You can also do those same motions as a press or a dab. Using effort shape is a way to take the movements you have and texturize them so that each movement can be sharp, gooey, tough, or anything else you want to share with your audience. Learning and using the effort shapes as descriptive terms will help you to remember and showcase these variations during your performance.

## Making the Most of Your Music

There is only so much that a dancer can do with a mediocre piece of music. Choose music that gives you a chance to show variety and to engage the audience. Always try to match your mood to your music and your music to your mood. If you are starting with an amazing song, you will need to match your presentation to what is appropriate for the song. You can vary your costuming based on the mood you want to set and style of music, not just in regional costume styles, but also in fabrics, flow, etc. By coordinating your mood, music, and costume, you will reduce any confusion or dissonance that your audience may experience in cases where the music and dancer seem completely unrelated. To choose the best music and make the most of it, you will need to know what the music is about. As a dancer, part of your job is understanding both the music and lyrics and interpreting that information for the audience. This is not a pantomime, but the audience should get a feel for the emotional content of the song from your performance. A bright and happy performance to a song about lost love can take your audience out of enjoying your performance and into second guessing your choices. Musicality and musical interpretation is a huge topic, but it is definitely one that all dancers should study.

## That Absolutely Mesmerizing Dancer Could Be You

Remember that mesmerizing dancer we talked about at the beginning? While these steps won't automatically turn you into that dancer, they will help you develop the skills to bring your performances to be more memorable and better at communicating with your audience. Dancers who spend time thinking about the variety of presentations available to them on staging, emoting, characters, movement quality, and things like music and costume choice are intentional dancers. Each one is in control and confident, knowing that he or she is performing and communicating to the best of their abilities. It looks like a natural gift, but all of these are skills that can be learned. Imagine the dancer you want to be and you can make it happen.

"When the soul wishes to experience something, she throws an image of the experience out before her and enters her own image" – Meister Eckhart

## References

Chi, Diane; Monica Costa; Liwei Zhao; & Norman Badler. *The EMOTE model for effort and shape Presentation*. Siggraph 00, New York, New York. 2000. Conference Presentation.

Dell, Cecily. *A primer for movement description using effort-shape and supplementary concepts*. (10th ed.). New York, New York: Dance Notation Bureau Press, 2007. Print.

Plutchik, Robert. *Emotions and life: Perspectives from psychology, biology, and evolution*. Washington: American Psychological Association, 2002. Print.

### Mahsati Janan

*Mahsati Janan is an instructor, performer, choreographer, and workshop instructor in Asheville, North Carolina. She began her journey in belly dance in 1996 and has studied and performed throughout the US. She specializes in classical and modern Egyptian styles, but also enjoys many other modern belly dance forms.*

# How to Balance Anything!
## by Stasha Vlasuk

**B**alance dances have been a fascinating staple in Middle Eastern dance for hundreds of years. An assortment of items can be balanced while dancing. I've seen an early 1900s film of a dancer balancing a chair, holding it with her teeth! This article will introduce basic techniques for achieving various feats of balance. Some simple exercises and my Harem Hints will inspire you to balance trays, jugs, swords, candles - anything! How about a hookah? Choose a balancing item that charms you: Research it, and make it your own.

### Balinese Candle Trick

My balancing career began in the 1970s. Although Belly dancing was certainly exotic, performers still needed feats of skill in addition to the dance to both captivate their audience and make themselves distinct from other performers. The more varied a performer's repertoire, the more likely they are to make big tips and be hired again. This hasn't changed! Haji Baba's, the Armenian restaurant where I performed at that time, featured cocktails in a flat-bottomed glass. When emulating the candle dancer in the Perfumes of Araby Dance Company (to which I belonged) it was natural and easy to balance the cocktail glass on my forehead or on the top of my head.

One evening, utilizing the cocktails of two customers, I implemented a balancing technique commonly called the Balinese Candle Trick, inspired by the Tari Lilin, originating from the Minangkabau people of West Sumatra. An open cup of liquid is held in one's hand and rotated 720 degrees, or any multiple thereof, without spilling the liquid!

You hold the cup with your right palm underneath it, straight out in front of you. Now circle it towards the left, counter clockwise, keeping your palm upward, circle below your right underarm, (awkwardly) around front with your elbow straight up in the air. That's 360 degrees, and you're a pretzel. Keep moving your hand, keeping palm up, around counterclockwise, this time circling your arm around over your head. At 720 degrees, the cup is back where it started, unspilled, and your arm is straight once more. Practice this so it becomes graceful. The challenge is to do this with both hands simultaneously, in opposition. This was a great success at garnering attention!

Next, I decided to add sword balancing to my repertoire, inspired by the Orientalist painting "Sabre Dance in a Cafe" by Jean Leon Gerome that features a dancer brandishing a sword while balancing another on her head. (Painting is portrayed elsewhere in this book.)

I've heard a theory regarding the Sword Dance ("Raqs al Saif") that this painting might depict: Dancers would spirit away the weapons of tipsy patrons. Notice that she uses what appears to be a scimitar, a heavier, more curved blade. The scimitar's weight precludes extravagant dancing; yet,

**Balancing drinks was a great success at garnering attention!**

it's fullness and its curve seem to make balancing easier. I decided I wanted to do a fusion of two elements: Both weapon brandishing and balancing. I purchased two Indian Tulwars (a less curved blade than the scimitar) whose lightness allowed me to perform martial arts maneuvers.

Another historical reference to Raqs al Saif is in a wedding dance: A woman would dance with her husband's sword as a symbol of both pride and a warning to other men. There's a description and drawing of this by Giovanni Belzoni in his "Narrative of the Operations and Recent Discoveries within the Pyramids, Temples, Tombs and Excavations in Egypt and Nubia", published in 1822.

He describes:

"In the evening we arrived at Meimond; and, hearing the tambourine, went to see an Arabic feast in the village. We were introduced in front of the spectators. The performers consisted of about thirty men, all in a row, clapping their hands in concert, so as to form a kind of accompaniment to their song, which consisted of three or four words; and with one foot before the other keeping a sort of perpetual motion, but without changing their positions. Before the men were two women with daggers in their hands, also in continual action, running toward the men and then returning from them with an extraordinary motion, brandishing their daggers, and waving their garments. In this, they persevered for such a length of time, that I wondered how they could support the exertion. This is a sort of Bedoween (Bedouin) dance, and is the most decent of all that I ever saw in Egypt…"

He then concludes:

"… but no sooner was it ended than, in order I suppose to please us, they immediately began another, in the fashion of the country, which fully compensated for the extraordinary modesty of the first; but we returned to our boat more disgusted than pleased with it."

Belly dance can be so controversial!

## Balancing Exercises

Before we talk more about swords, let's start balancing! To begin, first, you may want to try balancing a book or a half-filled, capped bottle of water on your head. Relax, breathe deeply, concentrate. No pressure: Let this practice object tumble many times as you become familiar with balancing, and once you achieve effortless balance with it, you'll be ready to graduate to a prop. Where is your personal balancing point? Experiment: You may find it's towards the front of your head. Chin up! You'll have to keep your head still and not tilt it forward or back, or to one side or the other. Don't attempt to move until you feel the object is well balanced. Once you sense where it balances, simply walk it around the house as if you were a crazy person. Walk into the kitchen, do your emails, drop to your knees and stand back up. The exercise here is for your object to become effortlessly balanced while you move around. Try to achieve this feeling of effortless balance before taking the next step: Dancing.

## Balancing Tricks and Techniques

The golden rule of balancing is: Practice makes perfect!

Because of the structure of your performance, warming up your upper body, legs and core is essential. Try dancing much slower than you normally would to start, until you feel confident and proficient in your balancing technique.

Generally, a balancing dance has four elements:

### Standing and Traveling
Learn to perform smooth and well-articulated hip work by isolating the movement of your chest and upper body from your head and neck. Lower torso flexibility extends your range of movement in the hips and pelvis; so pivot in a big hip circle under an object without losing it. Isolated big hip shimmies are quite impressive while balancing something, and are exceptionally easy. With your object balanced on your head, try a horizontal chest circle; proceed to vertical chest circles and the resulting full-body regular and reversed undulations.

### Descending and Reclining
Now for the hardest exercise! With an object on your head, kneel, lie down and roll on the floor. (I love to prop myself on one arm and perform belly rolls in time with the music.)

### Ascending
Here's where your costuming can trip you; be sure that your skirts or harem pants are not tangled beneath you as you rise! Likewise, make sure your costume isn't so brief that you unintentionally flash your audience!

### Big Finish
When you have become proficient in balancing, the dynamics of juxtaposing fast and slow moves is hypnotic. I love speeding up to a spinning finish with a big flourish as I remove the object from my head. This becomes my "Ta-dah!" moment. Are you using candles? Have the kids (or the birthday person) in the audience help blow them out.

### Add Drama
Once you have learned how easy it is to balance something, make it look difficult! Drama comes from allowing the audience the time to fully appreciate how difficult it is to accomplish what you are doing. Bring a movement to it's fullest point, then pause, and drop dramatically into a new movement. In the floor work of my Candle Dance, I perform a few seated undulations, then suddenly hinge back to a full layout, and I pause. In my Sword Dance, even a swift (yet simple) change from horizontal blade position to vertical is dramatic.

Ready to try a prop? Pick your favorite, plop it on your head, and go back over the exercises, tricks, and techniques.

### Pot Balancing
The Pot dance, (Raks al Juzur) balancing a fired clay jug or urn, is a popular folkloric dance from the south of Tunisia, featuring dramatic hip-twisting movements. A headscarf, which is also authentic for North African folkloric dance, may make your pot more stable. Peel-and-stick velcro applied to the bottom of the pot may help it stay in place.

**Raks al Juzur (Tunisian Pot Dance)
by Helene Eriksen**

**John Compton performs at the Ethnic Dance Festival in San Francisco.**

If you're performing with a group, keep a quantity of dried beans in the urn, and pour them out of and into one another's urn, it indicates to the audience that there's actually something in the urns. It also helps weight the urns at the bottom, resulting in easier balance.

## Tray Balancing

Tray dancing (Raks Al Senniyya), involving the balance of a large circular tray that usually has a tea set or lit candles balanced on top of it, is performed as a North African folkloric dance. The trays are usually brass or some kind of metal in various sizes. The larger the tray, the more impressive-looking they are; yet, if you are petite, a large tray may look overwhelming. Select a tray that suits your height. Look for them at swap meets or thrift and import stores.

To find the best-balanced position of your tray, put it on your head and tilt your head slightly right to left, then front to back, turn the tray a quarter turn and repeat. You will notice that the tray wobbles less in a particular orientation. When you have found this position, mark the "Front" on the underside of your tray with a marker or a sticker so you can put the tray on your head "Front side forward" during each performance.

Many tray dancers use a product called "Stick-um", or Play-Dough, to affix their tray objects so that they resist sliding. However, it is more intriguing to indicate the difficulty at the beginning of your tray dance by lifting items off the tray, showing the audience that you are not using trickery. Harem Hint: Affix your tea glasses evenly in a circle around the perimeter of your tray, and leave the urn free-standing in the center, where it will be most likely to balance easily. Lift off the big urn, pantomime pouring into one of the cups, replace the urn, and put the tray on your head. On my tray, I have applied clear shower curtain material, held on the surface with double-sided sticky tape, this discourages the items from sliding.

## Candle Balancing

Mahmoud Reda has stated that Turkish court dancers of Egypt's Ottoman rulers introduced the candelabra dance (Raks al Shamadan) to Egypt. Originally the "shamadan" had no headband to support them, making balance a true feat. Modern shamadan from Egypt feature a structured headband to help hold them on your head. I found my classic brass candelabra at an Asian import store, and removed a piece of the lower stem to make it less top-heavy. It has the added serendipity of my initial in the design! Whether your candelabra has a headband or not, dancing with live fire requires practice, expertise, and common sense. The lighted shamadan features real fire, thus it is one of the most dramatic props in Oriental dance, because live flames are always potentially dangerous, and balancing the shamadan is not easy. Core strength is essential in this feat.

## Safety Tips

Check fire regulations for the place where your performance will take place. Sometimes a fire marshal needs to be present, sometimes having a fire extinguisher is enough to allay any concern. Watch out for door frames or low hanging objects!

My favorite Harem Hint for removing dripping melted wax from your candelabra is to place it on a piece of newspaper, turn the hair dryer on the blobs and watch them fly off! Polish with a soft cloth; then, use brass-cleaner to keep that gleam.

## Cane Balancing

Light bamboo Egyptian dancing canes are used in folkloric Saidi dance, or sometimes as part of a cabaret show for the Cane Dance (Raks al Assaya). They are swung around in a manner similar to, but not the same as, twirling a baton.

**Core strength is essential in balancing feats.**

However, when using a cane, most of the swinging action will come from the wrist, not the shoulder. During the dance, they can also be balanced on the head, although because they are light and rounded, this can be challenging. To successfully get one to balance on your head, you must keep your shoulders, neck and head very stable. Get a cane that is straight, not bent or curved, and is appropriate for your height, coming up to your hipbone. Canes can be stored flat under the bed, or standing up crook side down.

If you have hair that is long enough to fall onto your shoulders, make sure it is out of the way if you decide to balance the cane on your shoulder while spinning. On my cane, I have determined the balance point, then circled that circumference with double-sided sticky tape to demarcate balance points. For safety (so the cane won't swing out of your hand) wrap a couple of rubber bands tightly around the straight end of the cane; you can get clear ones meant for hair that virtually disappear.

Interestingly, there actually are differing masculine and feminine forms of cane dancing. This is because the women started cane dancing in mimicry of the folkloric men's martial arts dance, the *Tahtib*, which is generally danced with straight sticks resembling staffs rather than the familiar crooked cane the women usually use. The *Tahtib* is more aggressive with emphasis on the cane/stick itself, than is the less combative dancing of the women's version. My Cane Dance teacher was also the coach for the Saudi Olympic Fencing team, and his version was a playful combination of both styles.

## Sword Balancing

In sword balance dancing (Raqs al Saif), the first thing to do is determine what can you do to encourage your sword to efficiently stick to your head? Some dancers notch the blade at the balance point mechanically, but I feel this shows to the audience too clearly, lessening the illusion. Some use double-sided sticky tape, but this makes your hair stick to the blade when you take it off. Other sticky residue has the same problem. Some rub a votive candle along the balancing edge to create a less slick surface. I've even heard of painting that area with clear nail polish and sprinkling sand on it before the polish dries; if you decide to go that route why not create a tiny strip from the peel and stick on the strip of sandpaper? Sandpaper is readily available at your local hardware store. However, my tried-and-true technique has worked for me for years. I suggest you clean the balance surface well with rubbing alcohol, let it dry and clean it again. Let it dry for a full day. Place transparent tape on the edge, a few inches to either side of the balance point, and trim to fit. Place another layer on top of this, and trim again. With a knife or the blade of a pair of scissors score the tape in a fine cross-hairs pattern, on both diagonals. Flick the tape up a bit here and there. This encourages the balance without sticking to too much hair, and doesn't seem to be

**Performing floor work during a sword balancing routine adds drama and suspence.**

that noticeable from the audience's perspective. Remember, you're offering an illusion.

Next, research and practice your dance to inspire unique balance points. Consider standing with one knee up, and balance the blade on top of your knee as you spin on the other foot. What unique presentations can you conjure up?

Store your sword in it's sheath (if it has one) flat under the bed or braced on a wall. You can use a silicone impregnated gun oil rag, found at sporting goods shops, to keep the the steel bright; stored in a ziplock bag, it can last for years.

## Shimmy on Glasses

Now we return to the beginning of this article, except that now, I'm on top of the glasses instead of beneath them!

GildedSerpent.com has a treasure trove of articles mentioning this balance specialty (indeed on all these props!) so I'll stick with the basics, and encourage you to research. Purchase your goblets based on strength, not beauty. I bought my sturdy goblets at a restaurant supply, and bought five of them in case of breakage. (Finger's crossed: I have had no breakage since 1979!) I don't wash them in a dishwasher because hot water can make them more fragile. I use three glasses, rim side down: Two under the ball and heel of my standing leg, and one under the ball of my working leg. Taxim movements are very appropriate, as are shimmies. In my presentation, I perform a drum solo whose rhythms alternate between several dynamic beats. Consider bringing a little Oriental carpet to place upon a hard surface on which you may be performing. I use my aforementioned tray to homogenize any dance surface; the clear shower curtain material on the surface of my tray keeps the glasses from slipping. However, some dancers enjoy the sliding quality, rotating in a circle during the performance, or performing the splits!

In closing, the unifying element in all balancing is the one-pointed concentration necessary to achieve balance. Practice, practice, practice will bring you to the effortless mindfulness that translates to a breathtaking moment of clarity and connection with your audience. This clarity, this connection, is what allows you, as a performer, to fully exist in, and share the timeless moment of now.

**Stasha is balancing on top of the glasses instead of beneath them!**

"When we dance, the journey itself is the point, as when we play music the playing itself is the point, And exactly the same thing is true in meditation. Meditation is the discovery that the point of life is always arrived at in the immediate moment." - Alan Watts

Now, I challenge you to resurrect the "Chair-Held-in-Teeth" Dance!

### Stasha Vlasuk

*Stasha has been joyfully performing and teaching Shamanic Middle Eastern Dance and costuming for over thirty-five years. From Folkloric to Contemporary styles, on stage and in film, her captivating performances since 1975 exceed fourteen thousand: across America, Europe, North Africa and the Middle East. That's a lot of balancing!*

**Melina of Daughters of Rhea Sword and Dagger Balance.
Shot on location at Victoria Theatre in Singapore.**

# Improvising With Ease
## Strategies That Work

**by Anthea "Kawakib"**

Imagine being so confident about improvisation that you:

- Dance without feeling "stuck" or blanking out.
- Dance "as one" with the music.
- Enjoying yourself!

Improvisation like this is the Holy Grail of belly dance, and it can happen for you! Here are three unique clues I've identified that can help you on your quest:

- Energy - powering your movement
- Rhythm - organizing your dance
- Style - your presentation onstage

## Working with Gravity

The secret here is your relationship with gravity. Discovering this relationship is like playing a videogame in which you suddenly unlock a new level. I wonder how many dancers understand and enjoy the feeling of their bodies moving with or against the pull of gravity? However, when you do understand it, it opens another world of sensation for you, taking your awareness out of your head and into feeling your dance.

The key is to become adept at harnessing and using the movement's energy: Focus on the feeling of moving both against and with gravity while dancing. Gravity manifests in, obviously, your weight; so you will want to become more aware of how your body-weight feels while you are dancing. Weight in motion creates momentum; the awareness of momentum is what we want to develop. It's one of those simple truths we might overlook.

**The Whirling Dervishess
by Jean-Leon Gerome**

Think of using your momentum as you swing your hips, snap your torso, swoosh your arms. It's especially fun to feel it in travel steps, turns, and foot patterns. You move across the floor, feeling the impact of your footsteps reverberate through your body. When you dance in place, shift your weight from foot-to-foot and feel your center of gravity change; feel the momentum move in your hips and into your torso, and as you move your shoulders, arms, and head.

I tune into this feeling often when improvising, catching my weight on one side and using the free or non-weighted side for my hip work, or enjoying the waves of energy flowing as I move my torso. It's delicious; a lovely way to experience dance movements! Instead of worrying about what to do next, you're enjoying the pleasure of moving in the moment, and certainly, the audience will see the difference!

## *Centering*

If you don't yet understand this concept of using momentum, you might need "centering". That means pulling your focus out of your head and into your body. I really began to connect with this awareness of center after learning chakra isolations, a form of combined movement meditation and body therapy. One of my former students, Shakti of Cinnamon Phoenix, taught me how to do circle isolations up and down my chakra energy centers, and I found it rooted me into my body awareness in a different way than belly dance by itself had done, and this was after I had spent twenty years in belly dance!

## *Timing, Rhythm and Pattern*

After you're comfortable feeling momentum as you dance, play with patterns of timing and create rhythms for your moves and steps. I don't mean to literally bounce your hips in a Beledi pattern, although you could but, rather, to create your own simple rhythms for both traveling steps and isolations in-place.

**Aurora**

For example, the patterns can be short; "fast-fast-slow, fast-fast-slow"; or longer, "slow-slow, fast-fast-fast, slow-slow, fast-fast-fast".

If you never noticed them before, you may begin seeing and hearing patterns now. They're in the music, both in the melody and, of course, the percussion. The only caveat for this tip is that your best results come from dancing to music that's based on typical belly dance rhythms; whether the music itself is classic, modern, or pop. Of course, you can create rhythms to a steady club-beat, but the process isn't as intuitive.

Your patterns can apply to your steps and movements not only in timing as above, but in the size of your steps and moves. I tell my students that, in many instances, "faster means smaller", meaning when our dancing speeds up, we can make our movements smaller, and vice versa. For instance, in the example above, substitute "small" for fast and "big" for slow, and see how that affects your moves and steps.

There are many more ways to create patterns (rhythms) in dance, for instance:
- Travel steps alternating with movements in place
- Three moves to the right, one move to the left
- A long shimmy ending with a hip snap, etc.

Anything that's organized, and then repeats, is a pattern. If you just did a couple of moves but then start blanking out, take those moves and make a pattern with them. Just let your body keep exploring, and you'll uncover treasures for your dance repertoire.

## Poses

When dancers perform, they are either dancing or posing. Whenever you or a part of your body isn't actually moving, it's posing, and who hasn't posed in a mirror? We all pose. (That's obvious whenever someone takes out a camera!). Use the mirror to find your best poses: Lift your chest, open your arms, with your legs and feet arranged gracefully. Your head and face are part of the picture too; so, tilt your head up, down, or turn your face toward one side or the other. Notice how the poses feel so you can recreate them without a mirror. Turn away from the mirror and find that feeling again.

Name your poses to make them easier to remember: For instance, having both arms extended up or out could be named "Open", while having your wrists crossed in front of you could be named "Closed", etc. Think of your favorite dancer and the pose she uses that comes to mind, and name it after her or him. Now you have a "Yasmine", "Tito", "Magda", etc. Move from one pose to another, slowly at first, then faster as you build your muscle memory. When you find several good poses, use them in your dancing. Do some of your moves in an "Open" pose, face another direction and do the same moves in a "Closed" pose. Decide which moves best fit each pose.

This exercise helps in improvisation because:
- A dynamic shift of focus overcomes that "stuck" feeling, and
- The strategy of posing impacts your whole body.

When you notice the first hint of asking yourself, "What do I do next?", change your pose and continue. Observe how using your best poses gives your moves and steps more variety. Plus, finding these style gems in the mirror is fun!

## A Living Work of Art

Can you imagine putting these three strategies to work at the same time? You will; they'll become easier the more you explore them.

- You'll enjoy the swing of momentum as you Shuffle-Step around the stage, arms flowing from one lovely pose to the next. (i.e. momentum, rhythm, style)
- You'll create a lovely pose to frame your rhythmic Hip lift, lift...drop-drop-drop, feeling each isolation reverberate through your core. (i.e. style, rhythm, energy)

A dancer's awareness goes beyond movements and steps. Her awareness also includes how she feels the movement; as well as how she appears from every direction; that's the difference between an integrated, organic improvisation and a mindlessly busy technical performance. A great dance artist gives the audience a living, three-dimensional work of movement art.

### Anthea

*Anthea ~Kawakib teaches, writes, and produces videos; focusing on both classic belly dance, and synchronized group improvisation. Her books and DVDS explain dance in simple concepts, giving students tools for their own composition or freestyle dancing. Her finger cymbal videos are among the most popular on YouTube.*

**Bacchus and Lynette**

# Shimmylab
## Muscle Activation Patterns in Belly Dance

**by Venus Marilee Nugent**

I began studying and teaching bellydance 30 years ago and soon discovered a fascination for analyzing human movement. Taking a movement analysis class in the contemporary dance program at SFU gave me new ways to think about how we use our bodies to create living pictures imbued with many different qualities of energy and expression. Taking a BSc in kinesiology gave me even more tools with which to think about and appreciate the infinite possibilities and variations in skilled human movement. This interest has led me to my current research as a PhD candidate at McGill Department of Kinesiology and Physical Education using bellydance movements to study voluntary control of the trunk.

Kinesiology is a broad field, encompassing everything to do with human physical performance. This includes such diverse areas of inquiry as cardiac, stroke or injury rehabilitation, physiological effects of exercise and training principles, obesity studies, injury in the work place, design of sport equipment and prosthetics and fall prevention in the elderly. My particular fields of interest are motor learning, motor control and biomechanics. These three disciplines are intimately related: the nervous system is genetically designed with many automatic movement coordination systems, but neuromotor function is also very plastic, i.e. modifiable through learning and experience. Although we artistic types don't like to think of the body as a machine, we must be able to analyze its movement characteristics as a physical object: a system of linked (through the joints) separate masses (the various segments - head, trunk, pelvis, upper limbs, lower limbs, feet, hands) which obeys the laws of Newtonian physics.

Much of the research on motor control explores reaching the arm to a target or automatic responses to loss of balance. The basic question behind motor control research is this: how is it possible, given so many muscles that can be recruited for so many different joint movements, that the central nervous system (CNS) is able to coordinate even the simplest of movements? Interpretation usually involves theories on how the CNS simplifies the control problem or how the goal of coordination is to minimize energy cost. Although much has been learned from these studies, whenever I read them I think, but what about more complex movements? What about movements for which the goal is artistic and success is not measured in speed or accuracy? I love that as bellydancers we use our intuitive understanding of biomechanics artistically to create emotional expression: we play with momentum to move our body parts in myriad interesting ways, we contrast motion in some segments against stillness in others, we resist or surrender to the force of gravity, we play with tension, making movements sharp and strong or soft and flowing. And we articulate many different parts in complex sequences, as with undulations or snake arms. We emphasize separation of body parts that are normally held still or have limited range of motion.

For my research I collect two types of data commonly gathered in movement studies. I record muscle activity (when a muscle is 'on' or 'off') and kinematics (motion capture, as used in animation and video games). To record body kinematics, reflective markers are placed on joints and other anatomical landmarks (see Figure 1a,b). Six or more cameras mounted around a darkened

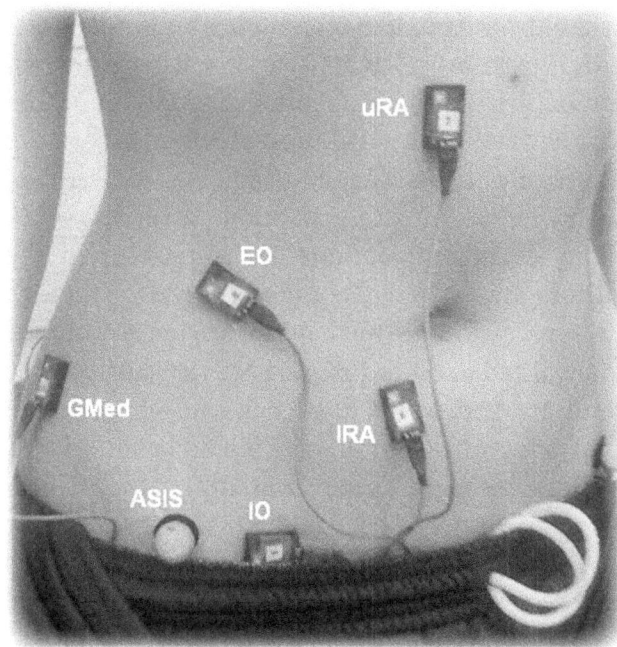

Figure 1a: EMG electrodes record muscle activity from electrical signals that travel to the skin surface. Infrared emitting cameras record positions of reflective markers placed on anatomical landmarks and joints to capture body motion. In this photo, electrodes placed to record from upper and lower rectus abdominis (uRA, lRA), external oblique (EO), internal oblique (IO), the hip abductor gluteus medius (GMed). Reflective markers can be seen on the anterior superior iliac spines (ASIS).

room emit infrared light which reflects off of the markers and is recorded by the cameras. Each camera records the position of each marker in 2-dimensional coordinates. Later, the data from all cameras is combined into a 3-D recreation of the marker positions (see Figure 1b). This position data can then be analyzed in various ways, such as assessing joint range of motion during particular tasks or analyzing gait patterns.

Electromyography (EMG) is used to record muscle activity. An electrode is placed on the skin over the muscle of interest (see Figure 1a), and as the contracting muscle issues a wave of electrical depolarization which travels through the tissue to the skin surface, the electrode picks up the electrical potential difference and the signal is recorded on a computer. Afterwords we look at these signals (plot them in graphs), process the data, and perform different kinds of mathematical and statistical manipulations to address specific research questions.

By recording from a number of different muscles at once during a motor task, we begin to get a picture of how movement is organized by the CNS. The muscle activation pattern represents the spatiotemporal coordination of muscles by the CNS, i.e. we can determine which muscles (the spatial element) are being activated when and in what sequence (the temporal component), and see whether these activations overlap in time or are clearly separated. For a given task or series of comparison tasks we can look at these patterns in tandem with the kinematic data to gain insights into the following questions:

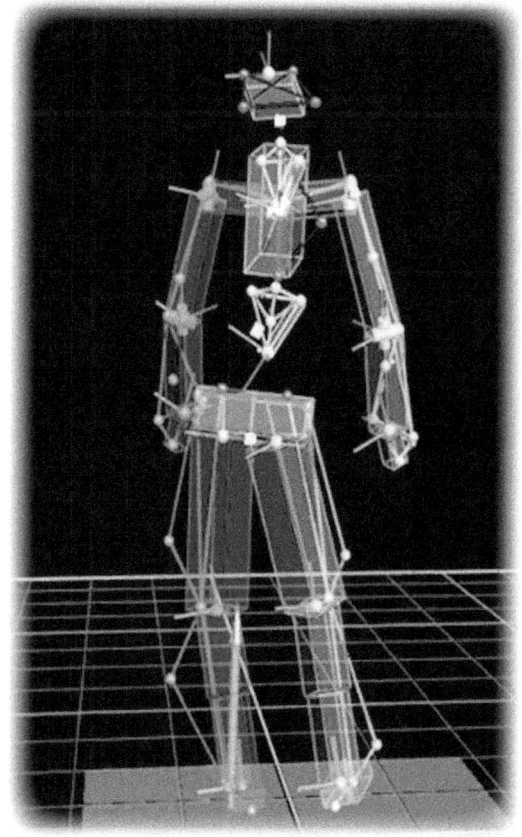

Figure 1b: Motion capture: 3D reconstruction of reflective marker positions. This subject is in mid-hipslide.

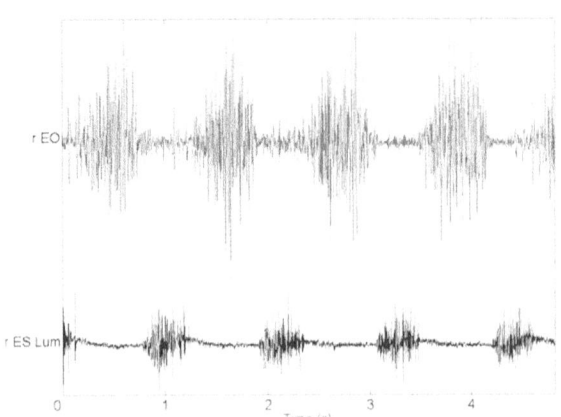

**Figure 2: Trunk extensors and flexors are antagonistic during pelvic tilts. Lumbar erector spinae, right side (r ES Lum), right external obliques (r EO).**

In which movements or joint angle range(s) does a particular muscle act as prime mover? Where does it switch to being a stabilizer (to limit movement) or to an antagonist (to slow the movement or change direction)?

Which muscles work together as synergists and how do these synergies shift when the movement task is altered?

What is the relationship between agonists and antagonists? Does this relationship change depending on the task?

What I like about EMG is that, like dance, the results are very visual and directly related to the physical activity performed (I was never a big fan of physiology... trying to envision processes going on inside cells was always too intangible for me). I use the non-invasive surface EMG electrodes, but some types of studies require insertion of needle or wire electrodes directly into the muscles for precision recording from smaller muscles. In many animal studies (using cats, frogs, rats), wire electrodes are permanently implanted in specific muscles for very targeted recording of muscle activity during a range of motor behaviors across multiple experiments. These kinds of studies have yielded much information about muscle activation patterning in locomotion and balance.

As a dancer, you, like me, might think it is interesting to know what muscles are working when you do a particular dance move, and you probably already have a good idea which ones they are (especially after a weekend seminar!) When I set out to record muscle activation patterns I think about what joint actions are important in the movement, and choose muscles to record which are representative. By that I mean, for example, if you wanted to record muscle activity during knee bending, you would just pick one of the three hamstring muscles (all three would be redundant and involve extra data processing), which are all prime movers for knee flexion, and assume that whenever it was active, the others would be also, as they generally work as a synchronized functional group. There are a few important limitations to surface EMG: we can only record from superficial muscles (the ones that are covered only by the skin/fat layer), not the deeper ones (covered by other muscles and/or organs). For example, the psoas is a prime mover for hip flexion, but it lies against the front of the spine underneath the viscera. We would only be able to record from it by surgically implanting an electrode. Instead, we try using the rectus femoris to capture this action, as being the quadriceps muscle that crosses the hip joint it has a dual function in hip flexion and knee extension. You need to know your muscle anatomy, as you want to make sure you are over the correct muscle and not on the border between it and another, in which case your signal of interest would be contaminated by crosstalk from the other muscle's signal. Also, with movement, the skin may shift, and with it, the electrode to slightly different locations (and perhaps different muscles). Finally, if the fat & skin layers over the muscle are too thick, the signal is degraded, as it dissipates while traveling through the fat. The results are unclear and difficult to analyze. Despite these limitations, with some skill, practice and well-chosen subjects, we can get surprisingly good and reliable results.

Figure 2 shows two signals recorded simultaneously and plotted as a function of time. What you see in one trace is the sum of all the electrical depolarization from active muscle fibers that was occurring and detectible within the range of the electrode. It does not tell us how much of the muscle was active because we do not have a technology to measure total muscle activity. However, it does tell us when a muscle was contracting or relaxed. Note the clear bursting where the signal amplitude increases, alternating with a very low baseline activity when the muscle relaxes (silent period). In Figure 2. you see the alternation of two muscles that are antagonists during the pelvic tilt. The abdominals (muscle recorded: right external oblique - rEO) contract when the pelvis is tilted backwards (lower back flattens) and they go silent when the pelvis is tilted forwards (the lower back arch increases). The lumbar back extensors (muscle recorded: right lumbar erector spinae - rES) have the opposite pattern, being active when the flexors are inactive. Often when we expect a movement to have bilaterally symmetrical activation (the same on right and left sides of the body) we only record from one side to simplify the experimental procedure (i.e. save time!). We assume the pattern will be very similar on the other side (although in reality this is often not quite the case as people tend to be somewhat asymmetrical in posture and muscle balance). In Figure 2 the EO signal is stronger (higher amplitude) than the ES signal. This does not mean that the EO is working

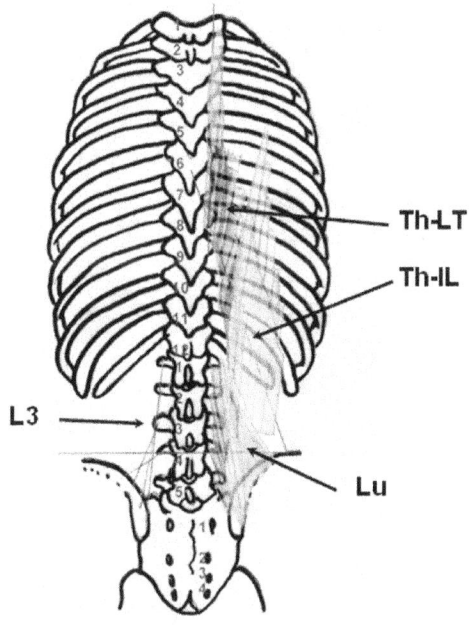
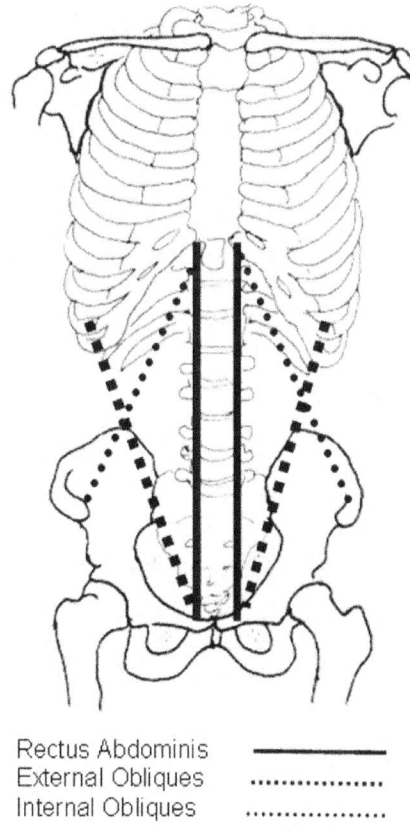

Rectus Abdominis ———
External Obliques ·········
Internal Obliques ·········

**Left Figure 3: Lumbar spine extensors: Layers of the erector spinae (ES) showing the thoracic (Th) and lumbar (Lu) (according to MacIntosh and Bogduk, 1987) portions. The lumbar portion is covered only by the tendons (removed in this picture) of the thoracic portion so EMG of the underlying lumbar portion can be recorded below the level of the 3rd lumbar vertebra (L3). The separate branches of the ES are identified as longissimus thoracis (LT) and iliocostalis lumborum (IL).**

**Right Figure 4: Schematic of the first three abdominal muscle layers, their relative points of attachment and lines of action.**

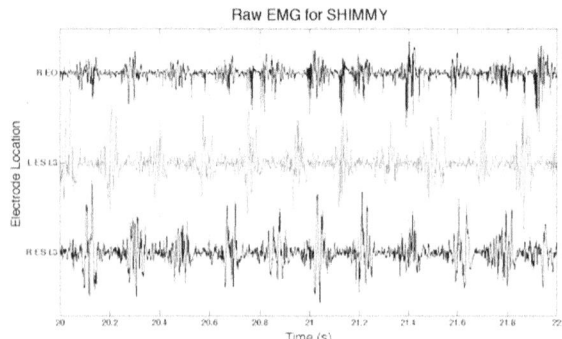

**Figure 5: Muscle patterns in the fast hip shimmy; right lumbar erector spinae (R ES L3) and right external oblique (R EO) are synergists. Right and left muscles are antagonistic during the shimmy. The signal for L EO was bad and not show here but it would be congruent with that for the left lumbar erector spinae (L ES L3).**

more strongly. It could simply mean that the electrode over the EO is closer to a greater number of active fibers than the one over the ES, or that the skin/fat layer was thinner at that location, allowing the signal to come through more strongly.

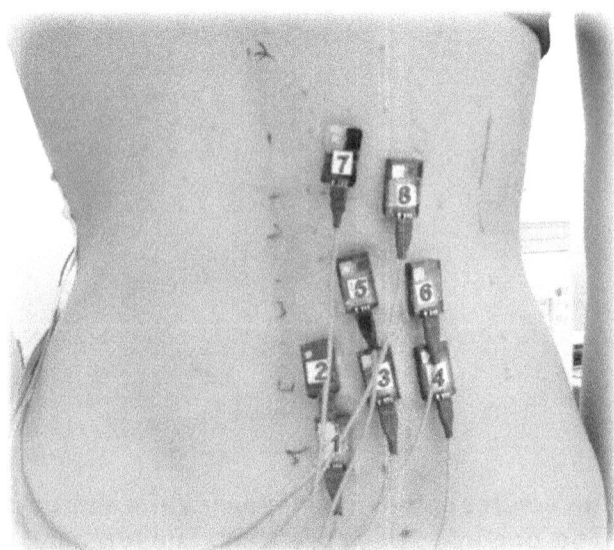

**Figure 6 Electrode placement according to MacIntosh and Bogduk 1987. Numbers written on the skin indicate approximate locations of the five lumbar vertebrae, determined through palpation**

Lets talk about the major muscles of the trunk that are involved in bellydance movements AND accessible to surface EMG. The muscles I have recorded from are the abdominals, going from most superficial to deep: rectus abdominus (RA), external obliques and internal obliques. The transverse abdominus is the deepest layer and is considered to have a very important role in lower back support and core stability. It cannot be recorded from using surface electrodes. Although the internal oblique is mostly covered by the external oblique, it is not covered at a spot just below the anterior superior iliac spine (ASIS) and towards the midline of the body, and can be recorded with an electrode placed here (see Figure 1a). The abdominals are functionally classified as spine flexors, bending the trunk forward when activated together. The major muscle group performing spine extension (straightening and arching of the spine) are the erector spinae (Figure 3). This group has two branches that span the lower back, the longissimus thoracis and iliocostalis lumborum.

A couple of things about muscle structure are important to note both for functional analysis and EMG technique: the location and placement of a muscle - where it attaches at both ends, and the direction of the muscle fibers give a very good indication of it's function (if active by itself). Contraction will cause the muscle to shorten in a direction parallel to the fibers, bringing the bones at the two ends closer together. Consider the schematic diagram of the abdominal muscles (Figure 4). The lines show approximate attachment sites for each muscle and the direction in which it acts. If you contract both internal and external obliques on both sides of the body simultaneously, what action will result? The net result will be to bring the ribs and pelvis closer together, as in a crunch. Of course, the rectus abdominis is also a synergist in this movement, as the forward crunch is its chief function. What if you contract the external oblique (dashed line) on one side of the body and the internal oblique (dotted line) on the other? You can see that they would be working

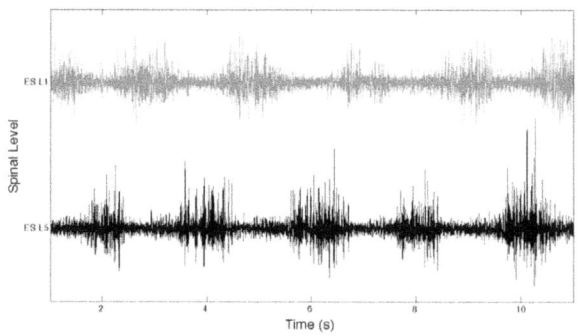

Figure 7: Activity of the erector spinae muscles (both right side) above and below L3 during maya.

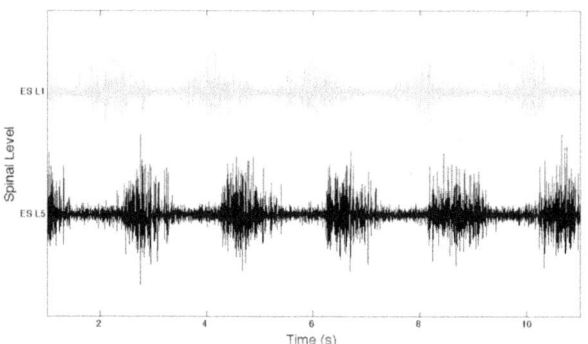

Figure 8: Activity of the erector spinae muscles (both right side) above and below L3 during serpentine.

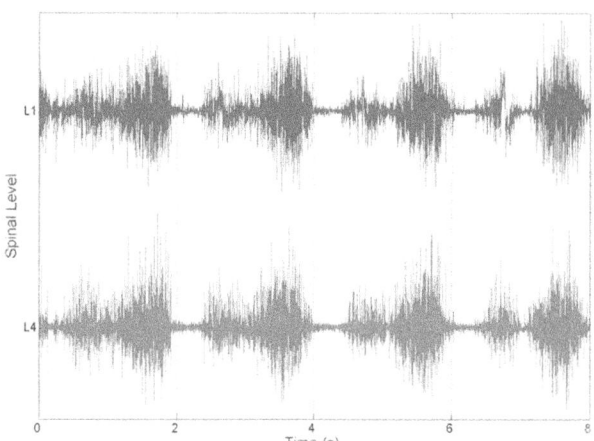

Figure 9: Activity of the erector spinae muscles (both right side) above and below L3 during forward bending and rising.

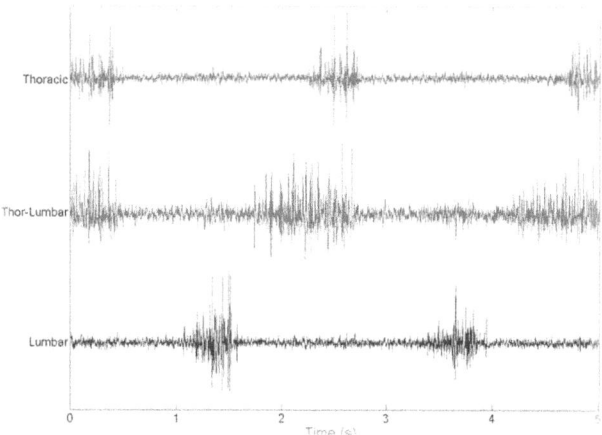

Figure 10: Activation of ES on one side of the spine at different vertebral levels during hip slide.

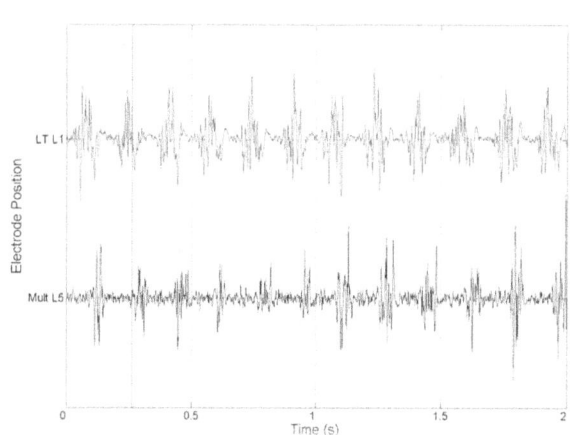

Figure 11: Activation of ES at first (L1) and fifth (L5) lumbar vertebral levels during the fast piston shimmy.

in parallel to rotate the ribcage (and upper spine) relative to the pelvis. To twist in the other direction, the opposite pair would be activated. If you kept the shoulders straight and allowed the pelvis to rotate, the same set of opposite EO/IO muscles would rotate the pelvis in the direction opposite to which they would rotate the ribcage if the pelvis is held still. In the case of twists, because external and internal obliques on one side have their fibers running in opposite directions (in an X), they are antagonistic. However, the right EO is antagonistic to the left EO on the other side, but synergistic with the left IO, and vice versa. If they are activated simultaneously, each cancels out the twisting effect of the other, leaving a net forward flexion force.

It may have been dubbed danse du ventre but the muscles of the back are no less involved in bellydance than those of the front of the body. In fact, for doing something like a twist, if the back muscles were inactive the twist would be combined with a crunch, that is, the abdominals would cause not only a rotation but a forward flexion of the spine. So for a nice twist with spine straight, the back extensors must be active to counter the unwanted spine flexion. Thus their activity becomes synergistic to the horizontal rotation by being antagonistic to forward flexion. If all trunk flexors and extensors were activated together, what movement would result? If the forces front and back were pretty much equal, the result would be no movement between the pelvis and ribcage. But more than that, the net effect would stiffen the trunk, providing stability to the lower back. This is what is meant by core support.

Here's another synergy scenario: what if right spine flexors and right spine extensors were contracted at the same? Both forward and backward bending would be cancelled. The result would bring the ribcage and the top of the hip on right side closer together (spine lateral flexion). If the pelvis is held stationary, this results in a side bend, but if the upper spine and shoulders are stabilized (by muscles in the upper back) and the pelvis is allowed to rotate in the frontal (door) plane, the result is a hip lift (with hip drop on the opposite side). Figure 5 shows EMG recorded during the fast hip shimmy. Right and left erector spinae muscles at the level of the 3$^{rd}$ lumbar vertebrae are antagonistic to each other, their contraction and relaxation phases alternating. The right EO is synergistic to the right ES, bursting at the same time. This right/left alternating pattern during the shimmy I have also recorded in the rectus abdominis muscles, however the signal is often quite small (compared to during forward crunch), which supports the idea that it merely assists and is not a prime mover for spine lateral bending.

In a detailed back muscle dissection study, MacIntosh and Bogduk (1987) described a deeper layer of the ES virtually overlooked by anatomy texts. Whereas the more superficial layer (Figure 3 Th) spans the pelvis and the ribs to pull the thorax laterally towards the pelvis (unilateral activation) or extend (bilateral action) the lumbar spine, they postulated that the deeper portion spanning only the lumbar vertebrae would have a more local action on the lumbar spine only. They provided guidelines for surface electrode placement (Figure 6) to record from these separate portions but did not suggest a movement that would illustrate this proposed specificity of function and action.

I recently published a study (Nugent, Stapley et al. 2012) in which I used bellydance movements to obtain results in support of MacIntosh and Bogduk's hypothesis. I asked beginners and highly trained dancers to perform the maya and serpentine, and recorded activity from the erector spinae muscles above and below L3. We found that there was a difference in timing between these two regions: in the maya (Figure 7), the part of the ES closer to the pelvis contracted sooner than that closer to the rib cage, whereas in the the serpentine (Figure 8), this timing pattern was reversed. In contrast, during forward bending and straightening (Figure 9), both regions had the same timing. These findings have some interesting implications: 1) this temporal separation of function suggests that we managed to record from distinct compartments (with separate innervation) of what is considered the 'same' muscle, that is the CNS is able to send separate messages to each to fine-tune control. 2) The CNS can flexibly alter relative activation timing of adjacent portions of the ES (on the same side of the spine, remember) so that portions that are synergists in one movement (forward bend, pelvic tilt) become antagonists in other movements (bellydance vertical figure 8s). I also recorded from these same muscle regions during hip slide (Figure 10) and piston shimmy (Figure 11), finding different timing of ES above and below L3 in these movements also.

In conclusion, I believe bellydance will continue to provide insights into motor control by virtue of its segmental specificity. Comparing the different types of movements also underlines the flexibility of the nervous system in patterning muscle activity to suit each task. Interestingly, we found no differences between beginners and trained dancers for separation of timing in back muscles. One possible measure of skill might be ability to control unwanted motion (such as twisting during maya). Perhaps I will find clues to skill in future studies.

## Glossary of Anatomical Terms

**Central nervous system** - The structures of the nervous system including the brain, brainstem and spinal cord.

**Kinematics** - Data collected to describe the motion of the body.

**Prime mover** - Main muscle or muscle group responsible for producing a particular joint action. E.g. biceps brachii is a prime mover for elbow flexion.

**Stabilizer** - A muscle performing the job of limiting or preventing motion at one joint so that the desired movement can be performed at another.

**Agonist** - The muscle that causes a joint motion. E.g. triceps is an agonist for elbow extension.

**Antagonist** - A muscle opposing a joint action. E.g. triceps is an antagonist to elbow flexion.

**Synergists** - Muscles contributing together to perform a joint action or series of coordinated joint actions.

**Flexion** - When contraction of a muscle decrease the joint angle, bringing the bones on opposite sides of the joint closer together.

**Extension** - When contraction of a muscle increases the joint angle, moving the bones on opposite sides of the joint farther apart.

**Superficial** - Refers to the location of an anatomical structure as being close to the surface of the body relative to other structures. E.g. the external oblique is superficial to the internal oblique.

**Deep** - Refers to the location of an anatomical structure as being farther from the surface of the body relative to other structures. E.g. the quadratus lumborum is deep to the erector spinae.

## References

Macintosh, J. E. and N. Bogduk. "1987 Volvo award in basic science. The morphology of the lumbar erector spinae." Spine 12.7 (1987): 658-668. Print.

Nugent, M. M., P. J. Stapley, et al. "Independent activation in adjacent lumbar extensor muscle compartments." *Journal of electromyography and kinesiology : official journal of the International Society of Electrophysiological Kinesiology* 22.4 (2012): 531-539. Print.

### Venus

*Venus ~ Marilee Nugent, owner of Venus Belly Dance, performed and taught full time for 20+ years. She has a BA, a BSc and a 20-episode TV series "Belly Dance Workout With Venus". Venus is currently a PhD candidate at McGill University using belly dance to study trunk control.*

# Are The Stars Out Tonight?
## Fitting Music & Dance to Your Gig

### By Najia Marlyz

As time rolls along merrily, more of the completion puzzle pieces find their rightful places in the big picture of belly dance for me. During my early years, I wondered why Arabic people kept gifting me tapes of nearly un-danceable songs with the suggestion that for anyone to be "a real dancer" (you can translate that into "Arabic person") any dancer should be thrilled to use these gift-tape compilations for her dance shows. For a while, they nearly had me convinced that they were correct.

I felt that someday, when I knew more about the Arabic, the Egyptian, the Lebanese, the Turkish—all the Middle Eastern cultures in general, including the language, I would appreciate the music that I was hearing on the cassette tapes. Somehow, my heart would automatically long to make it part of my repertoire of recorded music, and the sounds would evoke my best dance performances, ever. Still, I found the tapes I had received to be dull musically—disappointing for the most part, predictable and common when compared to the wealth of complexities I relished in the orchestrated music of Egypt.

Nearly all of the tapes I had included a single strong vocalist who had made each song popular in Lebanon, Egypt or wherever, and I also noticed that the gift cassette tapes were nearly always poorly reproduced with muffled fidelity because they were copies of copies (of copies?). However, when I purchased the originals from vendors, the quality of the sound reproduction was heightened--while the lackluster dance quality of the tunes became even more evident. I was puzzled! What was it that my Arabic fans were hearing that I could not seem to appreciate?

### A Dancer's Dilemma

Once, back in the '80s, a dancer from the San Francisco Bay area came to her coaching session with me, bringing just such a taped compilation from one of her employers. She said he was suggesting that this was a currently popular recording of musical tracks (from his particular ethnic background) that she should record into her shows—precisely because the tunes were so popular and new. Perhaps because I was more removed from the problem than I had been in the past when it was my show that the music would impact, I listened to the recording from a new perspective.

For the first time, I began to understand that there was a deep schism between listening music and dancing music, and that there is a corresponding divide in different jobs of dancing in public as well. For many occasions a dancer has to be aware that some performers are hired simply to be "background dancers" or "atmosphere enhancers" (especially in restaurants where only ambiance is needed) while other dancers are hired to be "star performers" in variety shows or showcases of talent.

**Rashid dances at the Arabian Nights restaurant in San Francisco**

## Are You a Star, Recreation Director, or Drapery Enhancer?

The answer to the question, "What music should I chose for this gig?" is in the nature of the gig. Starring dancers are the center of attention; they know how to gain attention and hold it. They are commanding and powerful in their presentations, so, they require music that is also powerful and dynamic. They feel deeply offended to have people carry on private conversations or look into their dinner plates while they, the dance star for

Rhea of Athens gets customers up to dance at Taverna Athena in Oakland, CA

the evening, are performing; that is why I would, in my role as the coach for dancers who are working towards Bellydance stardom, recommend that they find an agent to represent them in finding suitable star-performer gigs. While it is perfectly reasonable to compile your own portfolio and contact material on the Internet to find your own gigs in restaurants, delicatessens, coffee houses, and home birthday parties, you must be content to be viewed as a visiting princess in someone's great room and/or settle for fun, a little payment, tips, and a warmed-over dinner after your sets are finished. You might as well forget the "really big bucks"!

Some employers hire dancers to be "background" dancers only. In that case, you can forget about my princess comment; you are just the hired help. Ambiance dancers are hired to carry out a theme, create atmosphere, and not be too obtrusive while doing it—even though she may have to transform herself into a recreation director sometime during her set; cajoling various members of the audience to leave their dinners and table mates to get up and shake their booties with the housedancer of the evening in a fake Bellydance lesson. (Worse things yet may befall you in life.)

Lynette wasn't sure what music to use to entertain at the Mr & Ms Leather contest in San Francisco.

When restaurant dancers are required to dance to recorded music, some may be heard to grouse, argue and carry on from time to time about weak and defective sound systems. They complain that they can barely hear any nuances in their music because it is tuned to a much lower volume than would be possible with a live band (or even just a couple of instruments such as a single oud with a drum). Sometimes, the dancer's recordings are in stereophonic sound while the employer only has a monaural speaker--aimed at the kitchen, by the way. (Say "Good-bye" to half of your musical cues!) Audiences are infinitely more amenable to a higher volume of music when it comes from a real instrument being played in their presence than medium decibels reproduced electronically from an audio speaker. Always!

**Linda dances at Couscous Royale in Berkeley.**

## Play Finger Cymbals or Not?

Many times, I had to put down my cymbals in a restaurant when I was performing because I could not hear the recorded music playing above the sound of my own finger cymbals. Sometimes, I have speculated that this is part of the reason so few dancers dare to perform with finger cymbals these days as was routinely expected and required, when we dancers were hired in the past. Whenever I had to perform with dimmed music, for whatever reason, I could not help but feel slighted and a little frustrated. Being unable to hear my music appreciably impaired the quality of my dance performance—when the real problem resided in my misunderstanding of the reality of my job in the first place.

**It can be very difficult to hear your music at a street fair.**

## Consider the Source

Choosing beautiful dance music at home on your technologically advanced sound equipment is no problem; the problem is choosing something that will appear to work on an archaic worn-out system that has beat-up speakers, placed in all the wrong cubbyholes of the rooms in which you are expected to perform. Generally in the US, we dancers have had little control over sound reproduction unless we bring our own equipment. Even then, the audience or the hostess will want the volume lower than they would accept from a live band. The fact is: If you want to dance as a star, but you have accepted a job dancing and blending with the draperies, you will neither satisfy yourself or your employer with whatever dance you do because your attitude will seep into your face and body language. On the other hand, audiences don't care much what you do—unless they have directly paid for a ticket just to see your dance; then they will care quite a bit and will observe all the fine points of your dancing that you can produce. However, I have seen audiences who were so happy about a family member's birthday and the smooth bottle of wine they have all imbibed, that they will clap and cheer for just about anything odd a dancer does when she stops bouncing one hip in their general direction.

Anyway, returning to the person who brought me her employer's music tape: I told my dance client that this recording was not music arranged for dance, but "listening music" that she had brought from her potential employer. Maybe I missed an opportunity for an explanation that perhaps she needed to look for a different dance position because she was being hired to star dancing with music that had no star qiuality.

## Assessing Gig Requirements

Sometimes we dancers have to compromise with the hiring client in order to secure the gig at all, but I think each dancer must assess the job as it appears. Are you on stage like a star or are you dancing around the tables of people who are tussling with their Shish Kabobs and couscous? Has the audience come to see you dance, or have they come to hear the singer, who just got off the plane from Lebanon or Egypt? Does the band perk up when you appear, or conversely, do the musicians go into a "bored musician stupor." Can this indicate passive-aggressive behavior related to deep culture-based disrespect for what they believe is a prostitute dancer? (It can be one and the same to them "back home"). Were you hired to be a star or a time-fill-in warm-up before the starring singer appears? You have to face facts even if they do not fit your fantasy: Were you hired to flit around tables with your veil or perform under Klieg lights to bring down the house?

Wisdom from an Egyptian Dance Star
In a interview printed in Al Mawed Magazine back in the '90s, Nagwa Fouad was quoted, saying that a panel of judges had told her that she would not

**Lynette entertains at a birthday party for a man from the Tartar community.**

**Lora interacts at an old folks home**

be accepted after auditioning to sing on the radio because she was trying to present "dance songs." She learned that she would have to sing "listening songs" if she wished to sing on the radio. She mused that she had wanted to sing "just enough to round out her art" and that if she had wanted to become "a singer rather than a dancer", she would have done it 30 years earlier. However, she did acquiesce to their advice, the interview said, and learned some little three-minute songs that were appropriate for the radio audiences in Egypt.

I think it is also important for us, as western Belly dancers, to remember that our mostly western audiences cannot respond strongly to lyrics they do not understand. Our audiences respond to the music, but only if they can hear it. If not, they respond to the performer as a beautiful idea, and it is enough just to fulfill their Oriental fantasy and create their evening atmosphere. One does not have to "dance one's fanny off", creating a false feeling of high energy, implying a star quality performance when none is required—or even desired.

## Planning Your Costuming

Before I leave this subject, I need to mention a word or two about costuming for your gig. Sometimes the gig does not call for a jacked-up, tricked out sparkler of a costume when you are dancing in the park at a kid's birthday party, and yet, that dull romantic restaurant or lounge gig demands a dazzling costume that can catch the dim light sources and let the audience see that at least there is movement in your body. It seems ridiculous, I know, to spend a thousand dollars or more on a costume that you are going to wear in a darkened restaurant with the wait-staff running back and forth across your dance space, serving the couscous, but it will be necessary to costume in a reflective bejeweled, bright hue—if you want to be seen at all. Choose your costume with the venue in mind so that you do not clash with the stage curtains, and in a home, try not to clash with the draperies.

Additionally, I would suggest that you not insert blank spaces between tracks of your recorded music to accommodate the anticipated clapping of your audience because their hands will be full of bread and hunks of dripping lamb; some evenings, they won't give a flying camel's flea whether you dance well or not—you will have to impress yourself. When they gaze into each other's eyes, the last thing they need is you sidling up to them, requesting them to dance in front of everyone. You have to be a little circumspect!

## Speaking of Costuming

Once, back in the day when Bert Balladine (my mentor and dance partner) and I were walking together one evening in the streets of Tangier, we fantasized about bringing the street-wear we were seeing back to the dance stages in the US, because being authentic and ethnic then was all the rage for so-called ethnic dancers of the Eastern genre. We laughed as we made our true and authentic list of must-have ethnic dance wear: A large straw hat, a cotton scarf draped (gracefully or not) beneath the nose—covering the lips and chin only, a red and white striped woven woolen straight skirt to mid-calf, and colorful plastic neon flip-flops. Well, it was only a fantasy based on a reality of what we saw then in

1975. I am somewhat relieved that we no longer expect ourselves as dancers to conform to the standards of ethnicity just to convey the beauty we find personally in Middle Eastern music.

Nevertheless, each time you commit to a gig, you need to ask yourself if you are correctly assessing your current dance situation, because each instance is different. Being asked to dance in a restaurant—under dimmed lighting, to Middle Eastern music made weak because it is tuned to impossibly low music decibels—should give you a clue what is expected from your presence! You need to choose recorded music that does not require quick and intricate movements that cannot be seen under the low lighting anyway and stick to movements that are broad with music that is more on the romantic side (almost what we might consider "movie music"-- yet not "lounge music") rather than the more raucous sounds of ethnic and traditional Bellydance sounds. By fitting your dance music to the actual gig, you may not find your perfect dance being published on YouTube by an astonished group of Bellydance fans, but you will have the satisfaction of adding another small cog into your shining, and hopefully, long and satisfying dance career.

### Najia Marlyz

*Najia has performed, taught, written, coached, and traveled in the Middle East during her career spanning 45 years. Partnering with her mentor, Bert Balladine, she taught in her Albany, CA, studio, "The Dancing Girl" (later, "Bellydance Arts") in the 1970s. Masterclass instructor in the '80s through '00s, she is recognized for dramatic improvisation, seamless movement, and inventive technique for coaching pros based on imaginative musical analysis.*

**Najia performs at the Rakkasah Festival in California in 1990**

Above:
Gilded Serpent Founders Meeting
November 1998,
Robyn, Najia, Lora, Wendy, Krista, Ryan
and taking the photo, Lynette

Right:
Since its inception in 1998, Gilded Serpent Online Magazine has grown to more than 2000 articles with more than 400 contributors with a global readership.

# THE BACKSIDE

**Maps**
**A Few Maqams & Rhythms**
**Glossary**

**References**
**Gig Form**
**Contributors**
**Photo Credits**
**More Photos**

Mish Mish

# Egypt
## Dance Zone Study Map

Sahra C. Kent - "Sahra Saeeda"
www.SahraSaeeda.com
JourneyEgypt@yahoo.com

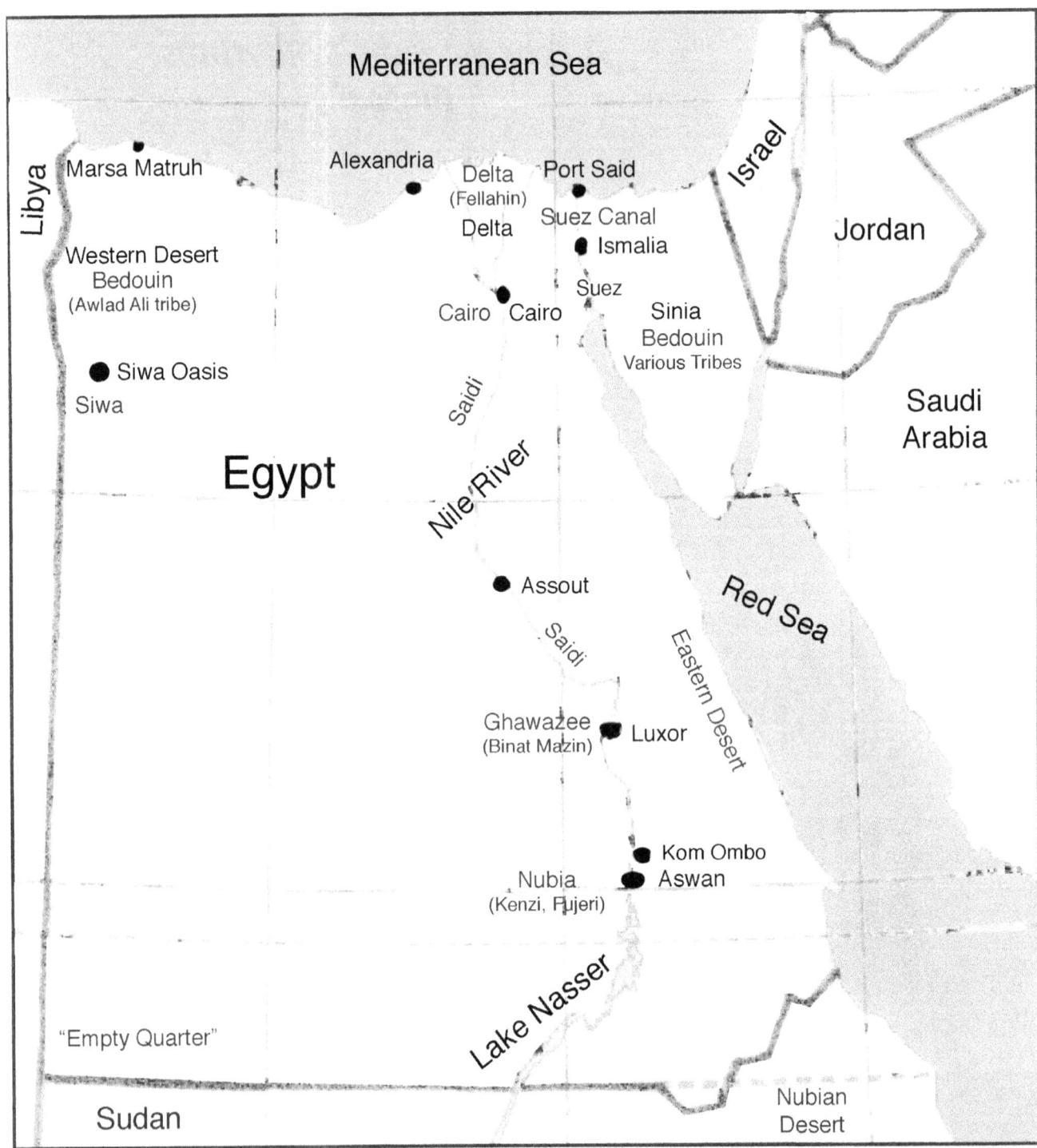

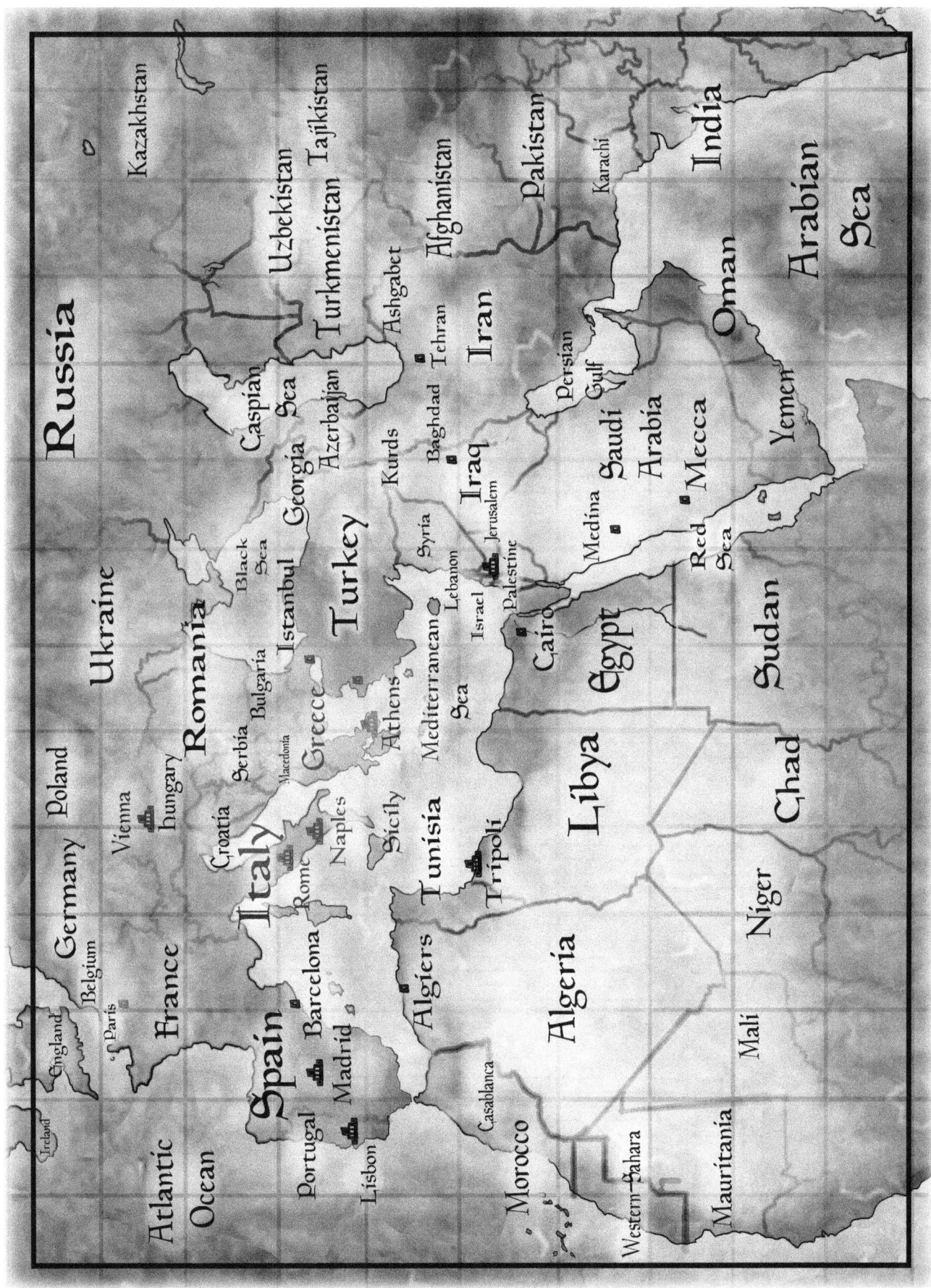

# A Few Belly Dance Rhythms

## Ayub

| 1 | & | 2 | & |
|---|---|---|---|
| D | ta | D | t |

## Beledi

| 1 | | 2 | | 3 | | 4 | |
|---|---|---|---|---|---|---|---|
| D | D | | tat | D | | | tat |

## Masmudi

| 1 | 2 | 3 | 4 | 5 | 6 | 7 | 8 |
|---|---|---|---|---|---|---|---|
| D | D | D | tat | D | tat | tat | tat |

## Cheftitelli

| 1 | 2 | 3 | 4 | 5 | 6 | 7 | 8 |
|---|---|---|---|---|---|---|---|
| D | tat | tat | tat | D | tat | tat | ( ) |

## Kashlima 9/8

| 1 | 2 | 3 | 4 | 5 | 6 | 7 | 8 | 9 |
|---|---|---|---|---|---|---|---|---|
| D | ta | D | ta | D | ta | D | t | t |

## References

Gilded Serpent has, at the core of it's mission, the goal of providing accurate information. To maintain the flow of the book, we've decided to keep the references with the essays and articles. If you are interested in further readings, references and bonus material, we encourage you to visit us on the web at www.gildedserpent.com.

## Bibliography Project

As part of our desire to share knowledge, we've begun building a bibliography to help researchers track down references and resources. This interdisciplinary reading list is presented in MLA format and we will be making regular additions as readers, editors and contributors send us submissions.

## Bonus material

Although we tried to include every submission, we reached practical limitations for the size of this publication. The editors have decided to include bonus features on our website so you can continue to further explore the themes in this belly dance reader.

## Disclaimers

Photographs throughout the book were submitted by the authors or were pulled from the Gilded Serpent Archive. For a complete list of photo credits see our Photo Credits page. URLs are current as of publication date.

## Errata

Errors and omissions will be corrected and adjusted on our website at
www.GildedSerpent.com/reader.

## GILDED SERPENT PRESENTS
# The Gig Form

Date: _____  Time: _____
Ocassion: ☐ birthday  ☐ surprise  ☐ holiday  ☐ anniversary
         ☐ other: _____
Contact person: _____  Phone #: _____
Get paid by: _____  Expect: ☐ check  ☐ cash
Deposit made: ☐ yes  ☐ no           Refered by: _____

**LOCATION:** _____
Directions:

**AUDIENCE:**
Size: # _____     Gender: ☐ mixed  ☐ male  ☐ female   Age: _____
Heritage: ☐ Arab  ☐ Greek  ☐ average American  ☐ Persian  ☐ Turkish
Honoree: _____

**PERFORMANCE AREA:**
Stage area raised? ☐ yes  ☐ no   Audience on: ☐ 1  ☐ 2  ☐ 3  ☐ all sides
☐ indoors  ☐ outdoors
Floor: ☐ wood  ☐ linoleum  ☐ carpet (secure? ☐ yes  ☐ no)
       ☐ concrete/brick  ☐ other: _____
Sound system: ☐ On premises  ☐ tape  ☐ CD   Bring portable? ☐ yes  ☐ no
Electrical outlet close? ☐ yes  ☐ no  ☐ bring cord

**THE DANCE:**
Style of dance: _____  Costume: _____
Specialties requested: ☐ snake  ☐ sword  ☐ cane
                      ☐ sultan  ☐ other: _____
Number of sets: _____  Length of set: _____
Other dancers: _____
Other performers (DJ, magician, etc): _____

**DRESSING AREA:**
☐ arrive dressed  ☐ mirror  ☐ light  ☐ lock on door

**QUOTED PRICE:** $ _____
**SEND PHOTO / BROCHURE TO:** _____

Debrief:
Client happy? ☐ Yes  ☐ No
Lessons learned:

---

**BRING**
snake-heating pad?
boom box
cord?
caftan
map
tapes
finger cymbals
costume/s
shoes
make-up
business cards
brochures
sword
sultan gear
greeting card
receipts
apprentice/assistant?

---

*Find this form online in our Bonus Features at www.gildedserpent.com/reader*

# A Glossary of Common Belly Dance Terms

This glossary includes definitions of all the significant terms found in this book, but includes also a few terms that you might encounter in your studies of belly dance. You may be aware that many of the Arabic terms have multiple spellings. Arabic is transliterated into English based on how the word sounds rather than on a letter-for-letter transcription. Because of that, there are multiple spellings for Arabic terms in English. For example, khaleegi can also be spelled khaliji; baladi might be found as beledi or beledy. In addition, the term "belly dance" can be found as a single word—"bellydance" and also capitalized—"Bellydance." Putting aside our personal choices, the contributors have tried to use consistent spellings throughout the text and in this glossary.

Definitions were contributed by many of the authors, though even there, many terms don't have agreed upon definitions. Even defining the subject of this book—belly dance—is fraught with historical and cultural debates. We have agreed upon these definitions, not because they are the objectively accurate but because they provide a common foundation from which to continue discussing these topics.

**American Tribal Style® (ATS®)** a modern American interpretation of traditional belly dancing in which two or more dancers improvise through the use of visual cues. Costume is brightly colored full skirt, pantaloons, coin bra, and layers of belts, scarves, coin belts, and an abundance of ethnic jewelry.

**Awalim** (alma, singular) Traditional female Middle Eastern entertainers who were often highly educated in the arts. They specialized in music, dance, and poetry and performed exclusively at women-only events for wealthy patrons.

**Awlad il-Balad** (ibn il-balad, singular, masculine) "Sons of the country." Concept of Egyptian identity characterized as savvy, good humored, hospitable, noble, honorable, resourceful, generous; can also imply lack of sophistication or conservative.

**Baladi** is an Arabic word that literally means "my country" or "of the country".

**Banat il-Balad** (bint il-balad, singular, feminine) "Daughters of the country." Concept of Egyptian identity characterized as honorable, modest, flirty, and tough. (They were frequently called "Awlad" because they were so admirable they were like sons rather than daughters.)

**Barbary Coast** Also called the Berber Coast, it originally referenced the Arabic nations on the Mediterranean and North African coasts who became infamous in the 17th century as a result of corsairs or pirates. Later, the name was given to the red-light district of old San Francisco created largely by the California Gold Rush.

**Bedlah** (Arabic word meaning "suit".) One way this term can be used is to refer to a particular type of costume for dance. The term can refer to either a two-piece costume consisting of a decorated bra top and belt with an attached skirt, or to an evening gown style of dress.

**Belly dance** (also bellydance) A dance form that originally developed in the Middle East, North Africa and Turkey. It includes a wide range of influences, among them, folkloric or regional dances. Primarily a woman's dance when performed in public for an audience, specialized versions of it are also danced by men. Today, belly dance may be performed as a solo improvisation or as a group choreography.

**Berber** Colonialist name derived from *"barbarian"*, considered a derogatory name by this group who prefer to be called *"Amazigh"*-singular or *"Imazighen"*-plural.

**Bouzouki** (also Bozuk) was originally a Turkish stringed instrument (with 3 pairs of strings – modern version has 4 pairs). It is in the same instrumental family as the Mandolin and the Lute. Originally the body was carved from a solid block of wood. It was introduced in Greece in the early 1910s.

**Burlesque** Nineteenth century American burlesque theater was derived from the British form which appealed to the working-class as it exaggerated and mocked respected and well-known high cultural forms in brief comic bits that relied on kitschy costumes, puns, double entendre, cross-dressing, and racial, gender, and ethnic stereotypes. Burlesque shows often included singing, juggling, comedy skits, acrobatics, dancing, and other performance art, and due to its liberal dose of sexual innuendo was considered a lower-class art directed towards male viewers. See Catherine Scheelar's article on Burlesque and Vaudeville.

**Cabaret** A European nightclub in which entertainment is offered accompanying a late-night supper. In Egypt, the term was used to refer to a type of entertainment experience geared solely to adults, at which alcohol would be served. When used to describe belly dance, it refers to a show or performance style dance suitable for use in nightclubs - similar to that introduced in Egypt by Badia Masabni in the 1930s, consisting of Turkish, Egyptian, and Lebanese dance steps and movements.

**Classical** A catch-all term used by dancers to indicate that the dance it describes is authentic, ethnic, and recognizable as belly dancing; it is usually accompanied by older, traditional North African and Middle Eastern music.

**Dalah** A particular attribute of Middle Eastern women, girls and little boys that shows naive. In dance its flirtatiousness is often employed to show that the dancer is cute and sweet, if also empty-headed. Men, young or old, are not accepted showing this quality.

**Danse du ventre** (French) a.k.a. "Dance of the stomach." A colonial French name for North African dancing; historically also known as Nautch, Contortion dance, Muscle dance, Oriental dance or "Dance of the Bee".

**Danse Orientale** See Oriental or Raks Sharqi.

**Debke** A spirited and intricate group or line dance popular in Lebanon and other Middle Eastern countries. Characterized by quick, rhythmical footwork, including hops, jumps, and especially, sharp stamping in unison.

**Deff drum** is a circular (sometimes decorated) frame drum with five sets of jingles similar to a Tambourine. Frame drums are among the most versatile and oldest drums. Other Middle Eastern frame drums, most without jingles, include: The Egyptian Rik, the middle eastern Tar, and Bendir.

**Dumbek** (also called Tabla) is an Arabic hand drum similar to the Darbukka. Usually made of clay, it may be made of various materials, including cast aluminum, hand hammered aluminum, and copper with hand-etched designs.

**Emad el Din Street** Cairo's theater and nightclub district.

**Fellah** Refers to people from the country or rural areas of Egypt, often farming along the Nile River. (**fellahin** - plural) (**Fellahi** - a negative term indicating some object that is considered gauche or too brightly colored, belonging to the colorful fellah.)

**Finger cymbals** Metal percussion instruments attached to the thumb and middle finger of each hand. Also called zhagat, sagat, or zills.

**Folklore dancing** A generic term for regional and folk steps taken from traditional folk dances, and often fused within belly dance show sets. A dance is said to be "folkloric" in belly dancing if it resembles or is reminiscent of some specific folk dance. See Saidi, Khaleegy, Ghawazi, Zikker and Zaar.

**Fusion** In belly dance, this term refers to blending various dance elements with unrelated movements, music, and costuming. Can also refer to incorporating belly dance movements with other dance forms such as Ballet, Hip-Hop, Sport-dance, or East Indian dance, or to blending different styles of belly dance, such as Cabaret and Beledi. See Shira's discussion of fusion in her article - Talking about Dance.

**Gallabiyya** A full length robe worn by men and women in Egypt and other Middle Eastern countries. See Shira's article on Ethnic Dresses.

**Ghawazi** (ghaziyeh, singular) A class of female singers and musicians in Egypt who performed for mixed audiences at public events as troupes and who were viewed as being lower class performers than the awalim. When modern western belly dancers perform in the Ghawazi style, they generally perform in groups. Few Ghawazi continue to perform today, with the notable exception of the Maazin family.

**Gothic Bellydance** A dramatic fusion form of belly dancing, merging the movement vocabulary and musicality of all styles of belly dance with the dark styles of the Goth subculture. The presentation of the performance is theatrical and often deals with macabre and mythic themes. Also known as "Raks Gothique" or "Dark Fusion."

**Hagallah** A celebratory folkloric dance performed in parts of Egypt and Libya. Usually involves a single female dancer and groups of men. It is a coquettish dance showing a dancer being "dalah", attracting and flirting with men who are courting her favor. The men vie for her favor as she plays between their affection. She displays her dowry by emphasizing or removing a piece of jewelry from her ensemble.

**Gypsy** Slang derived from "Egyptian", considered a derogatory name by this group of people, who prefer to be called "Rom". See Romany.

**Hafla** (Arabic word meaning "party".) Today this term has been modified by Western belly dancers to refer to a dance event that is generally less formal than a show in a theatre or stage setting, featuring student dancers.

**Harem** Women's and children's quarters in a palace or other large enclave.

**Haram** Arabic word meaning "sinful" or "forbidden".

**Kanoon** Arabic Kanoon (Kanoone, Kanoun or Qanun). The Kanoon or Kanoune, predecessor of the piano, is a stringed instrument that is popular in all parts of the Middle East. It's played flat on the knees or a stand and is plucked with finger picks made of metal. It has a shape similar to a harp.

**Khaleegy** (Arabic word meaning "gulf".) The term is often used to Indicate the region of the Arabian Gulf, including countries such as Saudi Arabia, Kuwait, and others, as well as cultural aspects (music, dance, etc.) of that region. Belly dancers often use the term "Khaleegy Dance" to refer to raqs al nashaat (also known as samri), which is a women's dance, but is actually only one of many dances from the region. Raqs al nashaat uses music with a specific 2/4 rhythmic pattern. The dance movements feature swaying, shoulder shimmies, head and hair tosses, and moving the hem of the thobe (an extremely long dance dress with big sleeves). Also spelled khaigi, khaligi.

**Khan El-Khalili** The tourist's shopping district in Cairo.

**Khawal** Egyptian male dancer.

**Levant** Ancient reference to regions in North Africa, the Mediterranean, and the Middle East. Obsolete except in archaeological and historical research.

**Maqam** A term in North African and Middle Eastern music that is somewhat related to scales. Each maqam has a mood or feeling associated with it. *See our Maqamat (pl) sheet included.*

**Middle East** (formerly called the "Near East") A vernacular reference with no agreed upon boundaries. Usually includes Iraq, Iran, the Arabian Peninsula, Israel, Pakistan, Afghanistan, Tajikistan, and other countries. It sometimes also includes about 20 other nations, including North African nations as well as Turkey and the Caucasus.

**Maghreb** (Arabic word meaning "west".) It is commonly used to refer to Northwest Africa along the Mediterranean coast, especially Morocco, Algeria, and Libya. Homelands of the Imazighen (formerly, Berber).

**Muhammad Ali Pasha** This former ruler of Egypt under the Ottoman empire is known to history as "the father of modern Egypt". He brought Egypt into the Industrial Revolution. In the late 1830's, he banished all female dancers from Cairo, sending them south to Upper Egypt where they found it very difficult to make a living. The ban ended in approximately 1860

**Muhammad Ali Street** Known as the "Street of Artists," this Cairo neighborhood is home to professional dancers, musicians, instrument makers, and costumers.

**North Africa** Home to the indigenous Berbers (who today call themselves Imazighen - plural or Amazigh - singular). Modern North African nations include Egypt, Tunisia, Morocco, Algeria, and Libya.

**Oriental Dance** Refers to a modern style of belly dance that developed during the "Golden Age" of Egyptian and Lebanese dance, around the 1940s, '50s, and '60s. In a 1966 interview, Badia Masabni said she created the Oriental dance we know today by combining traditional dance with influences from Turkish, Spanish, and Persian dance.

**Orientalism** The western tendency to treat aspects of north African and Middle Eastern life as being exotic, sensual, and "other". Also a movement in fine arts and literature that is characterized by eroticism and colonialist attitudes. See Brigid's article on Orientalism.

**Ouled Nail** (pronounced: wal'ed na'eel) A tribe of Algerian dancers.

**Oud** is a forerunner of the Lute family, without frets, and is the most important and popular of the Middle Eastern stringed instruments. Today, the Oud is known as Ut or Ud in Turkey, Laouta in Greece, Udi in Africa and Barbat in Iran. It has a large pot-bellied soundboard and a short neck - eleven strings are common, in five pairs with one single 'drone string' or 'bam teli'.

**Performative** A term initially coined by academics to suggest that we perform language on the basis of a specific cultural background. It has come to mean the way in which we express our identity including our ethnicity, gender, religious affiliations, or sexual preferences. In regards to belly dance, this means how a dancer expresses her social and cultural identity through his or her dance. The term has also come to mean the way we express our identity in general.

In regard to belly dance, one could suggest that an individual dancer is performing her social and cultural identity through how she improvises.

**Raqs** (Arabic word meaning "dance"). Also spelled "raks." See also raqs al assaya, raqs beledi, raqs shaabi, raqs sharqi.

**Raqs al Assaya** A folkloric style of women's dance from Egypt that is performed to Saidi music, with Saidi movements, using a stick or cane as a prop. It is thought to have been influenced by the "*tahtib*" or martial arts stick. See also tahtib.

**Raqs Beladi** (Arabic term meaning "country dance") The traditional folk dance and core rhythm of Egypt, Lebanon, Syria, and other cultures of the region. Egyptian beladi dances are typically non-narrative, solo improvisations performed by women.

**Raqs Shaabi** (Arabic term meaning "dance of the people")

A style of music and dance from the streets of Cairo and other urban centers in Egypt and other parts of North Africa and the Middle East. Characterized by fun, lively, lyrics and movements.

**Raqs Sharqi** (Arabic term meaning "Eastern dance"). An urban elaboration of beladi, often referred to as dance of the cabaret, Oriental dance or traditional solo dance. Traditionally performed as a solo, improvised dance, raqs sharqi now often includes choreography or group performances. The costume is typically a long fitted dress or skirt and bra and a belt heavily embroidered with sequins and beads. See also Cabaret, Oriental, and Belly dance.

**Rebab or Rabab** (Spike Fiddle, also Kemenche) is a bowed string instrument that is part of the Lute family, and has 2 or 3 strings typically. It is considered the earliest ancestor of the violin. There are two basic types of Rebab: Wooden fiddles with pear-shaped bodies, and spiked fiddles, named for the spike on the bottom of the instrument on which it stands while being played. Spiked Rebabs typically have no frets, but instead, the fingers of the musician's left hand become movable bridges

**Romany** A population of people who trace their ancestry back to the Punjabi region in India and who migrated through and settled in parts of the Middle East, North Africa, western Asia, Europe, and the Americas. Still also known by local and tribal names such as "travellers" in England and "Gitano" in Spain. "Gypsy" is now considered derogatory though it is still used in popular Western culture. See also Gypsy.

**Saz** is a stringed instrument that is a member of the long necked Lute family. The Saz is the most important instrument of the Turkish folk genre. Its general shape is similar to the Bouzouki Oud. The traditional method of playing the Saz is to pluck with the fingers of the right hand or a plectrum and note the strings (typically 7 divided into courses of two, two and three) with the fingers of the left hand.

**Shamadan** A candelabrum fitted to the dancer's head. Dancers sometimes perform with a lighted shamadan balanced on the head, particularly during the *zeffah* or wedding dance.

**Saidi** The Said is a region of upper Egypt. People from the Said are referred to as "Saidi," which can also be a derogatory term for someone from the country. In belly dance, it refers to a regional or folkloric dance style with traditional steps. It is often performed to a 4/4 rhythmic pattern in music that features the mizmar, mizwij, (wind instruments) and rhababa.

**Steampunk Bellydance** Steampunk began as a science fiction literary genre in the 1980s and has developed into its own subculture with unique costuming, role-playing, and art. When it is blended with belly dance, the result is a fusion performance dance that has deep roots in story-telling with a powerful aesthetic rooted in both the Steampunk subculture and belly dance. See also Fusion and Belly dance.

**Tahtib** A men's martial art that utilizes a large staff or stick. This martial art serves as the inspiration for a men's dance based on its movement vocabulary. The movements tend to be powerful and athletic, alternating strikes and blocks.

**Takht** (alternatively spelled **Takhat**) is the representative musical ensemble, the orchestra, of Middle Eastern music. In Egypt, Syria, Lebanon, Palestine, and Jordan, the ensemble consists of the *oud*, the *qanun*, the *kamanjah* (or now alternatively *violin*), the *ney*, the *riq*, and the *darabukkah*. The word *takht* means "bed", "seat", or "podium" in Arabic.

**Taqsim** Also "taqseem", "taxeem", "taxim". In belly dance, traditionally referred to as a style of performance in which the musician improvises and the dancer follows the musician. Dancers often incorrectly use the term to refer to a technique of belly dance that allows the dancer to express the content of the musical taqsim, emphasizing improvisation and emotional expressiveness, often with isolations and little or no traveling movements.

**Tribal** An adjective and a shortened way of referring to American Tribal Style Belly dance that developed around the 1980s. The adjective is used to describe a faux-country fusion fantasy in both movements and costuming. The effect is reminiscent and perhaps a derivation of Orientalist visions in the graphic fine arts. See also ATS®.

**Tribal Fusion** inspired by ATS®, these forms also draw from techno music and current day Goth culture. Costume follows ATS® but is usually either black or antique brown. See ATS®.

**Vaudeville** was a British and North American stage performance genre consisting of a variety of popular entertainment acts, mostly farcical, meant to appeal to a general audience from about 1880 until the 1930s. Compared to lower-class burlesque theater, vaudeville tended to offer a "cleaner" show without sexual innuendo and was therefore considered more suitable for middle-class family audiences. However, many performers played both the burlesque and the vaudeville circuit.

**Zaar** (also spelled zar) the *zar* is performed to placate possession spirits. Participants dance themselves into a trance to communicate with a blood-loving sub-species of jinn called the *Zar*. *Zar* is also the name given to the trance inducing movements performed during the ritual. These movements, particularly the wild head tossing, are what belly dancers find so fascinating about this possession cult ceremony. For more information see Yasmin's article on the zaar.

**Zeffah** Wedding procession generally led by a belly dancer wearing a shamadan or by children carrying large candles. See also shamadan. See Sahra and Leila's articles on weddings.

**Zhagareet** Middle Eastern ululation.

**Zhagat, Sagat, Zills** A set of four metal cymbals worn on the thumb and middle finger of both hands. Often played by belly dancers while they are dancing, and also played as part of a band in the percussion section. See finger cymbals. (Note: zhagat and Sagat are both plural as the set contains four objects.) Zills is short for a brand-name of cymbal much sought after: Zildjian.

# Contributors

### Alia Thabit
An Arab-American and a Vermont Juried Artist, Alia draws from four decades of technique, history, regional and folkloric styles, props, theatre, fusion, costuming, music, choreography, improvisation, and performance. She specializes in solo and group performance, improvisation, and choreography, developed with collaborative, narrative, symbolic, and movement-based structures. Alia has danced on three continents, in six countries, and fifteen states; she champions creativity and self-expression grounded in tradition, uniting dancers, musicians, and audience in a radiant oasis of warmth and delight.

*www.earth-goddess.com*

### Alisha
Alisha Westerfeld is a Bay Area dance artist who has a passion for photography. She was one of the founding members of the Bay Area chapter of MECDA and was instrumental in growing the organization and supporting the greater belly dance community through outreach and event planning. She is currently working on a book entitled "The Cloth of Egypt: All About Assiut" as the principle photographer. For more information about her dance and photographic arts, you can find her on Face Book -

*www.facebook.com/pages/Zemira/118582709029*

### Amera Eid
Amera Eid is a well known Australian belly dancer of Egyptian and European background, beginning her professional training in Sydney in 1983, working the restaurant and Arabic nightclub circuit. In 1990, Amera began her rise to fame, performing continuous year round contracts throughout the Middle East. Amera returned to Australia after reaching international stardom, continuing as a professional belly dancer. She recently retired from the dancing circuit and teaches and hosts international workshops and produces Belly Dance albums. Amera is the founder and owner of Australian belly dance Boutique and school, Amera's Palace, where she hosted The Farha Tour to Australia in 2008 among others.

*www.ameraspalace.com.au*

### Andrea Deagon

Andrea Deagon began teaching and performing belly dance in 1975. After receiving her Ph.D. in Classical Studies from Duke University in 1984, she taught at Victoria University of Wellington, New Zealand, where she continued teaching and performing, and finally settled in Wilmington, NC where she directs the Classical Studies program and teaches in the Women's Studies programs. She has published widely on the Western reception of belly dance in both dancer-oriented and academic journals.

She is currently at work on a book, Belly Dance: An Intimate History, the lively tale of belly dance across the ages, revealed through the lives and words of the dancers, audiences, lovers, aficionados, entrepreneurs, and adventurers who lived it.

*www.people.uncw.edu/deagona/raqs/aboutme.htm*

### Anthea Poole

Anthea "Kawakib" shares her passion for belly dance through teaching, writing, and performing with her PRISM Dancers. She teaches both classic belly dance, and synchronized group improvisation. She's honed her teaching methodology in the classroom since 1988; and was also a professional belly dancer in Washington DC's top Middle Eastern venues for twenty years. Besides writing, Anthea has produced instructional videos breaking down the complexities of dance into simple patterns and concepts; tools students can use in their dance journey whether their interest is choreography or freestyle. Her finger cymbal videos are among the most popular on YouTube.

*www.kawakib.com*

### April Rose

An educated and traveled belly dancer of 13 years, April Rose tours globally with Bellydance Superstars and is a former member of UNMATA. April Rose holds a Masters degree in Culture and Performance from UCLA's World Arts & Cultures & Dance Department, where she also holds a BA in Dance. Her research explores the transnational history of belly dance since the mid-19th century and the many incarnations of belly dance practice in the post-1960's US. She is particularly interested in Improvisational Tribal Style belly dance and it's potential for thoughtful self-expression, community formation, and challenge of social convention.

*www.aprilrosedance.com*

\* Photographs throughout the book were submitted by the authors or were pulled from the GildedSerpent Archive. For a complete list please see the following photo credits section.

### Athena Nile

Athena has loved belly dance since childhood. Raised in a primarily Lebanese neighborhood, she began to learn how to dance from childhood. In 2005, her mother began to take formal belly dance classes. After a lot of cajoling from Athena, she was allowed to take belly dance classes with her mother at 15. Soon after that, the two began to perform together. To this day, her mother is one of her biggest supporters. Athena loves working on her mountain of belly dance costume projects, performing throughout the US, and is 4 classes away from a Business Administration degree.

*www.athenanile.com*

### Azura

Azura dances, writes, sings, and teaches belly dance workshops and classes. When she's not doing that, she's organizing events and helping community-based groups at the local, provincial and national levels. Azura has performed in Egypt, Seattle, and Canadian communities between the western prairie and the eastern seaboard. Her performances feature rippling veils, dynamic level changes, and audience interaction, and her workshops focus on good technique and musical interpretation. Azura has been a featured artist at dance festivals, served the dance community as the president of the Regina Association of Middle Eastern Dance, and contributes to belly dance journals.

*www.azura-bellydance.com*

### Barbara Grant

Barbara Grant was born in Los Angeles and grew up in Northridge, California. Her performing arts background includes training in acting and Middle Eastern dance. She received an M. S. degree from the College of Optical Sciences at the University of Arizona, and published two books as author or co-author in her professional field of optical radiant energy. She performed Middle Eastern dance in the San Francisco Bay Area, Tucson, Arizona, and Athens, Greece. She taught classes in the Bay Area and in Tucson, where she formed the "Wings of the Desert" dance troupe at Davis-Monthan Air Force Base.

### Barbara Sellers-Young

Barbara Sellers-Young was appointed Dean of the Faculty of Fine Arts and a Professor in the Dance Department at York University in July 2008. Prior to that, she was a professor at the University of California, Davis where she served as Chair of the Department of Theatre and Dance and as executive director of the Robert and Margit Mondavi Center for the Performing Arts. She is an interdisciplinary scholar with an international research profile in the fields of dance, theatre and performance. Her interest in all forms of art and diverse performance styles informs her research on the moving body and globalization, which has taken her to Sudan, Egypt, Nepal, Japan, China, England and Australia.

*www.yorku.ca/finearts/faculty/profs/sellers-young.htm*

### Beatrice Parvin

Beatrice Parvin grew up in Oxford, England where she first wrote poetry on her bedroom wall. She first studied acting then received her BA in English and History of Art at Goldsmiths College, London. She discovered Arabic dance and trained in the Maghreb style with Amel Tafsout, who continues to be an inspiration. For the last 15 years she has performed and taught at numerous events and festivals, mostly with Balkan maestros, 'Mukka' – including the Queen's Golden Jubilee Celebrations at Buckingham Palace gardens. Her style is mixing the movements of the Maghreb with Turkish, Bulgarian and Romanian Gypsy traditions. She is currently on the MFA Creative Writing program at Kingston University.

### Brad Dosland

Brad has produced and co-produced major events, including Unmata's Blood Moon Regale, the San Francisco Mecca Revue, the national Spark Tour (featuring Urban Tribal and Ultra Gypsy), Tribal Throwdown, the uniquely Unmata Rodeo, the Undulation shows, Nouveau Nights, and Kosmos music and dance camp. Brad has worked with artists including Rachel Brice, Ansuya, Heather Stants, Amy Sigil, Zoe Jakes, Ariellah, Kami Liddle, Aradia, Jill Parker, Cera Byer and more on original photography and design. But most know his work photographing performances such as Tribal Fest, Shadowdance, Tribal Massive, Las Vegas Bellydance Intensive and countless sets at after parties and more intimate venues.

*www.taboomedia.com*

### Brigid Kelly

Brigid Kelly ~ Zumarrad is based in Christchurch, New Zealand. She started studying Middle Eastern dance in 1998 with oriental dancer Gendi Tanner and continues to perform, teach and research. Brigid graduated with a MA (Distinction) in Cultural Studies from the University of Canterbury in 2008, having completed New Zealand's first masters-level academic inquiry into belly dancing – Belly dancing in New Zealand: Identity, hybridity, transculture - under the supervision of Rosemary Du Plessis and Dr Nabila Jaber. Her thesis concentrated on how belly dancing intersects with concepts of a New Zealand identity. By night Brigid works as a subeditor.

*www.zumarrad.co.nz*

### Carl Sermon

Carl Sermon is the premier photographer to the San Francisco Bay Area Middle Eastern Dance community. He has over 30 years of performance photography experience, knowledge of the music and the dance form, and the expertise to anticipate the best moment to photograph the most favorable image of the dancer. "I look for that special sparkle of personality that twinkles in their eyes, the subtle smile of satisfaction and happiness, and that look of pure joy from feeling they are performing to their utmost. I look for veils and skirts floating about the performer framing them in rich color and texture. I look for the mystery and drama created in the moment and conveyed to the audience in a flash."

*www.ReelSoundandLight.com*

### Catherine Barros

Catherine lives in Dallas, Texas and has been studying Middle Eastern dance for over 20 years. Her latest effort to further her understanding of Middle Eastern music involves taking doumbek classes and the accordion. Catherine is teaching on a private and semi-private basis.

*www.catherinebarros.us*

## Catherine Scheelar

Catherine Mary Scheelar is a social science researcher out of Edmonton, Alberta, Canada. While particularly drawn to Tribal Fusion and its various manifestations, she also partakes in various Cabaret/Raqs styles as well as folkloric dances and has studied Arabic music through tabla, sagat, vocals, and dance with the University of Alberta's Middle Eastern and North African Music Ensemble (MENAME). Her contribution to this volume was adapted from her Master of Arts thesis in Cultural Anthropology entitled "The Use of Nostalgia in Genre Formation in Tribal Fusion Dance", which focuses on the proliferation of the Victorian/Vintage/Vaudevillian Aesthetic in modern Tribal Fusion.

## DaVid of Scandinavia

Known for his precise technique, delicacy in artistry and expressive range along with his refined musical sense; DaVid of Scandinavia is an internationally touring Middle Eastern and Indian dance artist, choreographer and dance coach based in San Diego, California and Oslo, Norway. He is the artistic director of the Ethnic Dance Academy. He has worked with high profile artists and dance companies along with coaching several dancers for competitions. He is featured on several internationally distributed DVDs. DaVid has authored 3 publications on the subject of Middle Eastern Dance and his articles have been featured in international dance magazines and webzines.

*www.davidofscandinavia.com*

## Dawn Devine ~ Davina

Dawn Devine aka Davina has degrees in Fashion Design (Mesa College), Visual Arts and Theater (UCSD). While in graduate school at UC Davis, Dawn realized that she could marry her passion for costume history, design and her love of dance and started her line of DIY costuming books. Her first, Costuming From the Hip, has sold 90,000+ copies since 1997. In 2011, Davina restructured her business, reformatted her books and began work on the upcoming publication on her passion, assiut. You can learn more about this book, The Cloth of Egypt: All About Assiut on her blog or Costumer's Notes bimonthly newsletter.

*www.davina.us*

### Denise of Pangia
Pangia plays exciting and dynamic arrangements of Egyptian, Armenian, Greek, Lebanese, Turkish and Persian dance classics as well as a varying array of original compositions. Very popular with Belly Dancers and Musicians alike, Pangia's music is sold world wide with 6 CDs and MP3s available. Be on the lookout for more from this diverse and popular band.

*www.pangiaraks.com*

### Dondi Dahlin
Dondi grew up in the world of healing, dance, and drama and has performed in over 20 countries. She has performed in the Middle East, India, Africa, South Pacific, Mexico, Spain, Greece and Europe and is a member of the Screen Actors Guild. She was chosen as the exclusive dancer for Omar Sharif on his 60th birthday, has won many dance titles and was an original member of The Belly Dance Superstars. Dondi still takes occasional contracts overseas and teaches at OMEGA. But, she now travels the world with her mom, renowned healer, Donna Eden. In 2009 she became a mama to the greatest project of her life, Tiernan Ray.

*www.DondiBellyDancer.com*

### Elianae
Elianae has studied ballet, jazz and Modern Dance since she was young. She was in the Pre-Professional Program at BalletMet (Columbus, Ohio) and performed in various professional productions, including the "Nutcracker". She majored in dance at Jacksonville University, earning scholarships and awards. She went on in 2004 to study the Art of Oriental Dance at Habeeba's Dance of the Arts in Columbus, Ohio. She is currently an Instructor there, and performs regularly with the Troupe, as a soloist, and in her student productions. She placed first in the Rising Star Category in the Personal Best Middle Eastern Dance Competition, and won Audience Choice Award in the "Let's Beat Cancer By Dancing!" benefit competition in Chicago.

*www.habeebas.com*

## Iana

Iana has been practicing belly dance since 2004. During 2007-2009 she performed with "Ishtar Dance Co" (Ukraine), and also choreographed for their main shows. In 2009 Iana won a belly dance championship "Bastet" in Ukraine (category "youth"). Also, she has attended numerous international dance festivals, including "Nile Group" (Egypt, 2010), "Turkish Delight Festival" (Turkey, 2011) and others. At the end of 2011 Iana moved to Canada and joined Arabesque Dance Co and Orchestra for the next year. At IBCC 2012 she both presented a lecture "The historical connections between Belly Dance and Ballet", and first performed a piece with Triple Isis Wings.

*www.ianadance.com*

## Izzah

Izzah lives in Canada. As well as being a psychologist, she has been studying Middle Eastern dance since 2003. Izzah became deeply involved in her belly dance community, organizing events and workshops, creating isis wings, and writing articles relating psychology to Middle Eastern dancing. Since 2009, Izzah started giving conferences on body language and the oriental dancer. She considers herself as a student who teaches, and a teacher who will never stop learning. She can't wait to connect with you and help you on your journey of discovering the belly dancer you were born to be!

*www.izzah.ca*

## Jalilah Lorraine Chamas

Jalilah (Lorraine Zamora Chamas) has danced and traveled through various Middle Eastern and North African countries, particularly Egypt. She toured Europe regularly with the "Musicians of the Nile" from 1990-1996. Through this experience, she was able to meet and spend time with some of the few remaining Ghawazee in order to learn about them and their dance. Her extensive experience in working with a variety of musicians and performing with live music enabled Jalilah to produce a series of six CDs of belly dance music entitled Jalilah's Raks Sharki.

*www.piranha.de/jalilah*

### Jezibell

Jezibell studied belly dance in Manhattan, New York with Serena, Elena, Anahid Sofian, Gamila el-Masri, Jehan, and others. She began teaching at Serena Studios in 1996. Her NYC credits include Lincoln Center Out-of-Doors, the Knitting Factory, Theatre for the New City, Taj Lounge and the New York Renaissance Faire. She has performed with the Egyptian/American Folkloric Group, the Serena Dance Theatre, Gamila el-Masri's Nileside Dancers, and PURE, and was a staff writer for Bennu Magazine. She moved to Augusta, Georgia in December 2007. She performs locally as a soloist, performing traditional and alternative dance, and directs Eastern Star Dance Theatre.

### Jillina

A Master Dancer, Instructor & Choreographer, Jillina has devoted her life to dance. In 1999 she founded The Sahlala Dance Company and served as Artistic Director and Main Choreographer for the Bellydance Superstars from 2003-09. In 2009 and 2010, Jillina was the first American to be a featured performer in the prestigious Closing Gala at Ahlan Wa Sahlan in Egypt. In the spring of 2009 she created Bellydance Evolution, a revolutionary full-production theatrical show with a storyline, which has toured in over a dozen countries. She owns Evolution Dance Studios in Universal City, California, USA. The studio provides rehearsal space to Hollywood's top artists and serves as a focal point for the Los Angeles Dance Community.

*www.jillina.com*

### Karen Proehl

Munira (Karen Proehl) has been dancing since the mid-1990's. Munira fell in love with cabaret style belly dance and has performed at many different venues. A student of Lynette's of Snake's Kin Studios, she helps out at GildedSerpent.com and various projects associated with Gilded Serpent. She is also studying the doumbek with Mary Ellen Donald, performing at various venues.

*www.gildedserpent.com/aboutuspages/karenproehl.htm*

## Lauren Michelle Boldt

Lauren Boldt holds a Bachelors degree in Percussion from Boston's world renowned Berklee College of Music, this combined with her extensive dance training make her an innovative performer and effective teacher. In 2006 Lauren moved to Los Angeles to train and perform with Jillina's Sahlala Dance company. From 2008-2012 she toured with the "Bellydance Superstars" and has appeared in many of their videos including: "Bombay Bellywood: BDSS live from Los Angeles". She is currently a part of the production team and cast of Bellydance Evolution and is excited to share her artistic passion and vision with this revolutionary new project.

www.laurenbellydance.com

## Leela Corman

Leela is an illustrator, belly dancer, and cartoonist, most recently author of the graphic novel Unterzakhn, published by Schocken-Pantheon. Originally from New York City, Leela now resides in Gainesville, FL, where she teaches both illustration and belly dance, and performs with Al Amoura Dance Company.

www.leelacorman.com

## Leila Farid

Leila is an American born dancer and rising star of the Egyptian dance scene. She is a sought after performer for weddings, parties and the nightclubs of Cairo's five star hotels, having collaborated with many superstar singers. Leila is a recognizable face from being featured on the covers of every major Egyptian fashion magazine to being on Arabic television, and acting in commercials. She recently made her cinema debut, acting and dancing in the blockbuster "Abu Araby Wasal." Leila has produced an oriental dance CD, "Helwa", and a video, "Bint al Balad", of her Cairo show. She teaches in Cairo with the Nile Group Festival and travels to perform and teach workshops abroad.

www.leilainegypt.com

### Leyla Lanty

Leyla has studied with both Arab and American dance masters in the USA and Egypt, where she travels often, to study with Raqia Hassan and others. Leyla is known for Egyptian style dancing and finger cymbal playing, which she teaches in the San Francisco Bay area. From 2006-2009, she taught cymbals at Ahlan Wa Sahlan in Cairo, Egypt. She has created a DVD "Habibi, You Are My... WHAT?! Leyla Lanty's Essential Arabic for Dancers", teaching Arabic words, phrases, gestures to help dancers interpret Arabic songs. She has also produced and recorded a music CD in Egypt, "Golden Days Enchanting Nights".

*www.leylalanty.com*

### Mahsati Janan

Mahsati Janan is an instructor, performer, choreographer, and workshop instructor in Asheville, NC. She began her journey in belly dance in 1996 and has studied and performed throughout the US. She specializes in Egyptian styles, but also enjoys many belly dance forms. She is available to teach workshops, private, or group classes in Classical Egyptian, Middle Eastern Folkloric, Turkish, Lebanese and techniques that are common to all styles. Her instructional DVDs, "Fabulous Fan VeilZZ I & II" and "Foundations of Raqs Sharqi Level 1", continue to be valuable resources for dancers around the world. Mahsati currently directs the Qamari Dance Collective and troupe Banat al-Qamar.

*www.mahsati-janan.com*

### Martha E Duran

Since age two, Martha attended MGM Dance studios in California directed by Marion G. Martha. In California at locally based dance schools in the 1980s and 90s she studied acting, ballet, jazz, tap and oriental dance classes. For the last 14 years Martha has been the director of her own school Danceme Academy in the city of Mexicali, Baja California. She was the first teacher to introduce belly dance seventeen years ago to her city. Martha received her masters degree in Communications in 2002, a degree in Arts and Education in 2004 and in 2010 a degree in Oriental Dance Education.

*www.danceme.20m.com*

## Mayada

Mayada (Meagan Hesham) is a belly dance instructor, performer, and writer based in Toronto, Canada with a background in fitness and personal training. She has taught belly dance classes across Toronto at various venues including Arabesque Academy, the Royal Ontario Museum, and Ryerson University, and opened her own studio, Fierce Fitness, in 2003. Mayada has performed with Arabesque Dance Company and Arabic restaurants, clubs, and special events. She currently hosts Bellydance Talk Radio, an online belly dance radio show that features interviews with stars, reviews, etc

*www.mayada.ca*

## Michael Baxter

Michael Baxter has been working with computers since he was nine, imprinted by a July 4, 1969 viewing of "2001: A Space Odyssey." He's also an experienced photographer who uses GNU/Linux for photo processing. Michael was more recently imprinted by the "Belly Dance Vortex," this time apparently on July 4, 2004 when he met Michelle Joyce in the photo studio. Since then he's met many new wonderful friends in the dance community and has taken over 80,000 studio and festival belly dance photographs.

*www.tribes.tribe.net/michaelbaxter*

## Najia Marlyz

Najia Marlyz performed, taught, wrote, coached, and traveled in the Middle East during her career spanning 45 years, beginning in 1970. Partnering with mentor, Bert Balladine, they taught in her California studio, "The Dancing Girl" (later, "Bellydance Arts") '73-'81. Masterclass instructor in the '80s through '00s, she is recognized for contributions to artistic dance concepts: dramatic improvisation, seamless movement, and inventive technique for coaching pros, based on imaginative musical analysis. During the 2000 decade and beyond, located in the SF East Bay Area, Najia has mentored—coaching performers in theatrical presentation. Najia maintains an enduring interest in dance journalism and related subjects; nearly one hundred articles are listed on Gilded Serpent.

*www.gildedserpent.com/najia.*

### Nancy Hernandez

Nancy Hernandez has devoted her life to her passion for ethnic jewelry, clothing, textiles and fabrics. Her company, Ojala, specializes in antiques from along the silk road, all one-of-a-kind and handmade by tribal people. She's also a collector and trader of rare and exotic books. Her extensive knowledge has led her to lecture on these topics in museums, schools and at dance events throughout Northern California. You can find Ojala each month at the Alameda Point Antiques Faire, each year at Rakkasah West, and Tribal Fest among others. For more information, contact Nancy via email:

*nan41herdez@sbcglobal.net*

### Pixie Vision

Pixie is a movement arts photographer based in Los Angeles. She has captured the essence of over 9,000 belly dancers in the past 10 years & been featured world-wide in various international publications.

*www.pixievision.com*

### Princess Farhana

Internationally acclaimed Princess Farhana has performed, taught and written about Oriental Dance since 1990. She has appeared in China, Egypt, across Europe and the United Kingdom, and throughout North America. An artistic chameleon and boundary-pushing pioneer, she performs many styles of dance, from traditional to contemporary. Trained in Egyptian style by Zahra Zuhair and Raqia Hassan among others, the Princess is known as a theatrical fusion performer, conceiving and executing fantasy tableaux in detail, dramatically recreating vintage styles of Oriental Dance from the Edwardian Era, the 1920's, and The Egyptian Golden Age.

*www.princessfarhana.com*

### Renée Rothman

Renée Rothman, PhD, a former modern dancer and aikidoka, began studying the art and history of belly dance in 2001. As a scholar, she taught anthropology of dance courses at San Jose State and the University of California, Santa Cruz. She currently maintains a blog 'dancedocsthinktank.wordpress.com' where she continues her ethnographic interests, providing readers with a new perspective on the pan-human activity of dance. She has published in Dance Research Journal, Journal of American Folklore, Zaghareet, The Belly Dance Chronicle, 'Fuse', and online magazines Journal of Folklore Research, Gilded Serpent, and Dance Advantage.

*www.dancedocsthinktank.wordpress.com*

### Sahra Kent

Sahra is a dancer, teacher and Dance Ethnologist. Sahra performs Orientale and Egyptian Folkloric worldwide and has taught Egyptian style Orientale and Folkloric dance on five continents. As a Dance Ethnologist, she has University degrees in Dance Ethnology (Master of Arts UCLA), Cultural Anthropology and Archeology (Bachelor UCSB), and Dance (Associate of Arts Palomar College). After living, researching and performing in Cairo for 6 years from 1989-1995 (with over 1600 shows) she returns to research in Egypt annually. Sahra developed and directs "JtE" series, "Journey through Egypt", applying Dance Ethnology concepts to a systematic overview of the Dance Zones of Egypt.

*www.SahraSaeeda.com*

### Samira Shuruk

As a full time dance performer and instructor, Samira has performed over 3,000 full shows including for royalty, diplomats, HBO events, international concerts, Turkish and Egyptian embassy events, museums, universities and more. Her depth of experience with the business and with cultures native to the dance provide her with first hand knowledge that she shares through mentoring, teaching and coaching beginners through professionals. She is a sought after performer, teacher and competition judge throughout the US. 2012 will bring Samira's first Pilates audio release and RaqFit DVD, which combines belly dance and Bollywood in fitness format.

*www.samirashuruk.com*

### Shelley Muzzy

Yasmela-Shelley Muzzy, began dancing in 1972 as a student of Jamila Salimpour and founded the Bou-Saada Dance Troupe in 1974. She was a staff writer for the original Habibi Magazine and a contributor to Arabesque Dance Magazine through the 1970's and '80's. Yasmela is an editor and advisor for the Gilded Serpent, and is currently working on a book about the Bou-Saada Dance Troupe, and a novel about San Francisco's Summer of Love. She holds a BA in History and Research with a concentration on the Middle East and North Africa from Fairhaven College/Western Washington University.

### Sierra Suraci

Sierra began her dance career in 1972 in the San Francisco Bay Area. Sierra (known professionally as Sadira), danced for many years with snakes; as well as dancing professionally in many popular clubs and restaurants. She is known for her knowledge in ethno regional dance from Egypt, North Africa, and the Pan-Arabic world. She has taught and lectured throughout California and the Pacific Northwest. Sierra directed her own dance troupe, Raks As Saidi, for 15 years with emphasis on traditional dances. She has been to Egypt to study the culture of Upper Egypt, Egyptology and the Mystery schools.

### Stasha

Stasha has been joyfully performing and teaching Middle Eastern Dance and costuming for more than thirty-five years. From Folkloric to Contemporary, solo or in a top notch dance team, she's performed continuously (over fourteen thousand shows!) across America, in Europe, North Africa, the Middle East - even on the Silver Screen. With a background in Cultural Anthropology, Stasha calls her style Shamanic: Inviting and holding the space for oneness of community. In her internationally popular manuals "Adventures in Belly Dance Costuming", she simply and clearly explains how to create "perfect fit" costuming; comfortable, adjustable, gorgeous costumes made by you!

*www.stashamania.com*

## Venus

Venus (Marilee Nugent) began belly dancing in 1981 and ran Venus Belly Dance full time, performing, teaching and event hosting for 20+ years in British Columbia. In 2008 Venus hosted the 20-episode TV series "Bellydance Workout With Venus". Venus has a BA in Art & Culture Studies and a BSc in Kinesiology. Currently a PhD candidate at McGill University, she uses belly dance to study voluntary control of complex spine movements. She has presented her research at both science and belly dance conferences. Venus has published cultural articles in Habibi Magazine and published her first science article in 2012 in the Journal of Electromyography and Kinesiology.

*www.venusbellydance.com*

## Yasmin Henkesh

Yasmin Henkesh, a professional belly dancer with forty years experience, has worked in Europe and Egypt alongside Arabic superstars Sabah, Walid Toufiq, Ahmed Adawia, Mohammed El Aizabi and Hassan Abou Saoud. She has a Masters degree in Arabic from the American University of Cairo and has been studying Egyptian sacred dance since 1981. Founder of Sands of Time Music, her first album, Zar – Trance Dancing for Women, is to date the only authentic compilation of Egyptian zar music on the market. Her first book, Trance Dancing with the Jinn, will be released by Llewellyn Worldwide in 2014.

*www.serpentine.org*

## Yasmina Ramzy

A highly acclaimed choreographer, Yasmina Ramzy is the founder and artistic director of Arabesque Dance Company & Orchestra, Arabesque Academy and the International Bellydance Conference of Canada. She received her training from leading masters in Egypt and Syria including Aida Nour of the Reda Troupe and Mohamed Khalil of the National Folklore Troupe of Egypt. Since 1981, she has performed throughout the Middle East, often for royalty and heads of state and taught in 60 cities on 5 continents. Her creative, unique choreography has been commissioned internationally by many including the Bellydance Superstars. Yasmina has produced many instructional and performance DVDs and music CDs that sell worldwide.

*www.yasminaramzy.com*

## Photo & Art Credits

Alisha Westerfeld ........................ 139-141, 260, 272
Amera Eid Archives ............................................ 260
Andras Meszaros ................................................ 100
Antoinette Khoury Archives ................................ 61
Asmahan Archives .............................................. 147
Avi Ohana ............................................................. 64
Barbara Grant Archives ..................................... 262
Barry Brown ........................................................ 149
Beatrice Parvin Archives .................................... 263
Ben Checkowy .................................................... 262
Bob Giles ............................... 57, 107, 154, 231, 268
Brad Dosland of Taboo Media .. 32, 35, 57, 151, 183, 189, 207
Carl Sermon ................... 34, 43, 68, 113, 114, 264, 270
Catherine Barros .......................................... 157, 264
Catherine Scheeler ............................................... 95
Catherine Yavorsky ............................................ 266
Cindy Martin ....................................................... 261
Dan Stone of Stone House Images .............. 44, 45
Dancers Eye ........................................................ 266
David Goodyear .................................................... 31
Dav Rue,
    Courtesy Goddess Motion, Singapore. ......... 227
Davina~Dawn Devine ................................ 159, 272
Denise Marino ..................................................... 120
Devyne.net ............................................................ 45
Dianne Dunya McPherson ................................ 260
Dorian Iribe ................................................. 211, 213
Dusti Cunningham .............................................. 272
Edward John Poynter ........................................... 27
Edward Frederic Wilhelm Richter .................... 104
Eee & Bee Photography ..................................... 265
Elianae Stone Archives ........................................ 46
Felix-Auguste Clement ....................................... 160

Frederick Goodall ................................................. 80
Fred Shaw ............................................................ 165
Gabriel Ray Morcillo ............................................ 84
George Melita ...................................................... 261
Gilded Serpent Archives .......................... 23, 118, 121, 137, 152, 152, 154, 155, 158, 158, 240, 241, 242, 243, 244, 249, 250, 251, 253, 255, 256, 257, 258
Gladys White ....................................................... 156
Guy Masson ......................................................... 190
Gustavo Simoni ................................................... 116
Gyula Tornai ......................................................... 24
Guy Vaiu ...................................................... 268, 269
Hanna St. John. ..................................................... 28
Helene Eriksen Archives .................................... 222
Hila Gvir ................................................................ 62
Iden Ford ............................................................... 30
Imad Allam ......................................................... 273
Jalilah Lorraine Chamas Archives .................... 267
Jean Baptiste Vanmour ........................................ 76
Jean Igres ............................................................... 72
Jean-Leon Gerome ...................... 26, 82, 101, 228
Jeff Glasser .......................................................... 122
Jeff Klukowski ...................................................... 94
JehanArts ............................................................ 204
Jen Yun ................................................................ 106
Jerry Case ............................................................ 265
Jezibell Archives ................................................. 209
Jillina Carlano Archives ................................ 54, 58
John Frederick Lewis ........................................... 93
John Singer Sargent ..................................... 87, 252
Joseph DeFelice ................................................... 152
Jules Kliot ....................................................... 10, 13
Julie Faisst ............................................................. 39
K. Craufurd ........................................................... 71

| | |
|---|---|
| Kateryna Kritsyna | 266 |
| Kelly Ting | 264 |
| Kristine Adams | 263 |
| Lauren Boldt Archives | 55 |
| Lee Corket | 179, 181 |
| Leela Corman | 52, 108, 269 |
| Leila Farid Archives | 117, 195, 196, 269 |
| Le'Paulle | 73 |
| Les Shuvanies | 186 |
| Lucie Vendittoli | 267 |
| Ludwig Hans Fischer | 70 |
| Lynette Harris | 8, 18, 23, 41, 133, 134, 135, 203, 229, 241, 245, 263, 271 |
| Marilee Nugent Archives | 275 |
| Martha Duran Archives | 40, 42, 270 |
| Mayada Archives | 271 |
| Michael Baxter | 111, 146, 154, 158, 225, 226, 265, 271, 274, 279 |
| Michelle Faithful | 152 |
| Mira Betz Archives | 99 |
| Monica Berini | 96 |
| Najia Marlyz Archives | 3, 12, 36 |
| Nakish Archives | 9 |
| Natalia Sokolovska | 125 |
| Natasha Reed | 145, 184 |
| Nomad | 33 |
| Norwegian Pearl Photography | 274 |
| Pangia Archives | 115 |
| Pepper Alexandria | 152 |
| Peter Koskenvoima | 212 |
| Pierre Filteau | 38, 49 |
| Pierre Marval | 275 |
| Pixie Vision | 215, 272 |
| Princess Farhana Archives | 130, 132, 136 |
| Public Domain | 53, 70, 74, 78, 89, 97, 102, 131, 161, 164, 166, 206, 221 |
| Rahma Haddad Archives | 69 |
| Ralph Thompson | 48 |
| Reed Burnam | 261 |
| Rhea of Athens Archives | 154 |
| Rod DelPoso | 66 |
| Rodin Eckenroth | 14 |
| R, Plutchik | 217 |
| Sahra Kent Archives | 199, 200, 248 |
| Samira Hafezi | 202 |
| Samira Shuruk Archives | 126, 129 |
| Sarah Skinner Photography | 266 |
| Serpentine Communications, Inc. | 172, 174, 175, 177, 275 |
| Shelley Muzzy Archives | 67, 273 |
| Shelly Rothman | 273 |
| Sierra Suraci Archives | 167 |
| Stasha Vlasuk Archives | 220, 224 |
| Stereo Vision | 129, 273 |
| Susie Poulelis | 223 |
| Sussi Dorrell | 162, 163 |
| Tracey Gibbs | 265 |
| US Library of Congress | 192, 193 |
| Venus Archives | 232, 233, 234, 235, 236, 237 |
| Vijay Rakhra | 142, 143, 144 |
| Vincenzo Marinelli | 90 |
| Walter Rasmussin | 153 |
| W. H. Frazer | 17, 156, 270 |
| Wikimedia Commons | 50, 169 |
| William H. Adams | 268 |
| William Logsdail | 110 |
| Yasmina of Cairo | 63 |
| Yen-Jun | 158 |
| Zanzibar Studio in Hollywood by Steven Arnold | 148 |

Thank you Sausan for creating the Dancer Trading Card Stats at the last minute! photo by Gerald Parker

## Late Additions

Jalilah's images for her article were too late to include within her article so here they are! Above: Jalilah performing with the Musicians of the Nile. Below: Nadia 1979

Photo & Art Credits

Sharifa and Muhara by Ken Keep

Delilah and Apollo, an albino Burmese python, photo by Jerry Johnson.

Tatseena with Kaa, a boa at her waist and and Kanari the ball python as a headress. by Michael Baxter

Surreyya Hada and Murjana have a talk. Photo by Michael Baxter

www.ingramcontent.com/pod-product-compliance
Lightning Source LLC
Chambersburg PA
CBHW080727230426
43665CB00020B/2649